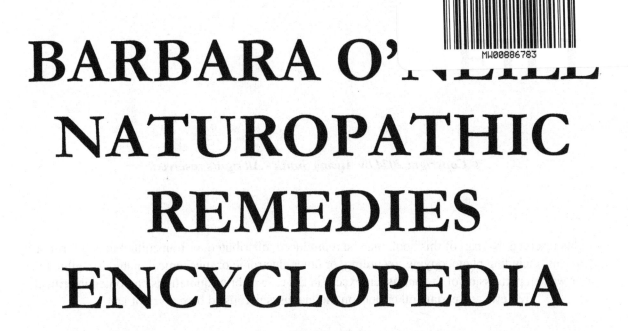

# BARBARA O'NEILL
# NATUROPATHIC REMEDIES ENCYCLOPEDIA

## THE LOST BOOK OF SELF-HEALING RECIPES AND HOLISTIC HEALTH SECRETS

## 30 BOOKS IN 1

Bonus: 40+ Hours of Exclusive Dr.Barbara Videos

and Success Stories

By Aiyana Smith

# TABLE OF CONTENTS

9

# INTRODUCTION

## A WARM WELCOME TO YOUR PATH OF SELF-HEALING

Hello and welcome! This guide serves as your starting point on a profoundly transformative path toward self-healing and holistic wellness. Here, you'll discover the insights, practical tools, and motivation to reclaim your health by tapping into nature's inherent wisdom. As you progress, you'll learn how to nurture your body in harmony with its natural cycles, empowering yourself to achieve lasting well-being.

Health is undeniably our most valuable asset, yet it's something many overlook until life throws unexpected challenges our way. The goal of this guide is simple: to empower you to understand your body on a deeper level and to make choices that nurture your health. By embracing natural remedies and holistic health practices, you'll embark on a healing path that complements your body's innate capacity to restore itself.

In today's fast-paced world, where quick fixes and synthetic treatments often dominate, this guide brings you back to the simplicity of nature. Healing doesn't have to be complicated or distant. In fact, it's a process that is often more intuitive than we realize, working in harmony with your body's needs rather than against them.

You'll find a wide range of practical insights here, from foundational nutrition and hydration principles to the powerful benefits of herbal medicine and specific strategies for addressing common health concerns. This isn't just a collection of remedies; it's a framework for developing a deeper connection with your body. Learning to listen to its signals and respond with care is the cornerstone of true healing.

As you progress, remember that healing is an individual experience. What works for one person may not be the perfect fit for another. This guide respects that individuality, offering flexible strategies that can be tailored to your specific needs. Whether you're managing an existing health condition or simply looking to enhance your overall vitality, these practices are designed to meet you where you are.

Take your time as you absorb the information, reflect on how it relates to your life, and implement the suggestions that resonate with you. Healing is a personal process—there's no universal formula, and that's what makes it powerful. As you embark on this path, let this guide support and inspire you to reclaim your health and embrace the vibrancy that comes with it.

You are fully capable of transforming your health and well-being. Welcome to your personal journey of self-healing. It starts now. Let's begin!

# ABOUT BARBARA O'NEILL: A TRAILBLAZER IN NATURAL HEALTH

Barbara O'Neill stands as a highly respected authority in the world of natural health and wellness. With decades of experience as a naturopath and wellness educator, she has devoted her career to empowering individuals to take charge of their health through the healing powers of nature. Her approach emphasizes the body's remarkable ability to heal itself, provided it is given the right tools and supportive environment.

Barbara's personal journey into natural health was born out of necessity. Like many, she faced health challenges that conventional medicine failed to address fully.

This experience led her to explore alternative solutions, diving deep into the world of nutrition, lifestyle changes, and natural remedies. Through years of dedicated research and practical application, she discovered the profound influence that these natural methods could have on the human body's ability to heal and maintain vitality.

Her philosophy is grounded in the principles of holistic health—a belief that true healing encompasses the body, mind, and spirit. Rather than just addressing symptoms, Barbara advocates for identifying and treating the root causes of illness. This fundamental idea permeates her teachings and is woven throughout this guide.

Barbara has inspired thousands to embrace natural healing as a way of life. Through her seminars, workshops, and online content, she has touched lives across the globe, offering practical insights and compassionate support to those seeking a sustainable, natural approach to health. Her message resonates with those looking for more than just temporary relief—it speaks to those in search of long-term wellness through evidence-based natural practices.

This book serves as a continuation of Barbara O'Neill's mission to educate and inspire others on their path to health. Within these pages, you will find her wealth of knowledge distilled into practical advice, supported by real-life examples. Whether you're new to natural remedies or already familiar with holistic practices, her insights will guide you on a journey toward deeper understanding and better health.

In the chapters ahead, you'll delve into the core principles of natural healing, learn how to nourish your body with essential nutrients properly, and discover the vast benefits of herbal medicine.

You'll also explore practical strategies for managing common health conditions and implementing everyday wellness practices alongside a curated selection of nourishing recipes designed to support your health goals.

As you embark on this path, you can be confident that a true pioneer in the field of natural health is guiding you. Let Barbara O'Neill's teachings inspire and empower you to take control of your well-being and tap into nature's healing potential.

# CHAPTER 01

## THE FOUNDATIONS OF NATURAL HEALING

Natural healing is a holistic approach to health that taps into the body's inherent ability to restore balance and well-being. Its foundation lies in several key principles, each deeply rooted in the alliance between nature and the body's extraordinary capabilities.

### 1. Holistic Health

Natural healing views health as a comprehensive state of physical, mental, and social well-being. It recognizes the connection between the body, mind, and spirit, emphasizing that all aspects of a person's life contribute to their overall health. This perspective ensures that care addresses the whole person rather than isolated symptoms, promoting long-term wellness rather than short-term fixes.

### 2. The Body's Innate Ability to Heal

At the heart of natural healing is the belief that the body possesses remarkable self-healing mechanisms. Given the right conditions—such as proper nutrition, hydration, rest, and emotional well-being—the body can effectively repair itself, regenerate tissues, and combat illness. The goal of natural healing is to support these intrinsic processes rather than overwhelm them with artificial interventions.

### 3. Emphasis on Prevention

In natural healing, prevention is a cornerstone. By adopting healthy lifestyle practices early on, you can significantly reduce the risk of disease. This includes maintaining a balanced diet, engaging in regular physical activity, managing stress, and incorporating routine health check-ups. Prevention is always more efficient and less burdensome than treatment.

### 4. Minimal Intervention

Natural healing prioritizes the least invasive treatments. When the body is in need, simple, natural methods such as dietary adjustments, herbal remedies, and lifestyle changes are used before more intensive medical interventions are considered. This encourages the body to heal in its own time and way.

### 5. The Healing Power of Nature

Nature offers an abundance of resources that can aid in the healing process. From medicinal herbs to nutrient-dense foods, these natural elements work in harmony with the body's systems. When used correctly, they provide effective, gentle solutions without the side effects often associated with synthetic drugs.

### 6. Personalized Care

Everyone's health journey is unique. Natural healing promotes personalized care, tailored to each individual's conditions, preferences, and lifestyle. This customized approach ensures that treatment is effective and specifically designed to support the individual's body, mind, and circumstances.

### 7. Empowerment Through Education

A fundamental aspect of natural healing is empowering people with the knowledge to manage their own health. By learning about how your body works and understanding the principles of natural healing, you can make informed decisions that support your well-being. Education fosters independence and confidence in taking control of your health.

### 8. Balancing the Body's Systems

Health is seen as a state of balance within the body's systems. Natural healing seeks to restore and maintain that balance through nutrition, movement, and mental wellness practices. When the body's systems are aligned, it can function optimally, resist disease, and recover more efficiently from illness.

### 9. Support for Detoxification

The modern world exposes us to environmental toxins, stress, and poor dietary habits that can overwhelm the body's detoxification systems. Natural healing emphasizes supporting these systems through diet, lifestyle changes, and herbal remedies that help cleanse the body and promote overall vitality.

### 10. Integration with Conventional Medicine

Natural healing doesn't reject conventional medicine but complements it. Integrative health practices blend the best of both approaches, using natural remedies alongside conventional treatments to enhance overall health and wellness. This ensures that you receive the most comprehensive care possible.

The principles of natural healing provide a roadmap to achieving and maintaining vibrant health. By embracing these practices, you can unlock the body's innate healing powers and foster a balanced, harmonious approach to well-being. As you move forward, this guide will show you how to apply these principles in practical ways to elevate your health and life.

## THE IMPORTANCE OF HOLISTIC HEALTH

Holistic health forms the bedrock of natural healing, focusing on the intricate connection between mind, body, and spirit. By addressing every facet of a person's well-being, holistic health creates a more comprehensive and sustainable approach to healing and wellness.

### 1. A Comprehensive View of Health

Holistic health considers the whole person—physically, emotionally, mentally, socially, and spiritually. It recognizes that a problem in one area often affects another. This broad view helps identify the root causes of health issues, offering more lasting solutions.

### 2. Mind-Body Connection

The link between mental and physical health is profound. Emotional distress, anxiety, and chronic stress can manifest as physical symptoms such as headaches or fatigue. By addressing emotional and mental health through mindfulness, meditation, or counseling, holistic health alleviates physical ailments and restores well-being.

### 3. Emotional Balance

Emotional well-being is essential to overall health. Practices such as meditation, mindfulness, and even therapy help achieve emotional balance, reduce stress, and improve quality of life. Maintaining this balance lowers the risk of stress-related conditions.

## 4. Physical Wellness

Your body thrives on movement, rest, and proper nourishment. Regular exercise, balanced nutrition, and quality sleep are critical elements of holistic wellness, which focuses on sustainable, natural ways to support your body's vitality.

## 5. Social Connections

Healthy relationships and strong social networks provide emotional support and reduce stress. Engaging in the community and fostering meaningful connections can enhance mental health and create a sense of belonging and purpose.

## 6. Spiritual Health

Spirituality doesn't necessarily mean religion—it involves a sense of purpose and meaning in life. Nurturing your spiritual side, whether through prayer, meditation, or time spent in nature, provides inner peace and resilience, helping you navigate life's challenges.

## 7. A Preventive Focus

Holistic health is about preventing illness, not just treating it. By building healthy habits, like balanced nutrition, exercise, and mindfulness, you can protect yourself from future health problems. Undoubtedly, prevention reduces the burden of disease and supports long-term vitality.

## 8. Personalized Care

Holistic health recognizes that everyone's path to wellness is different. It tailors interventions to fit individual needs, preferences, and circumstances, ensuring that each person receives care that is uniquely suited to their health journey.

## 9. Integration with Conventional Medicine

Holistic health doesn't dismiss modern medicine but integrates natural practices with it. This ensures you receive the best possible care. It draws on the strengths of both conventional and natural treatments without unnecessary side effects.

By embracing the holistic approach to health, you can achieve a more balanced, fulfilling life. The principles outlined here empower you to address your current health concerns while preventing future problems, and fostering a more profound sense of well-being.

# THE BODY'S INNATE HEALING POWER

Your body is a remarkable organism with incredible self-healing capabilities. Natural healing principles emphasize supporting the body's natural processes of repair, regeneration, and balance.

## 1. Understanding the Body's Healing Mechanisms

The body's ability to heal is guided by complex processes that include cellular regeneration, immune responses, and inflammation management. Each of these systems works together to restore health, whether from minor injuries or illnesses.

**Cellular Regeneration:** Every day, millions of cells are repaired or replaced. This regeneration is essential for wound healing, recovery from illness, and maintaining overall vitality.

**Immune Response:** The immune system detects and destroys harmful pathogens, repairs tissue damage, and removes toxins, all while keeping the body safe.

**Inflammation:** While chronic inflammation can harm the body, acute inflammation is an essential part of the healing process. It isolates damaged areas, prevents infection spread, and initiates tissue repair.

## 2. Supporting the Body's Healing Processes

The body needs certain conditions to facilitate these natural processes—nutrition, hydration, rest, and stress management all play critical roles.

- **Nutrition:** A nutrient-rich diet fuels cellular regeneration and immune function, supporting the body's self-healing processes.

- **Hydration:** Water is critical for cell function, waste removal, and maintaining temperature balance.

- **Rest and Sleep:** Quality sleep is when the body undergoes significant repair, tissue regeneration, and immune strengthening.

- **Stress Management:** Chronic stress impairs the body's ability to heal. Managing stress through mindfulness or physical activity enhances the body's healing potential.

## 3. Incorporating Natural Healing Practices

In addition to nutrition and rest, natural practices like herbal remedies, physical activity, and mind-body techniques can complement the body's healing power.

- **Herbal Remedies:** Herbs like turmeric and chamomile boost immune function, reduce inflammation, and promote overall wellness.

- **Physical Activity:** Regular movement improves circulation, strengthens immunity, and releases endorphins, enhancing the body's natural healing processes.

- **Mind-Body Practices:** Yoga, tai chi, and acupuncture balance the body and mind, reducing stress and supporting physical health.

By embracing the body's innate ability to heal, you can create the ideal environment for wellness. Supporting these processes with natural practices empowers your body to thrive, recover, and maintain optimal health.

# CHAPTER 02

# NUTRITION AND HYDRATION

The cornerstones of wellness are essential nutrients. Our bodies are marvelously designed, and like any finely tuned system, they require specific resources to function properly. At the heart of this system are essential nutrients, which are the building blocks of life.

These nutrients, primarily obtained through food, are critical for everything from tissue repair to energy production. By understanding these nutrients and where to find them, we can make dietary choices that enhance our overall well-being and vitality.

## 1. Macronutrients: The Foundation of Health

- **Proteins**

Proteins are essential for building and repairing tissues, creating enzymes and hormones, and maintaining a strong immune system. They are made up of amino acids. Some of which our bodies cannot produce and must be obtained through food.

Good sources include lean meats, fish, eggs, dairy, legumes, nuts, and seeds. Including a variety of these in your diet ensures your body gets the full range of amino acids it needs to function optimally.

- **Carbohydrates**

Carbohydrates are your body's primary energy source. They are broken down into two categories: simple carbohydrates (sugars) that provide quick energy, and complex carbohydrates (starches and fibers) that offer a more sustained energy release.

Complex carbs like whole grains, vegetables, fruits, and legumes are ideal for maintaining stable energy levels throughout the day. They also contribute to digestive health by providing necessary fiber.

- **Fats**

Fats have been misunderstood for years, but they are essential to your health. They serve as an energy reserve, support cell structure, and aid in the absorption of vital fat-soluble vitamins (A, D, E, and K).

Focus on healthy fats like those found in avocados, nuts, seeds, and oily fish, which provide beneficial monounsaturated and polyunsaturated fats. However, limit your intake of processed foods that often contain harmful saturated and trans fats.

## 2. Micronutrients: The Subtle Yet Vital Components

- **Vitamins**

Vitamins play a key role in nearly every bodily function, from immune defense to bone strength. They are divided into two categories:

- Water-soluble vitamins like Vitamin C and the B vitamins, which are not stored in the body and need to be replenished regularly.

- Fat-soluble vitamins like Vitamins A, D, E, and K, which are stored in the body's fat tissue and can be drawn upon as needed.

- **Minerals**

Minerals are equally crucial, supporting functions like bone health, nerve signaling, muscle contraction, and maintaining fluid balance. Key minerals include calcium, potassium, magnesium, iron, zinc, and selenium.

These nutrients are found in foods such as dairy, leafy greens, nuts, seeds, meat, and whole grains. Eating a varied diet rich in these foods ensures that your body gets the necessary support for these essential processes.

## 3. The Lifeblood of Wellness: Hydration

Water is the most overlooked yet essential component of good health. Our bodies are composed of about 60% water. It plays a critical role in countless processes, from regulating body temperature to transporting nutrients and removing waste. Without sufficient water intake, your body cannot function at its best.

**Why Water is Critical:**

-**Cellular Function:** Every cell in your body needs water to maintain its structure and operate effectively.

- **Temperature Regulation:** Sweating and respiration are your body's natural cooling systems, both of which require water.

- **Nutrient Transport and Waste Removal:** Water aids in delivering nutrients to cells and flushing toxins out of the system.

**Hydration Tips:**

- Aim to drink at least eight glasses of water a day, and more if you are physically active or live in a hot climate.

- Include water-rich foods like fruits and vegetables in your diet.

- Limit dehydrating beverages like caffeinated drinks and alcohol, which can increase your body's need for water.

## 4. Choosing Organic and Non-GMO Foods: Why It Matters

- **Organic Foods**

When it comes to what you put on your plate, choosing organic can make a significant difference. Organic foods are grown without synthetic pesticides, fertilizers, or genetically modified organisms (GMOs). As a result, they often contain higher levels of essential nutrients and lower levels of pesticide residues, which support not only your health but also the environment.

- **Non-GMO Foods**

Non-GMO foods are those that have not been genetically modified in a lab. By choosing non-GMO options, you reduce your exposure to potentially harmful additives and ensure you are consuming food in its most natural form. This choice can also help minimize exposure to allergens and toxins, making it an intelligent option for long-term health.

- **How to Make Better Choices:**

- Look for certified organic and non-GMO labels.

- Opt for whole foods over processed ones, which often contain additives and lower nutrient density.

- Support local farmers by shopping at farmers' markets, where fresh, organic produce is more readily available.

## 5. Putting it All Together: Integrating Nutrients Into Your Diet

Focusing on balance and variety is the best way to ensure that your body gets all the nutrients it needs.

- **Balanced Meals:**

- Breakfast: Start your day with a nutrient-dense meal like eggs or a smoothie packed with leafy greens and a quality protein source.

- Lunch and Dinner: Aim for plates that are colorful and filled with vegetables, lean proteins, and whole grains, ensuring a broad spectrum of nutrients.

- Snacks: Choose healthy options like nuts, seeds, yogurt, or fresh fruit to keep your energy levels stable throughout the day.

- **Practical Tips for Success:**

- Plan meals ahead to ensure you're meeting your nutrient needs and avoiding unhealthy last-minute choices.

- Keep a food diary if needed to track your intake and identify any gaps in your nutrition.

- Experiment with new recipes and ingredients to keep your diet diverse and exciting.

By prioritizing essential nutrients and hydration, and making thoughtful choices like incorporating organic and non-GMO foods, you create a strong foundation for your body to thrive. Your diet is the fuel that powers every function in your body, so make it count.

With the right nutrients and hydration, you're not just feeding your body—you're supporting its natural ability to heal, grow, and perform at its best.

# THE VITAL ROLE OF HYDRATION IN WELLNESS

Water is the foundation of life, an essential element that powers every function within our bodies. With approximately 60% of the human body composed of water, hydration is key to maintaining optimal health.

Understanding how water influences our physical, mental, and emotional well-being is crucial for those seeking vitality through natural health practices. This chapter explores the multiple roles water plays in supporting overall wellness.

## 1. Cellular Function and Energy

Water is at the core of cellular health. Every single cell in the body depends on water to perform its daily functions, including:

- Cell Structure: Water helps maintain cells' shape and integrity, creating the environment necessary for cellular processes to occur.

- Facilitating Biochemical Reactions: Water acts as a solvent for many of the body's chemical reactions, ensuring that nutrients, enzymes, and hormones can function effectively.

- Nutrient and Oxygen Transport: Water enables the transportation of essential nutrients and oxygen to cells while assisting in the removal of waste products.

When the body is dehydrated, these processes are impaired, leading to reduced energy production and fatigue. Proper hydration keeps your energy levels stable, allowing your cells to perform at their best throughout the day.

## 2. Temperature Regulation

Water plays a vital role in managing body temperature, especially during physical exertion or exposure to heat:

- Sweating: As your body heats up, it cools itself through sweat, which is mostly water. When sweat evaporates from your skin, it dissipates heat, helping maintain a safe body temperature.

- Respiration: Water vapor is also lost through breathing, particularly in dry environments or when exercising, which aids in temperature control.

Maintaining hydration allows your body to efficiently regulate its temperature, preventing heat-related illnesses and supporting overall comfort, especially during strenuous activities or hot climates.

## 3. Nutrient Transport and Waste Removal

Water serves as the body's transport system, moving nutrients to where they're needed and assisting in the removal of waste.

- Nutrient Delivery: Vitamins, minerals, and other nutrients dissolve in water, enabling them to be absorbed by the body's cells.

- Detoxification: Water facilitates the removal of waste products through urine and feces, supporting the body's natural detoxification processes.

By ensuring proper hydration, you allow your circulatory system to function optimally, delivering essential nutrients to tissues and efficiently removing metabolic waste.

## 4. Joint Lubrication and Muscle Function

Water is crucial for keeping joints and muscles functioning smoothly:

- **Joint Lubrication:** The synovial fluid that lubricates your joints is primarily made of water. Adequate hydration helps cushion your joints, reducing friction and preventing stiffness or injury.

- **Muscle Performance:** Muscles rely on water for efficient contraction. Dehydration can lead to cramps, reduced performance, and an increased risk of injury.

For those who engage in physical activity, maintaining hydration is vital to prevent injury and enhance performance.

## 5. Skin Health and Appearance

Water is a key factor in maintaining healthy, vibrant skin:

- **Elasticity and Smoothness:** Well-hydrated skin is more elastic and smooth, while dehydration leads to dryness, flakiness, and an increased appearance of wrinkles.

- **Detoxification:** By helping flush out toxins, water reduces the likelihood of skin conditions such as acne.

Adequate hydration gives your skin a radiant, youthful appearance by supporting its structure and detoxifying processes.

### 6. Cognitive Function and Emotional Well-Being

The brain, like the rest of the body, requires sufficient hydration to function optimally:

- **Cognitive Function:** Dehydration can impair concentration, short-term memory, and alertness, as the brain depends on adequate water levels to process information efficiently.

- **Mood Stability:** Research shows that even mild dehydration can negatively impact mood, leading to anxiety, irritability, and heightened stress.

Drinking enough water supports mental clarity and emotional stability, which is crucial for maintaining focus and reducing stress in daily life.

## HYDRATION TIPS FOR SUSTAINED VITALITY

Achieving optimal hydration is more than just drinking water when you're thirsty. It's about building habits that ensure your body stays well-hydrated throughout the day. Here's how:

- **Daily Water Intake:** Aim for at least eight 8-ounce glasses of water per day (about 2 liters), though individual needs may vary based on activity levels, climate, and overall health. Listen to your body's signals and drink water regularly.

- **Water-Rich Foods:** Incorporate fruits and vegetables high in water content, such as cucumbers, watermelons, oranges, and strawberries. Soups, broths, and smoothies can also contribute to your hydration goals.

- **Limit Dehydrating Beverages:** Caffeinated and alcoholic drinks can dehydrate the body. Make it a habit to compensate by drinking an additional glass of water for every cup of coffee or alcoholic beverage you consume.

## PRACTICAL HYDRATION ROUTINE

To make hydration a seamless part of your routine, follow these practical tips:

- **Morning Kickstart:** Begin your day with a glass of water to boost your metabolism and replenish fluids lost during sleep.

- **Carry Water with You:** Invest in a reusable water bottle and keep it with you throughout the day, especially during work, exercise, or travel.

- **Set Reminders:** If staying hydrated tends to slip your mind, set reminders on your phone or use apps designed to track your water intake.

# THE FOUNDATION OF VITALITY

Water is the single most crucial element for maintaining health and vitality. From supporting your cells and joints to enhancing your mental clarity and skin health, hydration is integral to every aspect of your well-being. By making water consumption a priority in your daily routine, you set the stage for a healthier, more energized life.

Adhering to Barbara O'Neill's principles, which emphasize hydration as a cornerstone of natural wellness, can profoundly impact your journey toward optimal health. Embrace the power of water—it's a simple yet transformative step toward long-term vitality.

# ORGANIC AND NON-GMO FOODS: WHY THEY MATTER AND HOW TO CHOOSE

In the world of health and wellness, food quality is everything. Barbara O'Neill, a leading voice in natural remedies and holistic health, often stresses the significant impact that organic and non-GMO foods can have on our overall well-being.

It's not just about what you eat—it's about how the food was grown, processed, and delivered to your table. For those of us committed to a healthier lifestyle, understanding the benefits of organic and non-GMO options is essential.

**Why Choose Organic?**

**1. More Nutrients, Fewer Chemicals:** Organic farming practices focus on building soil health, which in turn nurtures the plants. This leads to produce that's often richer in vitamins, minerals, and antioxidants.

When you consume organic foods, you're getting a more nutrient-dense product compared to conventionally grown counterparts. It's one of the simplest ways to give your body more of what it needs while avoiding harmful additives.

**2. Less Exposure to Pesticides:** One of the biggest draws of organic produce is the drastic reduction in pesticide use. Organic foods are grown without synthetic pesticides or fertilizers, lowering your exposure to chemicals that have been linked to various health issues. If you're serious about long-term health, reducing these toxins is an easy win.

**3. Avoiding GMOs:** Organic certification prohibits the use of genetically modified organisms (GMOs). This aligns with a holistic, nature-based approach to health. By choosing organic, you can rest assured that your food hasn't been genetically altered in ways that may not fully align with your body's natural needs.

**4. Superior Flavor:** Anyone who has tasted a fresh, ripe organic tomato or a crisp organic apple can attest to the difference in flavor. These foods are often grown in healthier soil and allowed to ripen naturally, which boosts their taste and quality. Enjoying flavorful, whole foods makes eating a nourishing experience rather than just a routine.

**5. Sustainability at Its Core:** Organic farming practices aim to be kinder to the planet. By minimizing the use of harmful chemicals, conserving water, and promoting biodiversity, organic farming helps maintain healthy ecosystems. Supporting organic means you're investing in a more sustainable future for food production.

**Why Non-GMO Matters**

**1. Preserving Natural Food Integrity:** Non-GMO foods retain their original genetic makeup, which means you're consuming food in its natural state. This not only supports biodiversity but also helps maintain the resilience of crops over time.

**2. Less Risk, More Balance:** Although the long-term effects of consuming GMOs are still under debate, many choose to avoid them to reduce potential risks. Sticking to non-GMO foods helps your body maintain its natural balance, aligning with holistic health principles that Barbara O'Neill emphasizes.

**3. Transparency and Trust:** Foods labeled as non-GMO ensure that you know exactly what you're eating. This transparency helps build trust between consumers and food producers, enabling you to make informed decisions that support your health goals.

**Making Smart Choices**

Now that we've covered the benefits, how do you actually make these choices part of your daily life?

**1. Get Familiar with Labels:** Look for certifications like USDA Organic or the Non-GMO Project Verified stamp when shopping. These labels guarantee that the food you're buying meets stringent standards. It's a simple but effective way to ensure the quality of what you're putting on your plate.

**2. Support Local Farmers' Markets:** Farmers' markets are treasure troves of fresh, locally grown organic and non-GMO produce. These markets allow you to interact with the people who grow your food, giving you insight into their practices and ensuring you're making healthy choices. Plus, local foods are often fresher, which means more nutrients.

**3. Consider a CSA Membership:** Community Supported Agriculture (CSA) programs provide an excellent way to receive regular deliveries of seasonal, fresh, and organic produce. By subscribing to a CSA, you not only support local farmers but also ensure that your fridge is stocked with high-quality, nutrient-rich foods throughout the year.

**4. Grow Your Own:** If you have the space, consider growing your own vegetables and herbs. Even a small garden can provide a steady supply of organic, pesticide-free produce. Gardening is not only a fulfilling hobby but also a practical way to ensure that what you're eating is as fresh and natural as possible.

**5. Prioritize When You Can:** Going completely organic or non-GMO may not always be realistic. If budget or availability is a concern, start by focusing on the items that matter most. The Environmental Working Group's "Dirty Dozen" list, for example, highlights produce with the highest pesticide residues—those are the foods you'll want to prioritize buying organic.

**Taking the First Step Toward Better Health**

Choosing organic and non-GMO foods isn't just about avoiding harmful chemicals; it's about embracing a healthier, more sustainable way of life. Every time you choose these foods, you support your own well-being while also contributing to the health of the planet.

Whether you're shopping more carefully, engaging with local farmers, or growing your own, each choice brings you one step closer to a more vibrant, balanced life.

As Barbara O'Neill reminds us, wellness is a journey, not a destination. Small, informed decisions in your daily routine can add up to significant improvements in your health.

Start with what feels manageable and build from there—your body will thank you, and so will the earth.

# CHAPTER 03

# THE POWER OF WHOLE FOODS

## SUPERFOODS FOR IMMUNITY AND VITALITY

In the realm of holistic health, few things are as impactful as superfoods—those nutrient-dense powerhouses that can transform your well-being when integrated into your diet. As Barbara O'Neill teaches, superfoods not only nourish but also help fortify the body's immune system and increase vitality, making them essential for those seeking to live more healthfully.

In this chapter, we'll explore what makes certain foods "super," their specific health benefits, and practical ways to incorporate them into your daily routine.

## UNDERSTANDING SUPERFOODS

Superfoods are natural, whole foods with exceptionally high concentrations of nutrients, such as vitamins, minerals, and antioxidants, that offer various health benefits. While no single food can supply all the nutrients your body requires, adding a variety of superfoods to your diet is one of the simplest and most effective ways to promote a well-balanced, healthy lifestyle.

## TOP SUPERFOODS FOR IMMUNITY AND VITALITY

### 1. Berries

- **Blueberries:** Packed with antioxidants like vitamin C and anthocyanins, blueberries combat oxidative stress and inflammation—two significant factors in chronic disease. They are a cornerstone of Barbara O'Neill's nutrition teachings for a reason.

- **Strawberries:** Known for their high vitamin C content and manganese, strawberries not only support immune function but also contribute to skin health.

- **Acai Berries:** Acai berries are famous for their ability to neutralize free radicals thanks to their high antioxidant content. They also promote heart health, making them a key food in any vitality-boosting diet.

### 2. Leafy Greens

- **Spinach:** A powerhouse of vitamins A, C, and K, along with essential nutrients like folate and iron, spinach is an excellent food for supporting immune function and energy production.

- **Kale:** With its high levels of vitamins A, C, and K, along with potent antioxidants such as quercetin and kaempferol, kale is a superfood you can count on to help reduce inflammation. Barbara frequently points to kale as a staple in anti-inflammatory diets.

- **Swiss Chard:** Rich in vitamins and minerals like magnesium and potassium, Swiss chard is great for maintaining overall health and vitality.

### 3. Nuts and Seeds

- **Chia Seeds:** Full of omega-3 fatty acids, fiber, and protein, chia seeds reduce inflammation and support cardiovascular health.

- **Flaxseeds:** With a high concentration of omega-3 fatty acids, fiber, and lignans, flaxseeds are excellent for supporting digestive health and balancing hormones.

- **Almonds:** High in vitamin E and magnesium, almonds provide healthy fats that promote heart health and offer long-lasting energy throughout the day.

### 4. Cruciferous Vegetables

- **Broccoli:** This veggie is loaded with vitamins C and K, as well as sulforaphane—a compound with strong antioxidant and anti-inflammatory effects.

- **Brussels Sprouts:** High in vitamins C and K, Brussels sprouts also provide fiber and antioxidants that support detoxification and immune health.

- **Cauliflower:** This cruciferous vegetable is rich in vitamins C and K and promotes digestive health with its high fiber content.

### 5. Healthy Fats

- **Avocado:** Full of monounsaturated fats, fiber, and potassium, avocados are a heart-healthy choice that provides anti-inflammatory benefits.

- **Olive Oil:** Rich in monounsaturated fats and antioxidants, olive oil is a staple for reducing inflammation and promoting cardiovascular health.

- **Coconut Oil:** Containing medium-chain triglycerides (MCTs), coconut oil offers quick energy and brain health support.

### 6. Fermented Foods

- **Yogurt:** Loaded with probiotics, yogurt supports gut health and enhances immune function.

- **Sauerkraut:** Fermented cabbage, high in probiotics and vitamins C and K, aids digestion and strengthens the immune system.

- **Kimchi:** This spicy fermented dish is packed with probiotics and antioxidants, making it excellent for gut health and reducing inflammation. Barbara often underscores the value of fermented foods in nurturing the gut microbiome.

### 7. Whole Grains

- **Quinoa:** A complete protein that contains all nine essential amino acids, quinoa is also high in fiber and magnesium, making it ideal for promoting digestive and overall health.

- **Brown Rice:** Rich in fiber, vitamins, and minerals, brown rice helps maintain digestive health and provides steady, long-lasting energy.

- **Oats:** High in beta-glucan, a type of fiber that helps regulate blood sugar and supports heart health, oats are a fantastic addition to any diet.

## 8. Legumes

- **Lentils:** Packed with protein, fiber, iron, and folate, lentils are key to energy production and digestive health.

- **Chickpeas:** High in protein, fiber, and essential vitamins, chickpeas promote fullness and contribute to heart health.

- **Black Beans:** Rich in antioxidants, protein, and fiber, black beans help regulate blood sugar and support overall health.

## 9. Herbs and Spices

**Turmeric:** This bright yellow spice contains curcumin, a potent anti-inflammatory and antioxidant compound that supports joint and immune health.

**Ginger:** Known for its anti-inflammatory and digestive properties, ginger also boosts the immune system.

**Garlic:** Rich in allicin, garlic offers antibacterial, antiviral, and antifungal benefits, helping to protect and boost immune function.

# PRACTICAL WAYS TO ADD SUPERFOODS TO YOUR DIET

**1. Start Your Day with a Superfood Smoothie:** Blend berries, leafy greens, chia seeds, and a dash of coconut oil for a nutrient-dense breakfast that provides energy and supports immunity.

**2. Incorporate Leafy Greens into Every Meal:** Add spinach, kale, or Swiss chard to salads, soups, or stir-fries to increase your daily intake of vitamins and minerals.

**3. Snack on Nuts and Seeds:** Keep almonds, flaxseeds, and chia seeds on hand for a quick, nutritious snack filled with healthy fats and protein.

**4. Cook with Healthy Fats:** Use olive oil or coconut oil in your cooking to enhance flavor while supporting heart health.

**5. Eat Fermented Foods Daily:** Include yogurt, sauerkraut, or kimchi in your meals to promote gut health and bolster your immune system.

**6. Swap Refined Grains for Whole Grains:** Choose quinoa, brown rice, or oats instead of refined grains to boost your fiber intake and improve digestive health.

**7. Incorporate Legumes into Your Diet:** Add lentils, chickpeas, and black beans to soups, stews, and salads for an extra dose of protein and fiber.

**8. Spice It Up:** Use turmeric, ginger, and garlic in your cooking to enjoy their anti-inflammatory and immune-boosting benefits.

## EMBRACE THE POWER OF WHOLE FOODS

Superfoods are an easy and effective way to upgrade your diet and improve your overall health. By integrating these nutrient-dense foods into your daily meals, you'll experience not only enhanced immunity and vitality but also a greater sense of well-being.

As Barbara O'Neill reminds us, embracing the power of whole foods can be a transformative step toward achieving long-term wellness. Make these choices part of your daily routine and witness their profound impact on your health.

## ANTI-INFLAMMATORY FOODS: A VITAL TOOL FOR LONG-TERM HEALTH

Inflammation is a natural defense mechanism your body uses to protect itself from injury or infection. However, when inflammation becomes chronic, it can lead to more serious health issues such as arthritis, heart disease, and even cancer. The good news?

You can take control of chronic inflammation through your diet by incorporating specific anti-inflammatory foods that support your body's healing processes. As Barbara O'Neill consistently reminds us, food is more than just fuel—it's medicine. Let's dive into how you can leverage the power of anti-inflammatory foods to enhance your health.

## UNDERSTANDING INFLAMMATION

Inflammation is your body's way of signaling that something is wrong. In cases of injury or infection, acute inflammation helps initiate the healing process by sending blood flow, immune cells, and nutrients to the affected area, resulting in temporary redness, swelling, and pain. Once healing begins, inflammation naturally subsides.

Chronic inflammation, however, is a prolonged, low-grade state of inflammation that can persist for months or even years. Instead of helping you heal, chronic inflammation contributes to the development of chronic diseases. Thankfully, your diet plays a crucial role in managing and reducing this harmful form of inflammation. Barbara O'Neill emphasizes the importance of choosing foods that aid in fighting inflammation to support your body's natural healing processes.

## TOP ANTI-INFLAMMATORY FOODS

## 1. Fatty Fish

Salmon, Mackerel, Sardines: These fish are rich in omega-3 fatty acids, known for their powerful anti-inflammatory properties. Omega-3s help decrease the production of inflammation-causing molecules in the body, supporting both heart health and reducing overall inflammation levels.

## 2. Leafy Greens

Spinach, Kale, Swiss Chard: These leafy greens are high in essential vitamins (A, C, and K) and antioxidants that help fight inflammation and oxidative stress. By including them in your diet, you can bolster your immune system while mitigating inflammation-related damage.

## 3. Berries

Blueberries, Strawberries, Raspberries: Berries are packed with antioxidants like anthocyanins, which are particularly effective at reducing inflammation. These powerful compounds neutralize harmful free radicals and prevent them from causing cell damage.

## 4. Nuts and Seeds

Almonds, Walnuts, Chia Seeds, Flaxseeds: These are excellent sources of healthy fats, fiber, and omega-3 fatty acids. The combination of these nutrients helps to reduce inflammation and supports heart health, making them a perfect anti-inflammatory snack.

## 5. Olive Oil

Extra Virgin Olive Oil: A staple of the Mediterranean diet, olive oil contains oleocanthal, a compound with anti-inflammatory effects similar to ibuprofen. It's an excellent choice for those looking to manage inflammation naturally while supporting heart health.

## 6. Turmeric

Curcumin: This active compound in turmeric is celebrated for its strong anti-inflammatory and antioxidant properties. Barbara O'Neill often emphasizes turmeric's role in reducing inflammation, particularly in joint health, where it can be especially beneficial.

## 7. Ginger

Gingerol: Ginger contains gingerol, a bioactive compound with potent anti-inflammatory effects. It's a natural way to ease muscle pain, soreness, and inflammation, whether due to exercise or chronic conditions.

## 8. Tomatoes

Lycopene: Tomatoes are rich in lycopene, a powerful antioxidant that helps reduce inflammation, particularly in the cardiovascular system. Cooking tomatoes enhances the bioavailability of lycopene, making them even more beneficial.

## 9. Garlic

Allicin: Garlic offers anti-inflammatory, antiviral, and antibacterial properties thanks to allicin, its active compound. Incorporating garlic into your meals is a simple way to boost your immune system and reduce inflammation.

## 10. Green Tea

**EGCG (Epigallocatechin Gallate):** Green tea is loaded with EGCG, a powerful antioxidant that helps reduce inflammation and protect cells from damage. It's an easy, daily addition to any anti-inflammatory regimen.

## PRACTICAL WAYS TO INCORPORATE ANTI-INFLAMMATORY FOODS

**1. Start Your Day Right:** Begin with a nutrient-packed smoothie blending berries, spinach, chia seeds, and almond milk. This easy breakfast helps reduce inflammation while boosting energy and immune health.

**2. Add Fatty Fish:** Aim to eat fatty fish like salmon or mackerel at least twice a week. Grilled or baked, these fish provide you with heart-healthy omega-3s that fight inflammation.

**3. Snack Smarter:** Keep a stash of almonds, walnuts, and flaxseeds handy for a quick, anti-inflammatory snack. They're rich in healthy fats and help stave off hunger while promoting heart health.

**4. Switch to Olive Oil:** Replace vegetable oils with extra virgin olive oil for cooking, drizzling over salads, or dipping bread. Its oleocanthal content is an easy way to introduce anti-inflammatory benefits into your meals.

**5. Add Turmeric and Ginger:** Incorporate these anti-inflammatory spices into soups, stews, or teas. Both turmeric and ginger not only add flavor but also actively reduce inflammation.

**6. Sip on Green Tea:** Swap out your regular beverages with green tea to boost your intake of antioxidants like EGCG and combat chronic inflammation.

**7. Prioritize Leafy Greens:** Whether you're making a salad, a stir-fry, or a smoothie, leafy greens like kale and spinach should be a daily staple to fight inflammation and support overall well-being.

**8. Use Garlic Often:** Garlic adds more than just flavor to your dishes. Its anti-inflammatory properties make it a go-to ingredient for any meal, helping you fight inflammation with every bite.

**9. Increase Your Tomato Intake:** Tomatoes are versatile and can be added to almost any dish—salads, soups, or sauces. Their lycopene content makes them a must for reducing chronic inflammation.

## FOODS THAT PROMOTE HEART HEALTH AND FIGHT DISEASE

While many anti-inflammatory foods also promote heart health, some additional options should be noted for their specific benefits:

- **Oats and Whole Grains:** High in fiber, oats, quinoa, and brown rice help reduce cholesterol and improve heart health. Start your day with oatmeal or add quinoa to your lunch for heart-boosting benefits.

- **More Berries:** Berries continue to shine for heart health. Their antioxidants and fiber help lower blood pressure and inflammation.

- **Fatty Fish:** Omega-3-rich fish not only fight inflammation but also reduce blood pressure and triglycerides, making them ideal for heart health.

- **Avocados:** Full of monounsaturated fats, potassium, and fiber, avocados support heart health while providing anti-inflammatory benefits.

- **Dark Chocolate:** A treat that's good for your heart! Dark chocolate with at least 70% cocoa contains flavonoids that reduce blood pressure and inflammation.

Adopting an anti-inflammatory diet is one of the most effective ways to protect your health and manage chronic conditions. By consistently incorporating these foods into your meals, you provide your body with the tools it needs to heal and thrive.

As Barbara O'Neill teaches, the right food choices can significantly impact your overall well-being. Embrace the power of anti-inflammatory foods and take proactive steps toward a healthier, more vibrant life.

## PRACTICAL TIPS FOR INCORPORATING HEART-HEALTHY FOODS

1. **Plan Balanced Meals:** Make sure your meals are designed with heart health in mind. Begin your day with something like a bowl of oatmeal topped with fresh berries. For lunch, try a quinoa salad with leafy greens and some nuts for a nutrient boost. At dinner, aim for lean proteins like grilled salmon, paired with a side of steamed vegetables for a complete, heart-healthy plate.

2. **Snack Wisely:** Ditch the processed snacks and choose options that support heart health. Reach for a handful of almonds or walnuts, fresh fruit, or vegetable sticks with hummus. These snacks not only satisfy hunger but also provide beneficial fats and nutrients.

3. **Cook with Healthy Fats:** Instead of butter or margarine, incorporate healthy fats like olive oil or avocado oil into your cooking. These fats help to lower bad cholesterol and are perfect for both cooking and salad dressings.

4. **Reduce Salt and Sugar Intake:** Excessive salt and sugar can elevate blood pressure and contribute to poor heart health. Use herbs and spices to add flavor without relying on salt, and when you need a sweet touch, go for natural alternatives like honey or maple syrup—but use them in moderation.

5. **Stay Hydrated:** Hydration plays a significant role in maintaining a healthy heart. Drink plenty of water throughout the day, and minimize sugary drinks and caffeine, which can negatively impact heart health.

## TAKE CONTROL OF YOUR HEART HEALTH

A heart-healthy diet is not just about preventing disease—it's about living vibrantly. By making conscious choices about the foods you eat daily, you can support your heart's function and enhance your overall well-being.

As Barbara O'Neill teaches, the decisions we make at each meal have lasting impacts on our health. Start integrating these heart-healthy foods into your routine today, and take proactive steps toward a healthier, more energetic life.

# CHAPTER 04

# INTRODUCTION TO HERBAL MEDICINE

## THE BASICS OF HERBAL MEDICINE: HISTORY AND EVOLUTION

Herbal medicine, also known as botanical medicine or phytotherapy, is a time-honored practice with deep roots in human history. From ancient civilizations to modern applications, herbs have always played an essential role in health and healing.

Barbara O'Neill emphasizes that understanding this rich history allows us to better appreciate how these remedies can support our well-being today.

## ANCIENT BEGINNINGS

The use of plants for healing dates back to the very beginning of human civilization. Archaeological discoveries suggest that humans have relied on plants for medicinal purposes for over 60,000 years.

Ancient cultures, such as those in Egypt, China, and India, documented their use of herbs extensively. The Ebers Papyrus, an Egyptian medical text from 1500 BCE, listed more than 700 plant-based remedies, offering one of the earliest examples of organized herbal medicine.

In ancient China, Shennong Ben Cao Jing (The Divine Farmer's Materia Medica), attributed to the mythical Emperor Shennong around 2800 BCE, cataloged medicinal plants and their uses.

Similarly, India's Ayurveda, a traditional system of medicine, has used herbs for over 5,000 years, with texts like the Charaka Samhita and Sushruta Samhita outlining plant-based therapies for various health conditions.

## THE GREEK AND ROMAN INFLUENCE

The Greeks and Romans significantly advanced herbal medicine. Hippocrates, the "Father of Medicine," promoted herbal remedies alongside lifestyle and dietary changes. His famous quote, "Let food be thy medicine and medicine be thy food," underscores the importance of natural healing.

In the 1st century CE, Greek physician Dioscorides wrote the influential work De Materia Medica, which documented over 600 plants and their medicinal uses. His work remained a cornerstone of herbal knowledge in Europe for centuries.

Another prominent figure, Galen, expanded upon Dioscorides' work and developed complex herbal formulas that influenced medical practices for generations.

## MEDIEVAL AND RENAISSANCE DEVELOPMENTS

Herbal medicine was preserved and advanced during the medieval period, particularly by monastic communities. Monks meticulously cultivated medicinal herbs in their gardens and documented their healing properties. Hildegard von Bingen, a 12th-century German abbess, wrote extensively about herbs in her works Physica and Causae et Curae, bringing a scientific lens to the healing powers of plants.

The Renaissance marked a revival in botanical medicine, spurred by new discoveries and the invention of the printing press. Herbalists like Nicholas Culpeper published works such as The Complete Herbal, which made knowledge of medicinal plants accessible to the general public.

## THE MODERN ERA AND SCIENTIFIC VALIDATION

The 19th and 20th centuries saw the development of pharmacognosy, the scientific study of medicinal plants. Researchers began isolating active compounds from herbs, leading to the creation of modern pharmaceuticals.

For example, aspirin was derived from salicin, a compound found in willow bark.

Barbara O'Neill emphasizes that while modern medicine has its place, the holistic use of whole plants can offer more balanced, gentle healing.

This perspective aligns with the growing field of integrative medicine, which combines conventional treatments with alternative therapies, including herbal medicine.

## HERBAL MEDICINE TODAY

In today's world, herbal medicine continues to be a vital part of healthcare for millions. According to the World Health Organization (WHO), 80% of the world's population relies on herbal medicine for some form of primary care.

In Western countries, there is renewed interest in holistic approaches, driven by concerns over the side effects of synthetic drugs and a desire for more sustainable, natural remedies.

Barbara O'Neill advocates for the safe and informed use of herbal remedies. She stresses the importance of sourcing herbs from reputable suppliers, ensuring purity, and consulting knowledgeable practitioners before using herbal treatments.

Herbal medicine should never be approached with a "one-size-fits-all" mindset, as individual health needs vary greatly.

## UNDERSTANDING YOUR BODY'S NEEDS

To fully benefit from herbal medicine, it's crucial to understand your body's unique signals. Barbara O'Neill often reminds us that our bodies communicate constantly, signaling when something is out of balance. Recognizing these signs allows us to address them effectively with appropriate herbal remedies.

**1. Identify Your Symptoms:** Start by keeping a journal of your symptoms. Record when they occur, their duration, and any potential triggers, such as specific foods or activities. This will help you identify patterns and better understand what your body is trying to tell you.

**2. Assess Your Lifestyle:** Take a close look at your daily routines, including your diet, exercise habits, sleep patterns, and stress levels. Each of these factors plays a significant role in how your body responds to herbal treatments.

**3. Evaluate Your Environment:** Your surroundings also impact your health. Consider how factors such as pollution, allergens, or even stressful social interactions might contribute to your symptoms.

# MOVING FORWARD

Herbal medicine is more than just a practice—it's a tradition steeped in wisdom, science, and nature. By learning from Barbara O'Neill's teachings and integrating this knowledge into your health regimen, you can embrace a balanced, holistic approach to healing. Understanding the historical context of herbal medicine enriches our appreciation of its power and potential in modern wellness.

In the next chapter, we will explore the practical aspects of preparing and using herbal remedies safely, ensuring that you can maximize their benefits while minimizing risks.

By paying close attention to your body's needs and working with knowledgeable practitioners, you can harness the healing power of herbs to support your journey toward optimal health and vitality.

# UNDERSTANDING YOUR CONSTITUTION

In the realm of herbal medicine, knowing your body type or constitution is key to creating effective, personalized remedies. Each individual responds differently to herbs, and recognizing your constitution helps tailor treatments to suit your specific health needs.

As Barbara O'Neill teaches, understanding your body is fundamental to reaping the full benefits of herbal remedies.

**1. Ayurvedic Constitutions**

Ayurveda, the traditional medical system of India, categorizes individuals into three main doshas: Vata, Pitta, and Kapha. Each dosha has distinct characteristics that influence an individual's physical and emotional tendencies, as well as their susceptibility to certain health conditions.

- Vata: Typically thin, energetic, and creative but prone to anxiety and digestive issues. They may benefit from warming, grounding herbs like ginger and ashwagandha.

- Pitta: Medium build, with a sharp intellect and strong appetite, but can experience inflammation and irritability. Cooling herbs such as peppermint and aloe vera are ideal for balancing this dosha.

- Kapha: Heavier build, with a calm demeanor, but may struggle with sluggishness and congestion. Stimulating herbs like cayenne and ginger help boost metabolism and circulation.

**2. Traditional Chinese Medicine (TCM) Constitutions**

In TCM, people are classified according to five elements: wood, fire, earth, metal, and water. Each element correlates with specific organs and health predispositions, and balancing these elements can prevent illness.

- Wood: Creative and ambitious but may face stress and liver issues. Herbs like dandelion or milk thistle support liver health.

- Fire: Passionate and energetic but prone to heart-related problems. Calming herbs like hawthorn or motherwort are beneficial.

- Earth: Stable and nurturing but often experiences digestive issues. Digestive-supporting herbs like ginger or fennel are ideal.

- Metal: Organized and disciplined but may suffer from respiratory conditions. Herbs like mullein and eucalyptus support lung health.

- Water: Reflective and adaptable but can face kidney or urinary problems. Diuretic herbs like nettle or horsetail are useful for these issues.

# PERSONALIZED HERBAL STRATEGIES

A deep understanding of your constitution allows for a more personalized approach to herbal medicine, enhancing the effectiveness of remedies. Barbara O'Neill advocates using this knowledge to create tailored herbal treatments and complementary lifestyle practices.

## 1. Customizing Herbal Blends

By aligning your herb selection with your constitution, you can better address your health concerns. For example, Vata types may benefit from calming herbs like chamomile or lavender, while Pitta individuals might respond well to cooling herbs like coriander and mint.

Kapha types, who often struggle with sluggish digestion, can benefit from warming, stimulating herbs like black pepper or turmeric.

## 2. Integrating Dietary Adjustments

Barbara O'Neill often emphasizes that dietary changes complement herbal remedies. Vata types thrive on warm, moist, and nourishing foods like soups and stews, while Pitta types do well with cooling and hydrating meals. Kapha individuals benefit from lighter, spicier foods to help invigorate their digestion and metabolism.

## 3. Adapting Lifestyle Practices

Herbal remedies work best when complemented by lifestyle practices that balance your constitution. Vata individuals may need routines that prioritize rest and reduce overstimulation, Pitta types benefit from stress-relieving techniques like meditation, and Kapha types thrive with regular physical activity to counter sluggishness.

# CASE STUDIES AND REAL-LIFE EXAMPLES

To better illustrate how understanding your constitution leads to effective herbal remedies, here are real-life examples of individuals who benefited from this approach:

- Case Study 1: Digestive Issues

Jane, a Pitta type, dealt with chronic acid reflux. After learning about her constitution, she incorporated cooling herbs like licorice root and adjusted her diet by avoiding spicy foods. Within weeks, her symptoms had improved significantly.

- Case Study 2: Anxiety and Insomnia

Tom, a Vata type, suffered from anxiety and insomnia. Understanding his Vata tendencies, he introduced calming herbs like valerian root and created a bedtime routine that included warm baths and gentle yoga. His sleep quality improved, and his anxiety levels decreased.

- Case Study 3: Respiratory Problems

Sarah, a Metal type, experienced recurring respiratory infections. She introduced respiratory-supportive herbs like mullein and adjusted her diet to reduce mucus-forming foods. Her respiratory health improved significantly over time.

# PRINCIPLES OF HERBAL WELLNESS

Barbara O'Neill teaches that herbal wellness revolves around the principle that nature provides everything we need to maintain and restore balance in the body. By harnessing the therapeutic properties of herbs, we can support healing and well-being in a way that respects the body's natural rhythms.

# HOLISTIC APPROACH TO HEALTH

True health goes beyond just treating symptoms—it's about achieving balance in the body, mind, and spirit. Herbal wellness addresses the root causes of health issues rather than merely masking symptoms.

- Treating the Root Cause: For instance, instead of using a quick fix like a painkiller for headaches, herbalists seek to uncover and address the underlying cause—whether it's dehydration, stress, or nutrient deficiencies.

- Balance and Harmony: Herbal remedies are designed to restore balance to the body's systems, including the digestive, nervous, and immune systems, empowering the body to heal itself.

# INDIVIDUALIZED CARE

Each person's health needs are unique, and Barbara O'Neill stresses the importance of personalized herbal care.

- Constitutional Analysis: By understanding your constitution—whether you're prone to coldness, warmth, dryness, or dampness—you can select herbs that complement your natural tendencies.

- Personalized Remedies: Customizing remedies based on individual constitutions ensures more effective treatment. This might include blending specific herbs or adjusting lifestyle factors such as diet and exercise.

## SYNERGY AND WHOLE PLANT USE

Another key principle is using the whole plant, rather than isolated extracts, to create a more balanced and effective remedy. Barbara O'Neill teaches that the various components of a plant work synergistically, enhancing its therapeutic effects and reducing the likelihood of side effects.

- Whole Plant Medicine: Utilizing the whole plant allows you to take advantage of its natural synergy. For example, using both the leaves and flowers of a plant may provide more balanced healing than using just one part.

- Herbal Combinations: Combining different herbs can enhance their effectiveness. For example, valerian root and passionflower together create a powerful remedy for insomnia, providing better results than using either herb alone.

## PREVENTION AND MAINTENANCE

Herbal medicine is not just for treating existing health problems; it's also a powerful tool for preventing illness and maintaining overall well-being.

- Daily Herbal Support: Incorporating herbs into your daily life, such as drinking herbal teas or taking supplements, can help maintain balance and prevent disease.

- Seasonal Adjustments: Tailoring your herbal remedies to the seasons can help maintain harmony. For example, using warming herbs like cinnamon in the winter and cooling herbs like peppermint in the summer helps balance your body's internal temperature with the external environment.

## INTEGRATION WITH MODERN MEDICINE

While herbs offer great health benefits, Barbara O'Neill emphasizes the importance of integrating them with modern medicine for comprehensive care. Informed choices are essential when using herbs alongside pharmaceutical treatments to avoid interactions and maximize benefits.

## PRACTICAL APPLICATION OF HERBAL PRINCIPLES

Integrating herbal remedies into your life doesn't have to be complicated. Start small and build up your herbal routine gradually. Here are some practical ways to begin:

1. Start with Herbal Teas: Herbal teas and infusions are simple yet effective ways to incorporate herbs into your routine. For example, chamomile for relaxation or peppermint for digestion.

2. Create a Herbal Medicine Cabinet: Stock your home with essential herbs like echinacea for immune support, ginger for digestion, and lavender for stress relief.

3. Daily Rituals: Incorporate herbal practices into your daily routine, such as a morning tea, using herbal oils for skincare, or adding fresh herbs to meals.

By understanding your body's constitution and applying these principles, you can achieve better health outcomes naturally.

# CHAPTER 05

# PREPARING HERBAL REMEDIES

Selecting and Sourcing Quality Herbs! One of the most critical aspects of crafting effective herbal remedies is selecting and sourcing the right herbs. The quality of the herbs you use directly impacts their healing properties, so understanding how to choose and store them is essential.

As Barbara O'Neill teaches, the more mindful you are about where your herbs come from and how they are grown, the more potent and beneficial your remedies will be.

## UNDERSTANDING HERB QUALITY

### 1. Organic and Non-GMO

Always prioritize organic and non-GMO herbs. Herbs grown without pesticides, herbicides, or genetic modification are not only safer but also retain their therapeutic properties more effectively.

Synthetic chemicals can diminish the natural potency of herbs and introduce toxins into your body. Barbara O'Neill stresses the importance of pure, clean herbs, reminding us that using high-quality ingredients is key to making remedies that work.

### 2. Freshness

Whenever possible, use fresh herbs. Fresh herbs tend to be more potent than dried ones, provided they are harvested and stored correctly. When selecting herbs, check their color, aroma, and texture.

Vibrant colors and strong scents are good indicators of freshness. Dried herbs that have been stored well should still have some of their original vibrancy. Herbs that look faded or smell weak may have lost their potency.

### 3. Harvesting Methods

The timing and method of harvesting play a vital role in herb quality. Ideally, herbs should be harvested at their peak, typically in the morning after dew has evaporated but before the sun is too hot.

This ensures that the plants retain their essential oils and active compounds. Sustainable and ethical harvesting practices are equally important to maintain the balance of ecosystems and ensure that plant populations continue to thrive.

# SOURCING HERBS

### 1. Reputable Suppliers

When purchasing herbs, seek out reputable suppliers who prioritize transparency about where and how their herbs are sourced. Barbara O'Neill suggests doing research or asking trusted herbalists or natural health practitioners for recommendations.

A supplier who specializes in medicinal herbs and is committed to ethical sourcing and high standards of quality is essential for making sure the herbs you use are effective.

### 2. Local Sources

Whenever possible, source your herbs locally. Herbs grown close to home are often fresher, and you can have more control over understanding how they were cultivated. Visiting local farms, farmers' markets, or herbalists allows you to see firsthand the growing conditions and learn more about sustainable practices. Plus, supporting local growers often means a fresher product in your hands.

### 3. Wildcrafting

Wildcrafting, or foraging for herbs in their natural habitats, can be a rewarding way to gather fresh plants. However, it requires a deep knowledge of plant identification and respect for the environment. Be sure to only harvest plants that you can confidently identify, and always practice sustainable foraging to protect wild populations. Avoid over-harvesting and leave plenty of plants to reproduce and thrive.

# ENSURING HERB POTENCY

### 1. Proper Drying Techniques

If you're drying your own herbs, use methods that preserve their active compounds. Herbs should be dried in a well-ventilated area out of direct sunlight to protect their potency.

Air-drying on a screen or rack is one method, or you can use a dehydrator set to a low temperature. Proper drying helps retain the herb's therapeutic value.

### 2. Storage

Once dried, herbs should be stored in airtight containers, preferably glass jars, away from light, heat, and moisture. Exposure to these elements can degrade the herb's active compounds over time.

Proper labeling is also important—note the name of the herb and the date it was harvested or purchased to keep track of shelf life.

### 3. Avoiding Contamination

It's crucial to ensure that herbs are free from contaminants such as dirt, mold, or pests. Washing fresh herbs before drying can help remove any surface contaminants.

Keep your storage area clean and check regularly for any signs of pests or spoilage to maintain the quality of your herbs.

# RECOGNIZING QUALITY HERBS

## 1. Visual Inspection

Quality herbs should look vibrant and healthy. Faded, discolored, or moldy herbs indicate poor quality or improper storage. Dried herbs should have a texture that is crisp but not overly brittle, which signals that they have been dried correctly and stored well.

## 2. Aroma

The aroma of an herb is a strong indicator of its quality. High-quality herbs have a fresh, strong scent that is characteristic of the plant. If the herb smells weak or stale, it may have lost its potency. Crushing a small amount between your fingers should release its essential oils and bring out a stronger aroma.

## 3. Taste

While some herbs may not have a pleasant taste, they should still taste strong and distinctive. If the flavor is bland or weak, this may indicate that the herb has lost its medicinal qualities over time.

Selecting and sourcing quality herbs is the foundation of effective herbal medicine. Barbara O'Neill teaches that by understanding and following the principles of herb quality—choosing organic and non-GMO varieties, sourcing locally or through reputable suppliers, and ensuring proper storage—you can create powerful, healing remedies that support natural wellness.

By paying attention to the quality of your herbs, you empower yourself to harness the full potential of nature's gifts and take charge of your health with confidence.

# CHAPTER 06

# PREPARING HERBAL REMEDIES

There are methods of Preparation: Teas, Tinctures, Oils, and More. The ability to properly prepare herbal remedies is key to fully harnessing the healing properties of herbs.

Each method of preparation has its own unique way of extracting the beneficial compounds from the plants, offering various options for both internal and external use. Barbara O'Neill consistently stresses the importance of precise preparation to ensure both the effectiveness and safety of herbal remedies.

## TEAS AND INFUSIONS

### HERBAL TEAS

Herbal teas are a simple, accessible way to consume herbs and can easily be customized to target specific health concerns.

1. Preparation:

- Basic Method: Boil water and pour it over dried or fresh herbs. Allow it to steep for 5-15 minutes depending on the herb, then strain and drink.

- Proportion: Use 1-2 teaspoons of dried herbs or 1 tablespoon of fresh herbs per cup of water.

2. Benefits:

- Hydrates the body while delivering the therapeutic compounds of the herbs.

- Commonly used for relaxation, digestion, and immune support.

### INFUSIONS

Infusions, similar to teas, are steeped for longer to extract more potent compounds from tougher plant materials like roots, seeds, or bark.

1. Preparation:

- Use 1 ounce of dried herb per quart of water. Pour boiling water over the herbs, cover, and let it steep for 4-10 hours, often overnight.

2. Benefits:

- More concentrated than teas, making them ideal for chronic conditions that require stronger doses of herbal compounds.

# TINCTURES

Tinctures are potent liquid extracts made by soaking herbs in alcohol or vinegar, providing a concentrated and long-lasting remedy.

1. Preparation:

- Ingredients: Use dried or fresh herbs along with alcohol (such as vodka) or apple cider vinegar.

- Method: Fill a jar with herbs, cover with alcohol or vinegar to submerge them completely, and seal the jar. Store in a cool, dark place for 4-6 weeks, shaking it daily. Strain and store in a dark glass bottle.

2. Dosage:

- Typically taken in small amounts (1-2 dropperfuls, or 20-40 drops) diluted in water or juice.

3. Benefits:

- Highly concentrated and easy to transport, making them convenient for daily use or travel.

- Longer shelf life compared to other preparations.

# HERBAL OILS AND SALVES

## Herbal Oils

Herbal oils are primarily used for external applications and can easily be transformed into salves by adding beeswax.

1. Preparation:

- Fill a jar with dried herbs and cover them with a carrier oil (such as olive or coconut oil). Seal and place the jar in a sunny spot for 2-6 weeks, shaking it daily. Strain the oil into a clean jar for use.

2. Uses:

- Applied topically for muscle pain, inflammation, and skin irritations.

## Salves

Salves are semi-solid mixtures of herbal oils and beeswax, used for treating skin conditions.

1. Preparation:

- Melt beeswax in a double boiler, then add herbal oil and stir. Pour into tins or jars and let it cool to solidify.

2. Uses:

- Ideal for healing wounds, moisturizing dry skin, and soothing rashes or burns.

# POULTICES AND COMPRESSES

**Poultices**

Poultices are made by applying mashed herbs directly to the skin for localized healing.

1. Preparation:

- Crush fresh herbs or mix dried herbs with hot water to form a paste. Spread the paste on a cloth and apply it to the affected area, then cover it with another cloth to secure it.

2. Uses:

- Effective for drawing out infections, reducing swelling, and soothing sore muscles.

# COMPRESSES

Compresses are herbal treatments that involve soaking a cloth in an herbal infusion or decoction.

1. Preparation:

- Soak a clean cloth in a strong herbal infusion or decoction, then apply the cloth to the skin.

2. Uses:

- Useful for inflammation, swelling, and skin irritations.

# CAPSULES AND TABLETS

For those who prefer a more convenient method, herbs can be encapsulated or pressed into tablet form.

1. Preparation:

- Capsules: Use a capsule machine to fill empty gelatin or vegetarian capsules with powdered herbs.

- Tablets: Mix powdered herbs with a binding agent and press them into tablets using a tablet press.

2. Benefits:

- Tasteless and easy to swallow, making them ideal for individuals who dislike the taste of teas or tinctures.

# VINEGARS AND OXYMELS

**Herbal Vinegars**

Herbal vinegars serve both culinary and medicinal purposes.

1. Preparation:

- Fill a jar with herbs and cover with apple cider vinegar. Let it steep for 2-4 weeks, then strain and bottle.

2. Uses:

- Can be taken internally, added to salad dressings, or applied topically for minor skin conditions.

**Oxymels**

An oxymel is a mixture of honey and vinegar that provides a sweet, tangy remedy.

1. Preparation:

- Mix herbal vinegar with honey in a 1:1 or 1:2 ratio. Shake well and store in a cool, dark place.

2. Uses:

- Taken by the spoonful to soothe sore throats, coughs, or to boost immunity.

# SAFE STORAGE AND SHELF LIFE OF HERBAL REMEDIES

To maintain the potency and effectiveness of your herbal remedies, it is crucial to store them properly. Barbara O'Neill emphasizes the importance of maintaining the integrity of remedies through careful storage.

# GENERAL PRINCIPLES FOR STORING HERBAL REMEDIES

**1. Temperature Control:**

- Store most remedies in a cool, dry place. Excessive heat can degrade herbal compounds, while moisture can lead to mold growth.

- Some preparations, like fresh herbal juices or infusions, may require refrigeration.

**2. Protection from Light:**

- Use opaque or dark glass containers to protect remedies from light, which can degrade sensitive compounds.

- Keep remedies in a closed cabinet to minimize light exposure.

**3. Air Exposure:**

- Ensure containers are airtight, especially for tinctures and oils, to prevent oxidation and maintain potency.

**4. Labeling:**

- Always label your remedies with the herb name, preparation method, and date to keep track of shelf life.

## SPECIFIC STORAGE GUIDELINES FOR VARIOUS HERBAL PREPARATIONS

- Herbal Teas and Infusions: Store dried herbs in airtight jars for up to one year. Teas and infusions should be consumed within 24 hours or kept in the refrigerator for up to a week.

- Tinctures: Store in dark glass bottles; alcohol-based tinctures last up to 5 years, while vinegar-based tinctures last 1-2 years.

- Herbal Oils: Store in dark, cool places. Most oils last about one year, but oils like flaxseed may need refrigeration.

- Salves and Balms: Store in glass jars or tins; these remedies can last 1-2 years.

- Capsules and Tablets: Store in airtight containers for up to 1-2 years.

- Poultices and Compresses: Best used fresh or within 24-48 hours if refrigerated.

- Vinegars and Oxymels: Due to the preservative properties of vinegar and honey, these can last up to a year or more.

By mastering these preparation and storage techniques, you can create safe, potent, and effective herbal remedies that meet your health needs. Barbara O'Neill's teachings emphasize the importance of these methods, empowering you to take charge of your health naturally.

## PRACTICAL TIPS FOR EXTENDING SHELF LIFE

**1. Regular Checks:** Regularly inspect your stored remedies for any signs of spoilage or degradation, such as changes in color, smell, or texture. Catching these signs early ensures you're only using remedies at their peak potency.

**2. Small Batches:** Prepare remedies in small batches to ensure you're using them while they're still fresh. This approach helps avoid waste and ensures that your remedies are effective and at their most potent.

**3. Desiccants:** Add desiccants (like silica gel packs) to your storage containers to absorb excess moisture and prevent mold growth. This is especially helpful in humid environments.

**4. Rotation:** Use the first-in, first-out method to ensure older remedies are used before newer ones. This practice helps maintain a cycle of freshness, ensuring your remedies don't expire before use.

Barbara O'Neill consistently emphasizes the importance of proper storage, as it preserves the therapeutic properties of herbal remedies and honors the time and effort invested in their preparation.

# CHAPTER 07

## COMPREHENSIVE HERBAL REMEDIES GUIDE

In this chapter, we explore the vast and rich world of herbal medicine, diving into the many herbs that have been used for centuries to promote health and healing. Barbara O'Neill, a strong advocate for natural health, has long emphasized the profound role that herbs play in our well-being. Inspired by her teachings, this guide offers a comprehensive approach to using herbal remedies effectively.

## UNDERSTANDING HERBAL SYNERGY

The power of herbal medicine lies not only in the individual properties of each herb but also in their ability to work together harmoniously. This synergy is at the core of effective herbal remedies, reflecting Barbara O'Neill's philosophy that our bodies are complex systems that thrive on balance. By using herbs in combination, we can support the body in a more holistic way, enhancing healing and overall wellness.

## BUILDING YOUR HERBAL TOOLKIT

Knowing which herbs to use for specific conditions is a fundamental part of herbal healing. This section provides detailed descriptions of key herbs, including:

- Historical Uses: How herbs have been traditionally used in various cultures.

- Active Constituents: The key compounds in each herb that provide its therapeutic effects.

- Herb-Body Interaction: How these herbs interact with the body to promote health.

We cover a wide range of herbs, from popular ones like ginger and turmeric, known for their anti-inflammatory properties, to more specialized herbs like ashwagandha, highly valued in Ayurvedic medicine for reducing stress and promoting mental clarity.

## SAFE AND EFFECTIVE USE OF HERBS

Safety is a top priority when working with herbal remedies. Drawing from Barbara O'Neill's balanced approach to natural healing, this section includes:

- Recommended Dosages: Guidelines for how much of each herb to take.

- Potential Side Effects: Information on what to watch for when using herbs.

- Contraindications: Warnings for when certain herbs should be avoided, particularly for individuals who are pregnant, dealing with chronic conditions, or taking prescription medications.

The goal is to ensure that herbal remedies are used effectively without compromising safety.

## CUSTOMIZING HERBAL TREATMENTS

Every person's health journey is unique, which means that herbal treatments should be personalized. This section offers insights into how to create customized herbal regimens based on individual needs.

Whether you're looking to support digestion, balance hormones, or boost immunity, we help you tailor your herbal approach to match your lifestyle and health goals, echoing Barbara's teachings about listening to the body and responding with natural, balanced solutions.

## INTEGRATING HERBS INTO DAILY LIFE

Making herbal remedies part of your daily routine is the key to long-term wellness. This section offers practical advice on how to integrate herbs into everyday life:

- Herbal Teas and Tinctures: Step-by-step instructions on preparing these remedies for daily use.

- Topical Applications: How to create herbal salves, ointments, and oils for skin care and healing.

- Cooking with Herbs: Easy ways to incorporate medicinal herbs into meals to boost health without disrupting your diet.

By making herbs part of your daily life, you can benefit from their healing properties in a sustainable, manageable way.

## CASE STUDIES AND SUCCESS STORIES

Real-life examples bring theory to life. This section includes case studies and personal success stories that demonstrate the transformative power of herbal remedies. These stories highlight how individuals have successfully used herbs to address health issues, much like Barbara O'Neill's experiences.

These practical applications of herbal knowledge offer inspiration and guidance to those looking to incorporate natural healing into their lives.

By following the principles laid out in this comprehensive guide, readers are empowered not just with knowledge, but also with the confidence to use herbal remedies safely and effectively.

This chapter serves as a testament to the power of natural healing and the profound role that herbs can play in promoting a balanced, healthy life.

# DETAILED PROFILES OF 150+ KEY HERBS: USES AND BENEFITS

## ACAI BERRY (EUTERPE OLERACEA)

- **Overview:** Native to the rainforests of South America, acai berries are known for their high antioxidant content, which exceeds that of most other berries. These dark purple fruits are used nutritionally and medicinally.

- **Active Compounds:** Rich in anthocyanins, polyphenols, vitamins A, C, and E.

- **Uses Against Diseases:** Acai berries are used to promote heart health, support weight loss, improve skin health, and enhance cellular function. They may also help manage cholesterol and offer anti-aging benefits.

- **Preparation & Dosage:** Commonly consumed as juice, pulp, or in smoothies. Available as pills or powders. Generally safe in moderation but can interact with blood thinners.

## AGAVE (AGAVE SPP.)

- Overview: A succulent native to Mexico and the Southwestern U.S., agave is widely used for its nectar as a natural sweetener.

- Active Compounds: Contains fructans, believed to have potential health benefits.

- Uses Against Diseases: Primarily used as a sugar alternative, suitable for diabetics due to its low glycemic index. It also has anti-inflammatory properties.

- Preparation & Dosage: Consumed as syrup or sweetener. Use in moderation due to high fructose content, which may affect liver health and blood sugar.

## ALFALFA (MEDICAGO SATIVA)

- Overview: Alfalfa is a nutrient-dense perennial flowering plant commonly used in herbal medicine.

- Active Compounds: Vitamins A, C, E, K4, potassium, phosphorus, iron, and saponins.

- Uses Against Diseases: Supports detoxification, urinary and kidney health, cholesterol reduction, and hormonal balance.

- Preparation & Dosages: Leaves can be eaten fresh, in salads, or brewed as tea. Seeds should be consumed in moderation due to potential toxicity. Avoid during pregnancy.


# ALOE VERA (ALOE BARBADENSIS)

- Overview: A tropical succulent well-known for its skincare and medicinal properties.

- Active Compounds: Vitamins A, C, E, enzymes, minerals (zinc, selenium), amino acids, and salicylic acids.

- Uses Against Diseases: Used to soothe burns, heal wounds, moisturize skin, aid digestion, and relieve constipation.

- Preparation & Dosage: Gel can be applied topically or consumed as juice. Avoid high doses internally due to potential laxative effects.


# AMARANTH (AMARANTHUS SPP.)

- Overview: An ancient grain praised for its high nutritional value and nutty flavor.

- Active Compounds: Fiber, protein, manganese, magnesium, iron, selenium.

- Uses Against Diseases: Supports cardiovascular health, reduces inflammation, aids digestion, and lowers cholesterol.

- Preparation & Dosage: Consumed as a grain or porridge. Gluten-free and suitable for those with gluten sensitivities.


# ANDROGRAPHIS (ANDROGRAPHIS PANICULATA)

- Overview: Known as "Indian Echinacea," Andrographis is used for its anti-inflammatory and antiviral properties.

- Active Compounds: Contains andrographolide, a potent anti-inflammatory and antiviral compound.

- Uses Against Diseases: Treats colds, flu, laryngitis, digestive issues, and cardiovascular problems.

- Preparation & Dosage: Available as tablets, teas, or extracts. Not recommended for pregnant or breastfeeding women.

# ANGELICA (ANGELICA ARCHANGELICA)

- Overview: Known for its sweet aroma, Angelica is widely used in Europe for both culinary and medicinal purposes.

- Active Compounds: Contains osthol, bergapten, and angelicin, with antispasmodic and anti-inflammatory properties.

- Uses Against Diseases: Used to treat indigestion, heartburn, poor circulation, colds, and rheumatic conditions.

- Preparation & Dosage: Used as tea, tincture, or dried herb. Not recommended for diabetics or pregnant women.

# ANISE (PIMPINELLA ANISUM)

- Overview: A flowering plant native to the Mediterranean, anise seeds are used for flavoring and medicinal benefits.

- Active Compounds: Contains anethole, which offers antifungal and antibacterial properties.

- Uses Against Diseases: Treats digestive issues like bloating, gas, and indigestion, as well as menopausal and menstrual discomfort.

- Preparation & Dosage: Typically consumed as tea or used as a spice. Should be used in moderation due to potential allergic reactions.

# APPLE CIDER VINEGAR (ACETIC ACID FROM APPLES)

- Overview: A popular home remedy made from fermented apple juice.

- Active Compounds: Contains acetic acid with antimicrobial properties, along with trace vitamins and minerals.

- Uses Against Diseases: Promotes weight loss, improves digestion, balances blood sugar, and detoxifies the body. It also helps treat skin conditions like acne.

- Preparation & Dosage: Dilute with water before drinking to protect tooth enamel. Use cautiously with kidney problems or diuretics.

# ARTEMISIA (ARTEMISIA ANNUA)

- Overvie: Known as sweet wormwood, it's famed for its role in treating malaria.

- Active Compounds: Contains artemisinin, effective against malaria-causing parasites.

- Uses Against Diseases: Treats fever, inflammation, bacterial infections, and malaria.

- Preparation & Dosage: Available in capsules, tablets, or tea. Not recommended during pregnancy due to potential toxicity.

**Ashitaba (Angelica keiskei)**

- Overview: A native Japanese herb known for its longevity properties and rapid growth.

- Active Compounds: Chalconoids, a type of flavonoid with strong antioxidant effects.

- Uses Against Diseases: Supports energy revitalization, blood cleansing, joint health, and endocrine health.

- Preparation & Dosage: Consumed as tea or in food. Regular moderate use is generally safe but should be used cautiously with anticoagulants.

## ASPARAGUS ROOT (ASPARAGUS RACEMOSUS)

- Overview: Known as Shatavari in Ayurvedic medicine, asparagus root is revered for its adaptogenic qualities.

- Active Compounds: Contains saponins, asparagine, and mucilage.

- Uses Against Diseases: Supports women's reproductive health, enhances fertility, regulates hormones, and treats digestive issues.

- Preparation & Dosage: Available as powder or supplement. Generally safe but consult a healthcare provider for use during pregnancy or with estrogen-sensitive conditions.

## ARNICA (ARNICA MONTANA)

- Overview: Arnica is a perennial herb known for its anti-inflammatory properties, often used in topical remedies.

- Active Compounds: Helenalin, thymol, and flavonoids.

- Uses Against Diseases: Primarily used for external application on bruises, sprains, muscle aches, arthritic pain, and swelling from fractures.

- Preparation & Dosage: Used in creams and ointments. Avoid applying to broken skin or ingesting it due to toxicity risks.

## ASHWAGANDHA (WITHANIA SOMNIFERA)

- Overview: A key herb in Ayurvedic medicine, ashwagandha is renowned for its adaptogenic properties that help the body manage stress.

- Active Compounds: Withanolides with anti-inflammatory, antitumor, and anxiolytic properties.

- Uses Against Diseases: Reduces stress, anxiety, boosts cognitive function, improves stamina, and strengthens immunity.

- Preparation & Dosage: Consumed as powder or capsules. Generally safe but consult a healthcare provider for proper dosage, especially if pregnant or taking other medications.

## ASTRAGALUS (ASTRAGALUS MEMBRANACEUS)

- Overview: A Traditional Chinese Medicine staple, astragalus is known for its immune-boosting and anti-aging effects.

- Active Compounds: Polysaccharides and saponins that support immune and cardiovascular health.

- Uses Against Diseases: Enhances immunity, promotes heart health, and increases vitality.

- Preparation & Dosage: Available as extract, tea, or capsules. Safe for long-term use, but avoid during acute infections or if on immune-suppressing medications.

## BACOPA (BACOPA MONNIERI)

- Overview: Also known as Brahmi, Bacopa is used in Ayurvedic medicine for its cognitive-enhancing effects.

- Active Compounds: Bacosides that improve neural communication and antioxidant activity.

- Uses Against Diseases: Improves memory, reduces anxiety, and enhances focus.

- Preparation & Dosage: Available as tea, tablet, or tincture. Safe for most, but may cause stomach discomfort in some.

## BARBERRY (BERBERIS VULGARIS)

- Overview: Known for its yellow roots and bark, barberry is valued for its antibacterial and digestive health properties.

- Active Compounds: Berberine, which is effective in treating infections and improving gut health.

- Uses Against Diseases: Treats digestive issues, UTIs, and helps manage diabetes by lowering blood sugar levels.

- Preparation & Dosage: Available in capsules, tinctures, or dried herb form. Use cautiously as high doses can cause stomach upset.

# BASIL (OCIMUM BASILICUM)

- Overview: A common culinary herb with medicinal benefits.

- Active Compounds: Eugenol, which provides anti-inflammatory and antibacterial properties.

- Uses Against Diseases: Treats digestive disorders, inflammation, and anxiety.

- Preparation & Dosage: Used fresh in meals, as tea, or essential oil. Generally safe when consumed in food amounts.

# BAY LEAF (LAURUS NOBILIS)

- Overview: Bay leaf is a culinary herb with digestive and respiratory benefits.

- Active Compounds: Cineole and parthenolide with anti-inflammatory and antioxidant effects.

- Uses Against Diseases: Improves digestion, relieves respiratory issues, and reduces inflammation.

- Preparation & Dosage: Used in cooking or brewed as tea. Whole leaves should be removed from food before consumption.

# BILBERRY (VACCINIUM MYRTILLUS)

- Overview: A close relative of the blueberry, bilberries are used for their vascular and eye health benefits.

- Active Compounds: Anthocyanins, which improve blood vessel health and enhance vision.

- Uses Against Diseases: Treats diabetic retinopathy, improves circulation, and enhances night vision.

- Preparation & Dosage: Consumed as fruit, extract, or capsules. Safe but consult with a healthcare provider, especially if on blood-thinning medications.

# BITTER MELON (MOMORDICA CHARANTIA)

- Overview: Known for its bitter taste, this fruit is widely used for its blood sugar-lowering properties.

- Active Compounds: Charantin, vicine, and polypeptide-p, known for their anti-diabetic effects.

- Uses Against Diseases: Manages diabetes and improves glucose tolerance.

- Preparation & Dosage: Consumed in meals or as a supplement. Should be used under healthcare supervision, especially for diabetics.

# BLACK COHOSH (ACTAEA RACEMOSA)

- Overview: A North American herb traditionally used for women's health issues.

- Active Compounds: Glycosides like actein, which have estrogenic effects.

- Uses Against Diseases: Relieves menopause symptoms and menstrual discomfort.

- Preparation & Dosage: Available in tablets, capsules, and tinctures. Should be used under medical guidance due to hormonal effects.

# BLACK SEED (NIGELLA SATIVA)

- Overview: Also known as black cumin, black seeds are widely used for their anti-inflammatory and immune-boosting properties.

- Active Compounds: Thymoquinone, an antioxidant and anti-inflammatory agent.

- Uses Against Diseases: Treats asthma, high blood pressure, and inflammatory conditions.

- Preparation & Dosage: Consumed as seeds or oil. Caution is advised for pregnant women and individuals on diabetes or blood clotting medications.

# BLACK WALNUT (JUGLANS NIGRA)

- Overview: Known for its strong antifungal and antiparasitic properties.

- Active Compounds: Tannins, which have astringent and anti-parasitic effects.

- Uses Against Diseases: Treats parasitic infections and skin conditions like eczema.

- Preparation & Dosage: Used as hull extract or tincture. High doses can be toxic and should be used cautiously.

# BLADDERWRACK (FUCUS VESICULOSUS)

- Overview: A type of seaweed high in iodine, often used for thyroid health.

- Active Compounds: Iodine, fucoidan, and algin.

- Uses Against Diseases: Supports thyroid function and promotes weight loss.

- Preparation & Dosage: Available as a dried herb or supplement. Should be used under professional supervision due to its iodine content.

# BLOODROOT (SANGUINARIA CANADENSIS)

- Overview: A traditional North American herb used for its antimicrobial properties.

- Active Compounds: Sanguinarine, which has antiseptic and antimicrobial effects.

- Uses Against Diseases: Treats skin conditions like warts and infections.

- Preparation & Dosage: Used topically. It is highly potent and can be toxic if ingested.

# BOLDO (PEUMUS BOLDUS)

- Overview: A Chilean herb valued for its benefits to the liver and gallbladder.

- Active Compounds: Boldine, which has antioxidant and liver-protective effects.

- Uses Against Diseases: Treats digestive issues and promotes liver health.

- Preparation & Dosage: Consumed as tea. Use with caution as excessive consumption can harm the liver.

# BORAGE (BORAGO OFFICINALIS)

- Overview: Known for its bright blue flowers, borage is used for its anti-inflammatory properties.

- Active Compounds: Gamma-linolenic acid (GLA), which reduces inflammation.

- Uses Against Diseases: Treats inflammatory conditions like arthritis and improves skin health.

- Preparation & Dosage: Typically consumed as borage oil. Monitor use for potential liver toxicity.

# BURDOCK (ARCTIUM LAPPA)

- Overview: A traditional herb known for its blood-purifying properties.

- Active Compounds: Inulin (a prebiotic) and polyacetylenes with antibacterial effects.

- Uses Against Diseases: Detoxifies the blood, treats skin conditions, and aids digestion.

- Preparation & Dosage: Consumed as root tea or extract. Generally safe but may cause allergic reactions.

# CALENDULA (CALENDULA OFFICINALIS)

- Overview: Renowned for its ability to heal skin wounds and inflammations.

- Active Compounds: Flavonoids and carotenoids, which offer anti-inflammatory and healing benefits.

- Uses Against Diseases: Treats cuts, burns, bruises, and skin infections. Also useful as a sore throat gargle.

- Preparation & Dosage: Used as creams, ointments, or tea. Safe for most people, including in skincare products.

# CARDAMOM (ELETTARIA CARDAMOMUM)

- Overview: Known as the "queen of spices," cardamom is not only a culinary favorite but also a medicinal herb, especially for digestive health.

- Active Compounds: Contains cineole, which aids in digestive enzyme secretion and reduces gas.

- Uses Against Diseases: Effective for treating nausea, bloating, acid reflux, and other digestive issues.

- Preparation & Dosage: Commonly used as a spice in cooking or brewed as tea. Generally safe, but excessive use may cause gallstone issues due to its high cineole content.

# CATNIP (NEPETA CATARIA)

- Overview: Known for its effects on cats, catnip also offers relaxation and sleep benefits for humans.

- Active Compounds: Contains nepetalactone, responsible for its calming effects.

- Uses Against Diseases: Used for alleviating stress, anxiety, insomnia, and cold symptoms.

- Preparation & Dosage: Typically consumed as a tea. Safe for most, but pregnant women should avoid it due to the risk of uterine contractions.

# CAT'S CLAW (UNCARIA TOMENTOSA)

- Overview: Indigenous to the Amazon rainforest, Cat's Claw is known for its immune-boosting and anti-inflammatory properties.

- Active Compounds: Contains oxindole alkaloids, which enhance immune function and reduce inflammation.

- Uses Against Diseases: Used to fight viral infections, boost immune response, and alleviate arthritis symptoms.

- Preparation & Dosage: Available in capsules, tea, or tincture. Not recommended for pregnant or lactating women, or for those with autoimmune conditions.

# CAYENNE (CAPSICUM ANNUUM)

- Overview: Famous for its heat and medicinal benefits, cayenne is a powerful circulatory stimulant.

- Active Compounds: Capsaicin, known for its pain-relieving and circulation-boosting properties.

- Uses Against Diseases: Used topically to relieve arthritis pain and muscle aches, and internally to improve circulation and digestion.

- Preparation & Dosage: Used in cooking or as a supplement. Caution is advised due to its intense heat, which may irritate the skin and mucous membranes.

# CEDAR BERRY (JUNIPERUS MONOSPERMA)

- Overview: Traditionally used by Native American tribes, cedar berry is known for its antiseptic and diuretic properties.

- Active Compounds: Contains volatile oils and flavonoids.

- Uses Against Diseases: Used to treat urinary tract infections and support kidney health.

- Preparation & Dosage: Typically consumed as a tea or tincture. Should be used cautiously, especially by individuals with kidney issues or pregnant women.

# CELERY SEED (APIUM GRAVEOLENS)

- Overview: Celery seeds are well-known in traditional medicine for their anti-inflammatory and diuretic properties.

- Active Compounds: Rich in volatile oils, flavonoids, and linoleic acid.

- Uses Against Diseases: Used to reduce hypertension, alleviate arthritis, and support urinary tract health.

- Preparation & Dosage: Consumed as a spice, in capsule form, or as tea. Use cautiously with kidney disorders due to its diuretic effects.

# CHAGA (INONOTUS OBLIQUUS)

- Overview: A fungus that grows on birch trees, known for its strong antioxidant properties.

- Active Compounds: Superoxide dismutase (SOD), beta-glucans, and melanin.

- Uses Against Diseases: Boosts the immune system, reduces inflammation, and may lower cancer risk.

- Preparation & Dosage: Typically consumed as tea. Important to source sustainably due to its slow growth. Generally safe, though long-term effects need further study.

# CHAMOMILE (MATRICARIA RECUTITA)

- Overview: Widely used for its calming properties, chamomile is commonly used for sleep and digestive support.

- Active Compounds: Bisabolol, flavonoids, and apigenin.

- Uses Against Diseases: Treats insomnia, digestive discomfort, skin irritations, and anxiety.

- Preparation & Dosage: Typically consumed as tea or used in creams. Generally safe, but individuals allergic to Asteraceae family plants should avoid it.

# CHASTE TREE (VITEX AGNUS-CASTUS)

- Overview: Chaste tree berries are often used to balance hormones, particularly for PMS and menopause symptoms.

- Active Compounds: Flavonoids, iridoid glycosides, and terpenoids.

- Uses Against Diseases: Used for menstrual cycle irregularities, PMS, and menopause symptom relief.

- Preparation & Dosage: Available in capsules or tincture. Should be used with caution, especially for those using hormone medications or pregnant women.

# CHLORELLA (CHLORELLA VULGARIS)

- Overview: A freshwater algae known for its detoxifying and nutritional properties.

- Active Compounds: Rich in chlorophyll, protein, iron, vitamins, and minerals.

- Uses Against Diseases: Detoxifies heavy metals, boosts immune function, and helps improve cholesterol levels.

- Preparation & Dosage: Typically consumed as a powder or tablet. Start with small doses due to its strong detoxifying effects.

# CINNAMON (CINNAMOMUM VERUM)

- Overview: Beyond its culinary use, cinnamon has potent anti-inflammatory and antimicrobial properties.

- Active Compounds: Cinnamaldehyde, responsible for its health benefits.

- Uses Against Diseases: Helps regulate blood sugar, lowers cholesterol, and may combat neurodegenerative diseases.

- Preparation & Dosage: Used in cooking or as a supplement. Ceylon cinnamon is preferred due to its lower coumarin content, which can be harmful in large amounts.

## CLOVE (SYZYGIUM AROMATICUM)

- Overview: Clove is best known for its powerful antiseptic and pain-relieving properties, especially for dental issues.

- Active Compounds: Eugenol, which has antimicrobial and pain-relieving effects.

- Uses Against Diseases: Commonly used for toothache, gum pain, and as an antimicrobial agent.

- Preparation & Dosage: Applied topically as an oil or consumed in small quantities in foods. Clove oil must be diluted before topical use to avoid skin irritation.

## CODONOPSIS (CODONOPSIS PILOSULA)

- Overview: Often called "poor man's ginseng," Codonopsis boosts energy and immune health.

- Active Compounds: Saponins, similar to ginseng, which promote energy and immune health.

- Uses Against Diseases: Increases energy, appetite, and boosts immune function.

- Preparation & Dosage: Used in soups, teas, or capsules. Safe for most but should be used cautiously by those with autoimmune diseases.

## COLEUS (COLEUS FORSKOHLII)

- Overview: Known for its ability to aid weight loss and support cardiovascular health.

- Active Compounds: Forskolin, which increases cAMP levels in cells.

- Uses Against Diseases: Aids weight loss, improves heart health, and helps manage asthma.

- Preparation & Dosage: Mainly available as a supplement. Should be used with caution, especially for those with cardiovascular conditions.

# COLTSFOOT (TUSSILAGO FARFARA)

- Overview: Traditionally used for respiratory conditions, coltsfoot soothes sore throats and coughs.

- Active Compounds: Mucilage, tannins, and flavonoids, which help support the respiratory system.

- Uses Against Diseases: Treats coughs, bronchitis, and asthma.

- Preparation & Dosage: Consumed as tea. Should be used cautiously due to pyrrolizidine alkaloids, which can be toxic to the liver.

# COMFREY (SYMPHYTUM OFFICINALE)

- Overview: Known for its wound-healing abilities, comfrey is commonly used for topical application.

- Active Compounds: Allantoin (promotes cell growth), rosmarinic acid, and mucilage.

- Uses Against Diseases: Used to heal bruises, sprains, and ulcers. Not recommended for internal use due to liver-toxic pyrrolizidine alkaloids.

- Preparation & Dosage: Used in creams, ointments, or as a poultice. Only apply to unbroken skin for short periods.

# CORIANDER (CORIANDRUM SATIVUM)

- Overview: Also known as cilantro, coriander is both a culinary herb and a medicinal remedy.

- Active Compounds: Linalool and pinene, which aid digestion and reduce anxiety.

- Uses Against Diseases: Lowers blood sugar, improves digestion, and helps reduce anxiety.

- Preparation & Dosage: Used fresh or as dried seeds in cooking. Generally safe, though essential oil should be diluted before use.

# CRANBERRY (VACCINIUM MACROCARPON)

- Overview: Cranberries are well-known for their role in preventing urinary tract infections.

- Active Compounds: Proanthocyanidins, which prevent bacteria from adhering to the urinary tract.

- Uses Against Diseases: Used to prevent and treat UTIs and support cardiovascular health.

- Preparation & Dosage: Consumed as juice, extract, or capsules. Typically safe in moderate amounts, but excessive consumption

## FENUGREEK (TRIGONELLA FOENUM-GRAECUM)

- Overview: A herb native to the Mediterranean, widely used as both a spice and a supplement due to its numerous health benefits.

- Active Compounds: Rich in saponins and fiber, with significant amounts of diosgenin, a compound that mimics estrogen.

- Uses Against Diseases: Known to enhance lactation, stabilize blood sugar, reduce cholesterol, and aid digestion.

- Preparation & Dosage: Available as whole seeds, powder, or capsules. Generally safe in both culinary and medicinal amounts, but it may interact with blood sugar medications. Caution is advised during pregnancy due to its potential hormonal effects.

## FENUGREEK SEED (TRIGONELLA FOENUM-GRAECUM)

- Overview: Focuses on the seeds, which are more intensively used for health benefits than the leaves.

- Active Compounds: High in dietary fiber, saponins, and diosgenin, contributing to its anti-inflammatory and glucose-regulation properties.

- Uses Against Diseases: Primarily used for its anti-inflammatory properties and its ability to help manage diabetes.

- Preparation & Dosage: Commonly used in managing blood sugar levels and reducing inflammation. Safe in dietary amounts, but pregnant women and individuals on diabetes medications should exercise caution.

## FEVERFEW (TANACETUM PARTHENIUM)

- Overview: A medicinal plant used for centuries for its anti-inflammatory properties, especially for preventing migraines.

- Active Compounds: Contains parthenolide, which can reduce inflammation and prevent migraines.

- Uses Against Diseases: Effective in preventing migraines, reducing arthritis symptoms, and alleviating digestive issues.

- Preparation & Dosage: Commonly consumed as dried leaves, capsules, or extracts. Should not be used by pregnant women as it can induce uterine contractions. Overuse may cause mouth ulcers and digestive upset.

## FIGWORT (SCROPHULARIA NODOSA)

- Overview: Figwort is known for its detoxifying properties and has been traditionally used to treat skin conditions.

- Active Compounds: Contains glycosides, flavonoids, and saponins, contributing to its therapeutic effects.

- Uses Against Diseases: Used to treat skin conditions like eczema and psoriasis and as a diuretic to flush toxins from the body.

- Preparation & Dosage: Typically consumed as tea or tincture. Not widely studied for safety, so it should be used under the guidance of a healthcare professional.

# FINGERROOT (BOESENBERGIA ROTUNDA)

- Overview: Also known as Chinese ginger, fingerroot is a medicinal herb from Southeast Asia used to improve digestion.

- Active Compounds: Contains essential oils and flavonoids with antioxidant and anti-inflammatory properties.

- Uses Against Diseases: Commonly used to relieve flatulence, improve digestion, and as an aphrodisiac. Investigated for its potential anticancer properties.

- Preparation & Dosage: Used as a spice or in supplements. Generally safe in food amounts, but the safety of medicinal doses is not well-documented.

# FIREWEED (CHAMERION ANGUSTIFOLIUM)

- Overview: Fireweed is a perennial herb traditionally used in Native American and European medicine for its anti-inflammatory properties.

- Active Compounds: Rich in vitamins A and C, and contains flavonoids and tannins.

- Uses Against Diseases: Used to treat urinary tract inflammation, prostate disorders, and skin conditions.

- Preparation & Dosage: Consumed as tea made from leaves and flowers. Generally safe when used appropriately, but there are limited long-term studies.

# FLAXSEED (LINUM USITATISSIMUM)

- Overview: Flaxseed is a nutritional powerhouse, rich in dietary fiber, omega-3 fatty acids, and lignans.

- Active Compounds: High in alpha-linolenic acid (ALA), fiber, and lignans, which have antioxidant and estrogenic properties.

- Uses Against Diseases: Known to improve cardiovascular health, aid digestion, and reduce cancer risks. Also beneficial for menopausal symptoms.

- Preparation & Dosage: Available as whole seeds, ground meal, or oil. Generally safe, though large doses may cause bowel obstruction. Pregnant women should consult a healthcare provider before using flaxseed in large quantities.

# FO-TI (POLYGONUM MULTIFLORUM)

- Overview: Known as He Shou Wu in Traditional Chinese Medicine, fo-ti is revered for its rejuvenating and anti-aging properties.

- Active Compounds: Contains stilbene glycosides, which have antioxidant effects, and anthraquinones, known for their laxative properties.

- Uses Against Diseases: Traditionally used to support liver and kidney health, improve vitality, and treat hair loss and premature aging.

- Preparation & Dosage: Commonly consumed as tea, tablets, or extracts. Fo-ti can cause liver damage in some cases, and individuals with liver conditions should avoid its use without medical supervision.

# FRANKINCENSE (BOSWELLIA SACRA)

- Overview: Frankincense is a resin from the Boswellia tree, historically valued for its aromatic and anti-inflammatory properties.

- Active Compounds: Contains boswellic acids, which have potent anti-inflammatory and analgesic properties.

- Uses Against Diseases: Commonly used to reduce inflammation in conditions like arthritis and asthma and for its benefits to inflammatory bowel diseases.

- Preparation & Dosage: Available in resin, oil, or capsule form. Generally safe when used as directed, though it may interact with medications and cause stomach upset.

# FENNEL (FOENICULUM VULGARE)

- Overview: Fennel is a flavorful and medicinal herb known for its antispasmodic and anti-inflammatory properties.

- Active Compounds: Contains anethole, which helps relax muscles and reduce digestive issues.

- Uses Against Diseases: Treats bloating, gas, and colic in infants. Also supports women's reproductive health.

- Preparation & Dosage: Consumed as seeds, oil, or tea. Safe in culinary amounts, but high doses of oil should be avoided by pregnant women as it can affect estrogen levels.

# GARLIC (ALLIUM SATIVUM)

- Overview: Garlic is both a culinary staple and a powerful medicinal herb with antibacterial and immune-boosting properties.

- Active Compounds: Allicin, along with other sulfur compounds, is responsible for its therapeutic benefits.

- Uses Against Diseases: Widely used to boost the immune system, reduce cholesterol, and protect against heart disease. Garlic also has anticancer properties.

- Preparation & Dosage: Eaten raw, cooked, or taken in supplements. Raw garlic may cause gastrointestinal upset, and caution is needed for those on blood thinners.

## GENTIAN ROOT (GENTIANA LUTEA)

- Overview: Gentian is a bitter herb that stimulates digestion and is often used in herbal bitters to promote appetite.

- Active Compounds: Contains bitter glycosides like gentiopicrin, which stimulate digestive enzymes.

- Uses Against Diseases: Used to treat indigestion, heartburn, and flatulence. Stimulates bile flow and aids digestive function.

- Preparation & Dosage: Consumed as a tea, tincture, or bitters. Avoid in cases of stomach ulcers, high blood pressure, or pregnancy due to its strong stimulatory effects on digestion.

## GOLDENSEAL (HYDRASTIS CANADENSIS)

- Overview: Goldenseal is a small, yellow-rooted plant that has been traditionally used for its antimicrobial properties.

- Active Compounds: Contains alkaloids such as berberine, hydrastine, and canadine, which have antibacterial and anti-inflammatory effects.

- Uses Against Diseases: Primarily used to treat skin disorders, digestive issues, and as a topical antimicrobial.

- Preparation & Dosage: Available in tinctures, capsules, and topical preparations. Goldenseal should be used moderately due to its potent effects on gut flora and nutrient absorption.

## HEMP (CANNABIS SATIVA)

- Overview: Hemp seeds and oil are celebrated for their rich nutritional profile, offering essential fatty acids and proteins.

- Active Compounds: High in omega-3 and omega-6 fatty acids, gamma-linolenic acid (GLA), and amino acids.

- Uses Against Diseases: Improves skin conditions like eczema, reduces inflammation, and supports heart health.

- Preparation & Dosage: Consumed as seeds, oil, or powder. Hemp products are generally safe, and they do not contain psychoactive levels of THC.

# HIBISCUS (HIBISCUS SABDARIFFA)

- Overview: Hibiscus is known for its vibrant flowers and tart flavor, often consumed as a tea with a range of health benefits.

- Active Compounds: Rich in vitamin C, minerals, and anthocyanins, which provide antioxidant and anti-inflammatory properties.

- Uses Against Diseases: Helps lower blood pressure, reduce blood sugar, and acts as a diuretic, which can aid in weight management.

- Preparation & Dosage: Typically consumed as tea. Safe for most people, but it may significantly lower blood pressure in some cases.

# HOLY BASIL (OCIMUM SANCTUM)

- Overview: Also known as Tulsi, holy basil is a sacred herb in Indian culture and a powerful adaptogen.

- Active Compounds: Contains eugenol, ursolic acid, and rosmarinic acid,

# HOREHOUND (MARRUBIUM VULGARE)

- Overview: A member of the mint family, horehound has long been used in traditional medicine, especially as an expectorant.

- Active Compounds: Contains marrubiin, which is thought to stimulate bronchial secretions, helping clear mucus from the lungs.

- Uses Against Diseases: Primarily used to treat respiratory conditions like coughs, bronchitis, and minor respiratory tract infections.

- Preparation & Dosage: Often consumed as a syrup or tea. Generally safe, but high doses can cause vomiting and diarrhea.

# HORSERADISH (ARMORACIA RUSTICANA)

- Overview: Known for its pungent flavor, horseradish is used as both a food and a medicinal root.

- Active Compounds: Contains glucosinolates, known for their antimicrobial and cancer-preventive properties.

- Uses Against Diseases: Traditionally used for sinus and urinary tract infections and as a stimulant to improve circulation.

- Preparation & Dosage: Commonly grated fresh as a condiment. Use with caution in medicinal amounts, as it may irritate the stomach and mucous membranes.

# HOPS (HUMULUS LUPULUS)

- Overview: Known for its role in brewing beer, hops also have sedative properties used in herbal medicine.

- Active Compounds: Contains xanthohumol (a potent antioxidant) and myrcene (which has sedative effects).

- Uses Against Diseases: Used to treat insomnia, anxiety, and menopausal symptoms due to its estrogenic effects.

- Preparation & Dosage: Commonly used in teas, tinctures, or as sleep aids in pillows. May cause drowsiness, so caution is needed when operating machinery. Not recommended during pregnancy.

# HORSETAIL (EQUISETUM ARVENSE)

- Overview: Known for its high silica content, horsetail is used to promote bone, skin, and nail health.

- Active Compounds: Rich in silica, which helps with tissue repair and has diuretic properties.

- Uses Against Diseases: Traditionally used to strengthen bones, improve skin health, and support urinary and renal health.

- Preparation & Dosage: Typically consumed as tea or capsules. Should be used with caution in people with kidney problems or those using diuretics due to the risk of electrolyte imbalances.

# HYSSOP (HYSSOPUS OFFICINALIS)

- Overview: A perennial herb used both in cooking and medicine for its antiseptic and antiviral properties.

- Active Compounds: Contains volatile oils and flavonoids that contribute to its expectorant and antimicrobial effects.

- Uses Against Diseases: Used to treat respiratory infections, aid digestion, and as a tonic for the nerves. Applied topically for skin infections and wounds.

- Preparation & Dosage: Available as tea, tincture, or essential oil. Should not be used by people with epilepsy or during pregnancy due to its thujone content, which may cause convulsions.

# JASMINE (JASMINUM OFFICINALE)

- Overview: Prized for its fragrant flowers, jasmine is used in both aromatherapy and traditional medicine for relaxation.

- Active Compounds: Contains linalool, known for its calming effects on the nervous system.

- Uses Against Diseases: Commonly used in aromatherapy to reduce stress and anxiety. Its oil is used in skincare for its moisturizing and anti-inflammatory properties.

- Preparation & Dosage: Typically consumed as tea or used as essential oil. Jasmine tea is safe for most people, while the oil should be diluted before topical use.

# JUNIPER (JUNIPERUS COMMUNIS)

- Overview: Known for its distinctive berries, juniper is widely used in culinary and medicinal applications.

- Active Compounds: Contains volatile oils like sabinene, limonene, and pinene, which have diuretic, antiseptic, and anti-inflammatory properties.

- Uses Against Diseases: Traditionally used to treat urinary tract infections, digestive issues, and relieve arthritis pain. Also supports heart health and improves skin conditions.

- Preparation & Dosage: Used in cooking, teas, or essential oil. Should not be used in large quantities or for prolonged periods due to the risk of kidney irritation.

# KAVA (PIPER METHYSTICUM)

- Overview: A plant from the Pacific Islands, traditionally used to promote relaxation and reduce anxiety.

- Active Compounds: Contains kavalactones, which have psychoactive properties that reduce anxiety without impairing cognitive function.

- Uses Against Diseases: Used for anxiety, sleep aid, and muscle relaxation.

- Preparation & Dosage: Typically consumed as a drink or in capsules/tinctures. Known for its liver toxicity risk, it should not be used with alcohol or medications that affect the liver.

# LAVENDER (LAVANDULA ANGUSTIFOLIA)

- Overview: Known for its pleasant aroma, lavender is widely used in aromatherapy, cosmetics, and medicine for relaxation.

- Active Compounds: Contains linalool and linalyl acetate, which help promote relaxation and reduce stress.

- Uses Against Diseases: Used to relieve anxiety, stress, and insomnia. Topically, it treats burns and insect bites.

- Preparation & Dosage: Can be used as essential oil, tea, or extracts. Essential oil should be diluted before topical use. Safe in general, but oral ingestion should be supervised.

## LEMON BALM (MELISSA OFFICINALIS)

- Overview: A lemon-scented herb in the mint family, lemon balm is used to reduce stress and anxiety.

- Active Compounds: Contains rosmarinic acid, terpenes, and tannins, which have antiviral, antimicrobial, and calming effects.

- Uses Against Diseases: Used to reduce stress, improve sleep, boost appetite, and ease indigestion.

- Preparation & Dosage: Commonly used as tea or extracts. Safe in culinary amounts, but excessive consumption may cause sedation.

## LAVANDIN (LAVANDULA X INTERMEDIA)

- Overview: A hybrid of lavender and spike lavender, known for its robust fragrance and higher oil yield.

- Active Compounds: Contains linalool, camphor, and terpineol, which contribute to its therapeutic properties.

- Uses Against Diseases: Commonly used in aromatherapy for stress relief and relaxation. Also has antiseptic properties.

- Preparation & Dosage: Used as essential oil in diffusers or topical applications. Should always be diluted before use to prevent skin irritation.

## LEMONGRASS (CYMBOPOGON CITRATUS)

- Overview: A tropical plant known for its lemony scent and flavor, commonly used in culinary and medicinal applications.

- Active Compounds: Contains citral, which has antimicrobial and anti-inflammatory properties.

- Uses Against Diseases: Used to relieve pain, reduce fever, improve digestion, and act as an insect repellent. Also helps reduce stress.

- Preparation & Dosage: Commonly used as tea or in cooking. Should be used with caution in medicinal amounts, as excessive consumption can cause stomach irritation.

This concludes the detailed profiles of these key herbs, providing a comprehensive understanding of their active compounds, medicinal uses, and safe preparation methods. Each herb offers unique benefits, making them valuable for both culinary and therapeutic purposes.

Always consult with a healthcare provider when incorporating herbal remedies, especially in medicinal doses or if you are pregnant, breastfeeding, or taking medications.

## LEMON VERBENA (ALOYSIA CITRODORA)

- Overview: Known for its intense lemon fragrance, lemon verbena is used both in culinary applications and traditional medicine for its soothing properties.

- Active Compounds: Contains verbascoside, which has antioxidant and anti-inflammatory properties.

- Uses Against Diseases: Commonly used to reduce inflammation, promote relaxation, and improve digestion. It is also believed to help with weight loss and reduce oxidative stress.

- Preparation & Dosage: Often consumed as tea or used in extracts. Generally safe when consumed in moderation, but high doses can lead to photosensitivity and gastrointestinal discomfort.

## LEMONGRASS (CYMBOPOGON FLEXUOSUS)

- Overview: Lemongrass is appreciated for its strong lemon aroma and is commonly used in herbal teas, culinary applications, and aromatherapy.

- Active Compounds: Rich in citral, a compound known for its antifungal and antimicrobial properties.

- Uses Against Diseases: Frequently used to ease digestive issues, reduce pain and inflammation, and combat anxiety. It is also used as a natural insect repellent.

- Preparation & Dosage: Typically brewed as tea or used as an essential oil in aromatherapy. Essential oils should always be diluted before application to the skin to prevent irritation.

## LICORICE ROOT (GLYCYRRHIZA GLABRA)

- Overview: Licorice root has a long history of use in herbal medicine, distinct from the flavoring used in candy.

- Active Compounds: Contains glycyrrhizin, a compound with anti-inflammatory and immune-boosting properties.

- Uses Against Diseases: Used to treat respiratory conditions, peptic ulcers, and liver problems. It also supports adrenal function and has shown antiviral properties.

- Preparation & Dosage: Available as dried root, teas, extracts, or powders. Long-term use or high doses can lead to side effects such as hypertension and electrolyte imbalances. People with high blood pressure or kidney issues should avoid it.

# LICORICE (GLYCYRRHIZA GLABRA)

- Overview: Widely used in traditional medicine across the world, licorice root offers a range of health benefits.

- Active Compounds: Contains glycyrrhizin, known for its antiviral, anti-inflammatory, and antimicrobial effects.

- Uses Against Diseases: Primarily used to treat gastrointestinal issues, respiratory infections, and adrenal insufficiency. It can also regulate cortisol levels, making it useful for managing stress.

- Preparation & Dosage: Licorice is available in teas, extracts, and capsules. Care should be taken with prolonged use due to potential risks like increased blood pressure and potassium depletion.

# LINDEN (TILIA EUROPAEA)

- Overview: The aromatic flowers of the linden tree have been used for centuries in European traditional medicine for their calming and anti-inflammatory properties.

- Active Compounds: Rich in flavonoids, mucilage, and volatile oils that provide soothing effects.

- Uses Against Diseases: Used to alleviate anxiety, promote relaxation, and reduce inflammation. It is also used to treat colds, high blood pressure, and digestive issues.

- Preparation & Dosage: Linden flowers are typically consumed as a tea. While generally safe, overuse may lead to heart complications in individuals with pre-existing conditions.

# MACA (LEPIDIUM MEYENII)

- Overview: Maca is a root vegetable native to the high Andes of Peru and is often considered a superfood due to its nutrient content and health benefits.

- Active Compounds: Rich in vitamins, minerals, and amino acids, including high concentrations of iron and calcium.

- Uses Against Diseases: Used to boost energy levels, enhance fertility, balance hormones, and improve mood. It has also been traditionally used to improve sexual health in both men and women.

- Preparation & Dosage: Maca is commonly consumed in powder form, mixed into smoothies or food. While generally safe, individuals should avoid it during pregnancy and breastfeeding due to limited research on long-term safety.

# MARIGOLD (CALENDULA OFFICINALIS)

- Overview: Often confused with ornamental marigolds, calendula is known for its medicinal properties, especially in treating skin conditions.

- Active Compounds: Contains triterpenoids, flavonoids, and carotenoids, which have anti-inflammatory and healing properties.

- Uses Against Diseases: Used to treat minor skin injuries, burns, rashes, and ulcers. It also helps reduce inflammation and may be taken orally to soothe a sore throat.

- Preparation & Dosage: Marigold can be used as creams, oils, or teas. It's generally safe but should be avoided by those with allergies to plants in the Asteraceae family.

## MARSHMALLOW (ALTHAEA OFFICINALIS)

- Overview: Marshmallow root is known for its high mucilage content, which makes it useful for soothing mucous membranes.

- Active Compounds: Contains mucilage, flavonoids, and pectin that provide anti-inflammatory, soothing, and immune-boosting effects.

- Uses Against Diseases: Used for soothing coughs, sore throats, and digestive issues such as ulcers and indigestion.

- Preparation & Dosage: Marshmallow root is typically consumed as a tea or extract. It is generally safe but may interfere with the absorption of other medications if taken too closely together.

## MILK THISTLE (SILYBUM MARIANUM)

- Overview: Milk thistle is best known for its role in supporting liver health and detoxification.

- Active Compounds: Contains silymarin, a potent antioxidant that helps protect and regenerate liver cells.

- Uses Against Diseases: Used to treat liver conditions such as hepatitis, cirrhosis, and fatty liver. It also helps to detoxify the body from harmful substances.

- Preparation & Dosage: Available in capsules, tinctures, and teas. Milk thistle is generally safe, though allergic reactions and mild gastrointestinal disturbances have been reported.

## MINT (MENTHA SPICATA)

- Overview: Mint is commonly used both in culinary dishes and for its medicinal properties, especially for digestive health.

- Active Compounds: Contains menthol, a compound known for its cooling and antispasmodic effects.

- Uses Against Diseases: Used to alleviate digestive issues such as bloating, nausea, and indigestion. It also has soothing effects on the respiratory tract.

- Preparation & Dosage: Mint can be consumed as tea, added to foods, or inhaled through essential oils. It is generally safe, but excessive consumption can lead to heartburn or allergic reactions.

## MOTHERWORT (LEONURUS CARDIACA)

- Overview: Motherwort is a perennial herb traditionally used to support cardiovascular and reproductive health.

- Active Compounds: Contains alkaloids, flavonoids, and tannins, which contribute to its calming, sedative, and heart-strengthening effects.

- Uses Against Diseases: Used to treat heart palpitations, high blood pressure, and anxiety. It is also used to alleviate menstrual cramps and symptoms of menopause.

- Preparation & Dosage: Typically consumed as a tea or tincture. Motherwort is not recommended during pregnancy, as it can stimulate the uterus. It may also cause photosensitivity in some individuals.

## MUGWORT (ARTEMISIA VULGARIS)

- Overview: Mugwort has a long history of use in both Western and Eastern traditional medicine for its digestive and calming effects.

- Active Compounds: Contains thujone, flavonoids, and coumarins.

- Uses Against Diseases: Used to stimulate appetite, ease digestion, and promote menstrual flow. In traditional Chinese medicine, it is used in moxibustion.

- Preparation & Dosage: Typically consumed as a tea or used in moxibustion. Mugwort should be avoided during pregnancy and by individuals with allergies to ragweed.

## MULLEIN (VERBASCUM THAPSUS)

- Overview: Recognized for its soft, woolly leaves, mullein is used primarily to treat respiratory issues.

- Active Compounds: Contains mucilage, saponins, and flavonoids that have soothing and anti-inflammatory effects.

- Uses Against Diseases: Commonly used to treat bronchitis, asthma, and coughs by reducing inflammation and promoting mucus expulsion.

- Preparation & Dosage: Leaves and flowers can be used to make teas or syrups. Mullein is generally safe, but the hairs on the leaves can be irritating if not properly filtered.

# NETTLE (URTICA DIOICA)

- Overview: Known for its nutrient-rich leaves, nettle has been used historically for food and medicine.

- Active Compounds: Rich in vitamins A, C, and K, as well as iron and antioxidants.

- Uses Against Diseases: Used to treat arthritis, anemia, and urinary tract infections. It is also known for its anti-inflammatory properties and support for prostate health.

- Preparation & Dosage: Nettle can be consumed as tea, in soups, or as a cooked green. Fresh nettles can cause skin irritation, so gloves are recommended when handling.

# OAT STRAW (AVENA SATIVA)

- Overview: Oat straw is derived from the green stalks of the oat plant and is known for its nourishing effects on the nervous system and bones.

- Active Compounds: Rich in silica, magnesium, and B vitamins.

- Uses Against Diseases: Used

# VALERIAN (VALERIANA OFFICINALIS)

- Overview: Valerian is a perennial plant native to Europe and Asia, primarily used for its root, which is known for its sedative properties and calming effects.

- Active Compounds: Contains valepotriates, sesquiterpenes, and isovaleric acid, believed to contribute to its sedative effects and anxiety-reducing properties.

- Uses Against Diseases: Most commonly used for treating insomnia, stress, and anxiety. It is also effective for easing tension headaches, muscle cramps, and even digestive issues caused by nervous tension.

- Preparation Methods, Dosage, Safety, and Precautions: Available in capsule form, as a tea, and in tinctures. While valerian is generally safe for short-term use, prolonged usage can cause side effects such as drowsiness, dizziness, and paradoxical reactions like increased anxiety or restlessness. It should not be used alongside alcohol or sedative medications and is not recommended for long-term use.

# VERVAIN (VERBENA OFFICINALIS)

- Overview: Vervain is an herb with a long history in European and Native American traditional medicine, used to treat various physical and emotional ailments.

- Active Compounds: Contains iridoid glycosides, flavonoids, and tannins, which give it anti-inflammatory, analgesic, and nervine properties.

- Uses Against Diseases: Commonly used to reduce symptoms of anxiety, mild depression, and insomnia. It is also believed to relieve pain from headaches, menstrual cramps, and kidney stones, and has been used to improve digestion and alleviate respiratory infections.

- Preparation Methods, Dosage, Safety, and Precautions: Typically consumed as a tea or tincture. Vervain is generally safe in moderate doses, but it should be avoided during pregnancy due to its ability to stimulate the uterus. It can also interact with sedatives or medications for anxiety, so use under medical supervision is recommended.

## PLANTAIN (PLANTAGO MAJOR)

- Overview: Plantain is a common herbaceous plant that grows in many regions, valued for its medicinal properties, especially for soothing irritated tissues.

- Active Compounds: Rich in mucilage, tannins, and aucubin, which provide anti-inflammatory, antibacterial, and astringent properties.

- Uses Against Diseases: Used topically to soothe insect bites, minor burns, rashes, and other skin irritations. When taken internally, it can help reduce coughing and soothe mucous membranes, making it useful for colds and respiratory issues.

- Preparation Methods, Dosage, Safety, and Precautions: Leaves can be used fresh in poultices or dried for teas and tinctures. It is generally safe when used appropriately, but some individuals may experience allergic reactions.

## POMEGRANATE (PUNICA GRANATUM)

- Overview: Pomegranate has been revered in many cultures for its health-promoting properties and is known for its nutrient-rich seeds and juice.

- Active Compounds: Contains high levels of antioxidants such as tannins, anthocyanins, and punicalagins.

- Uses Against Diseases: Known to support heart health by reducing blood pressure, cholesterol, and oxidative stress. Its anti-inflammatory properties may also help in preventing certain types of cancers, including prostate and breast cancer. Additionally, pomegranate has antimicrobial properties that can benefit oral and digestive health.

- Preparation Methods, Dosage, Safety, and Precautions: Pomegranate can be consumed as seeds, juice, or extract. It is generally safe in food amounts but should be used with caution by those on blood-thinning or blood pressure medications.

## RED CLOVER (TRIFOLIUM PRATENSE)

- Overview: Red clover is a perennial herb traditionally used to balance hormones and detoxify the body.

- Active Compounds: Contains isoflavones, which mimic estrogen in the body, and can help regulate hormonal imbalances.

- Uses Against Diseases: Primarily used to alleviate menopausal symptoms such as hot flashes and night sweats. It has also been used to support skin health, ease respiratory conditions, and detoxify the blood.

- Preparation Methods, Dosage, Safety, and Precautions: Available in teas, tinctures, and capsules. It should be used cautiously by those with hormone-sensitive conditions or those undergoing hormone therapy.

# RHODIOLA (RHODIOLA ROSEA)

- Overview: Rhodiola is an adaptogenic herb native to cold climates like the Arctic and mountainous regions of Europe and Asia.

- Active Compounds: Contains rosavin and salidroside, which are believed to help improve physical stamina and mental clarity while reducing fatigue and stress.

- Uses Against Diseases: Rhodiola is primarily used to combat stress, improve mental performance, and reduce symptoms of depression and anxiety. It may also support endurance and physical recovery in athletes.

- Preparation Methods, Dosage, Safety, and Precautions: Rhodiola is commonly consumed as an extract or in capsule form. It is generally safe for most people but can cause dry mouth, dizziness, or increased energy in some individuals, which may exacerbate anxiety. It should be used cautiously in individuals with bipolar disorder or those on antidepressants.

# ROSE (ROSA SPP.)

- Overview: Roses are known for their beauty and fragrance, but their petals also offer a range of health benefits, especially for skin care and emotional well-being.

- Active Compounds: Contains essential oils, polyphenols, flavonoids, and vitamin C, which contribute to its calming and skin-healing properties.

- Uses Against Diseases: Rose petals and rose water are often used to treat minor cuts, abrasions, and burns, and to enhance skin health. In aromatherapy, rose is used to reduce stress, promote relaxation, and combat symptoms of depression.

- Preparation Methods, Dosage, Safety, and Precautions: Rose can be used in teas, syrups, or topically as rose water. The essential oil should be diluted before use to avoid skin irritation.

# ROSEMARY (ROSMARINUS OFFICINALIS)

- Overview: Rosemary is a fragrant evergreen herb native to the Mediterranean region, known for its culinary and medicinal uses.

- Active Compounds: Contains rosmarinic acid, carnosic acid, and essential oils such as cineole, which have powerful antioxidant, antimicrobial, and anti-inflammatory properties.

- Uses Against Diseases: Often used to enhance memory and concentration, support digestive health, and relieve muscle pain. Rosemary is also applied topically to improve scalp health and promote hair growth.

- Preparation Methods, Dosage, Safety, and Precautions: Commonly used as a culinary herb, in teas, or as an essential oil. While generally safe, rosemary oil can be toxic in large doses and should be used with caution.

## SAGE (SALVIA OFFICINALIS)

- Overview: Sage is an aromatic herb used both in cooking and herbal medicine for its digestive and calming effects.

- Active Compounds: Contains volatile oils like thujone and camphor, along with flavonoids and phenolic acids.

- Uses Against Diseases: Used for its antibacterial, digestive, and calming properties. It is also effective as a mouthwash for soothing sore throats and gum infections.

- Preparation Methods, Dosage, Safety, and Precautions: Sage is commonly used in teas, culinary dishes, and supplements. High doses of sage essential oil should be avoided, particularly by pregnant women and individuals with seizure disorders due to its thujone content.

## ST. JOHN'S WORT (HYPERICUM PERFORATUM)

- Overview: St. John's Wort is a perennial herb best known for its use in treating mood disorders.

- Active Compounds: Contains hypericin and hyperforin, which are thought to have antidepressant and antiviral properties.

- Uses Against Diseases: Primarily used to alleviate mild to moderate depression, anxiety, and seasonal affective disorder (SAD). It has also been explored for its antiviral effects against certain infections.

- Preparation Methods, Dosage, Safety, and Precautions: St. John's Wort is available in capsules, teas, and tinctures. It can interact with a variety of medications, including antidepressants, birth control pills, and blood thinners, so it should only be used under the guidance of a healthcare provider.

## SAW PALMETTO (SERENOA REPENS)

- Overview: Saw palmetto is a small palm tree whose berries are used to treat various conditions, particularly those related to men's health.

- Active Compounds: Contains fatty acids and plant sterols that may influence testosterone and estrogen pathways.

- Uses Against Diseases: Most commonly used to treat symptoms of benign prostatic hyperplasia (BPH) in men, including urinary issues and inflammation. It may also help reduce hair loss and improve sexual health.

- Preparation Methods, Dosage, Safety, and Precautions: Typically consumed as an extract or capsule. While generally safe, saw palmetto can cause mild side effects like stomach upset and should be used cautiously in individuals on hormone therapy or blood thinners.


By extending these herb profiles, you have a comprehensive overview of their medicinal uses, active compounds, and safety precautions, helping ensure proper application in both traditional and modern contexts.


# VANILLA (VANILLA PLANIFOLIA)

- Overview: Vanilla is a widely cultivated spice known for its sweet aroma, derived from the seeds of orchid plants. It is often used in culinary, cosmetic, and therapeutic products.

- Active Compounds: The primary compound in vanilla is vanillin, which has antioxidant properties.

- Uses Against Diseases: Beyond its culinary uses, vanilla is believed to have mild anti-inflammatory and calming effects. It may help reduce anxiety and provide a sense of relaxation when used in aromatherapy.

- Preparation Methods, Dosage, Safety, and Precautions: Vanilla is commonly used as an extract or through vanilla beans in cooking. It is generally safe when consumed in food quantities, but synthetic vanillin in large doses can cause allergic reactions or headaches.

# VETIVER (CHRYSOPOGON ZIZANIOIDES)

- Overview: Vetiver is a tall grass known for its aromatic roots, often used in perfumery and traditional medicine.

- Active Compounds: The essential oils extracted from vetiver contain zizanol, khusimol, and other compounds with anti-inflammatory, antiseptic, and calming properties.

- Uses Against Diseases: In traditional medicine, vetiver is used to relieve stress, anxiety, and insomnia. It is also applied to reduce joint and muscle pain.

- Preparation Methods, Dosage, Safety, and Precautions: Vetiver oil is typically used in diffusers or applied topically in diluted forms. It is safe when used appropriately but should be diluted for topical use to avoid irritation.

# VIOLET (VIOLA ODORATA)

- Overview: Violet, with its delicate and fragrant flowers, has been used medicinally for its soothing effects, particularly on skin and respiratory issues.

- Active Compounds: Contains mucilage, salicylic acid, and flavonoids that provide anti-inflammatory and expectorant effects.

- Uses Against Diseases: Used to treat skin conditions such as acne and eczema. It is also used as an expectorant to ease coughs and other respiratory conditions.

- Preparation Methods, Dosage, Safety, and Precautions: Typically consumed as a tea or used in topical creams and salves. The essential oil should be diluted before use to prevent skin irritation.

## WHITE WILLOW (SALIX ALBA)

- Overview: White willow bark has been used for centuries to relieve pain and inflammation, often considered a natural alternative to aspirin.

- Active Compounds: Contains salicin, which the body converts into salicylic acid.

- Uses Against Diseases: Commonly used for pain relief, particularly for headaches, arthritis, and lower back pain. It also has anti-inflammatory properties.

- Preparation Methods, Dosage, Safety, and Precautions: White willow bark is available as capsules, tablets, or dried herbs for tea. It should not be used by those allergic to aspirin, taking blood thinners, or by children due to the risk of Reye's syndrome.

## WITCH HAZEL (HAMAMELIS VIRGINIANA)

- Overview: Witch hazel is a shrub native to North America, renowned for its skin-soothing properties.

- Active Compounds: Contains tannins and flavonoids, which have astringent and anti-inflammatory effects.

- Uses Against Diseases: Primarily used topically to soothe irritated skin, heal minor wounds, and reduce inflammation. It is also used for hemorrhoids and varicose veins.

- Preparation Methods, Dosage, Safety, and Precautions: Commonly applied as a distilled liquid or ointment. It is generally safe for topical use but should not be ingested.

## WORMWOOD (ARTEMISIA ABSINTHIUM)

- Overview: Best known as the key ingredient in absinthe, wormwood has a long history in herbal medicine for digestive and antiparasitic purposes.

- Active Compounds: Contains thujone, which can be toxic in large amounts, and sesquiterpene lactones that stimulate digestion.

- Uses Against Diseases: Used to treat digestive issues, liver problems, and parasitic infections.

- Preparation Methods, Dosage, Safety, and Precautions: Typically used in tinctures or infusions. Caution is necessary due to thujone's neurotoxic effects, so wormwood should not be used in high doses or over long periods.

# YARROW (ACHILLEA MILLEFOLIUM)

- Overview: Yarrow is a versatile flowering plant used for its wide range of medicinal benefits, including wound healing and anti-inflammatory effects.

- Active Compounds: Contains flavonoids and salicylic acid derivatives, which contribute to its anti-inflammatory and astringent properties.

- Uses Against Diseases: Used to treat wounds, fever, digestive issues, and various skin conditions. Yarrow is also effective for stopping bleeding due to its astringent properties.

- Preparation Methods, Dosage, Safety, and Precautions: Can be used topically or consumed as a tea. It is generally safe, but individuals allergic to the Asteraceae family should avoid it, and it is not recommended during pregnancy.

# YELLOW DOCK (RUMEX CRISPUS)

- Overview: Yellow dock is a perennial herb used for its detoxifying properties and to support liver health.

- Active Compounds: Contains anthraquinones, which have mild laxative effects, and is rich in iron.

- Uses Against Diseases: Commonly used to treat constipation, skin issues, and as a blood cleanser. It is also beneficial for anemia and supporting liver function.

- Preparation Methods, Dosage, Safety, and Precautions: Typically used as a tincture or decoction. Due to its laxative effect, it should be used with caution to avoid cramping or diarrhea.

# YUCCA (YUCCA SCHIDIGERA)

- Overview: Yucca is a desert plant known for its anti-inflammatory and antioxidant properties.

- Active Compounds: Contains saponins, which are believed to have anti-inflammatory effects.

- Uses Against Diseases: Used primarily to treat arthritis and joint pain, as well as to purify the blood.

- Preparation Methods, Dosage, Safety, and Precautions: Available in capsule, powder, or extract form. Excessive consumption can cause stomach irritation, so it should be used as directed.

# ZIZIPHUS (ZIZIPHUS JUJUBA)

- Overview: Also known as jujube or red date, Ziziphus is prized for its nutritious fruit and medicinal properties, especially in traditional Chinese medicine.

- Active Compounds: Contains vitamin C, flavonoids, saponins, and polysaccharides, which offer immune-boosting and sedative effects.

- Uses Against Diseases: Used to improve sleep, alleviate anxiety, and strengthen the body. It also has anti-inflammatory and liver-protective properties.

- Preparation Methods, Dosage, Safety, and Precautions: The fruit is consumed fresh, dried, or as an extract. Generally safe in food amounts, but extracts should be used cautiously to avoid interactions with medications.

# COMBINING HERBS FOR MAXIMUM EFFECT

Understanding the synergistic effects of combining herbs is crucial to maximizing their therapeutic benefits. Many traditional medicine systems, including Ayurveda and Traditional Chinese Medicine, have long emphasized herbal combinations for enhanced efficacy, broader therapeutic effects, and reduced side effects.

## BENEFITS OF COMBINING HERBS

1. Enhanced Efficacy: Combining complementary herbs can enhance their individual effects. For example, ginger and turmeric both have anti-inflammatory properties, but when used together, they may provide even greater relief from inflammation.

2. Broader Therapeutic Range: Using combinations of herbs can help address multiple symptoms or the underlying causes of health issues. For instance, a combination of echinacea (immune support) and elderberry (antiviral) can be effective during cold and flu season.

3. Side Effect Mitigation: Some herbs can counterbalance the side effects of others. For example, licorice can be paired with herbs like peppermint to help soothe the stomach while supporting digestive health.

By understanding how to pair herbs effectively, individuals can create well-rounded, potent remedies that support various aspects of health.

## PRINCIPLES OF EFFECTIVE HERBAL COMBINATIONS

1. Complementary Actions: Combining herbs with complementary actions can enhance their efficacy. For example, Echinacea strengthens the immune system, while elderberry has antiviral properties, making them a potent duo for fighting colds and flu.

2. Balancing Properties: Pairing herbs with opposing properties can create a balanced remedy. A stimulating herb like ginseng can be combined with calming chamomile to create a more harmonious blend, ensuring energy without overstimulation.

3. Sequential Use: In some cases, it's beneficial to use herbs sequentially rather than simultaneously. For example, milk thistle can be used first to detoxify the liver, followed by nettle to nourish and restore the body.

## POPULAR HERBAL COMBINATIONS

1. Turmeric and Black Pepper: Turmeric's curcumin is known for its powerful anti-inflammatory effects, but its absorption is low. Black pepper, containing piperine, enhances curcumin's absorption by up to 2000%, increasing its effectiveness.

2. Echinacea and Goldenseal: This powerful combination strengthens the immune system (Echinacea) and provides antimicrobial support (Goldenseal), making it an excellent choice for respiratory infections.

3. Valerian and Hops: Both herbs have sedative properties, making them an ideal natural remedy for anxiety, stress, and insomnia.

4. Ginger and Lemon Balm: Ginger aids digestion and has anti-inflammatory properties, while lemon balm is calming and supports digestion, particularly in cases of stress-induced gastrointestinal discomfort.

5. Ginseng and Astragalus: Both adaptogens, ginseng helps the body cope with stress, and astragalus supports the immune system, making them a perfect combination for improving physical endurance and resilience to stress.

## PRACTICAL APPLICATIONS

1. Tinctures: Combining herbs in liquid extracts (tinctures) makes them easy to use. For instance, a tincture combining echinacea, elderberry, and goldenseal can be an effective remedy during flu season.

2. Teas: Herbal teas are a popular and accessible way to combine herbs. A tea made from peppermint, ginger, and fennel can address various digestive complaints such as bloating, gas, and nausea.

3. Capsules and Powders: For convenience, herbs can be combined in capsule or powdered form. For example, a blend of ashwagandha, rhodiola, and holy basil in capsule form is ideal for supporting adrenal health and reducing stress.

4. Topical Applications: Herbal combinations can be used in topical forms, such as salves or ointments. A salve made from calendula, comfrey, and St. John's Wort can help heal wounds and reduce inflammation.

## DOSAGE, SAFETY, AND PRECAUTIONS

- Dosage: When combining herbs, start with lower doses to see how your body responds. Always follow standard guidelines for individual herbs but begin with half the recommended dose for combined herbs.

- Safety: Be aware of potential herb-herb or herb-drug interactions. For instance, combining blood-thinning herbs like garlic and ginkgo with anticoagulant medications can increase the risk of bleeding.

- Precautions: Pregnant or breastfeeding women, and individuals with chronic health conditions, should consult with a healthcare provider before using herbal combinations.

# INTEGRATING HERBS INTO DAILY LIFE

## EMBRACING HERBAL WELLNESS

Integrating herbs into your daily routine can lead to better health and well-being. Barbara O'Neill emphasizes the importance of consistency in using natural remedies to experience their full benefits.

## STARTING YOUR DAY WITH HERBS

1. Herbal Morning Teas: Start your day with a cup of herbal tea made with ginger, lemon balm, or peppermint to boost metabolism and prepare your digestive system. Ginger tea is particularly warming and supportive during colder months.

2. Herbal Infused Water: Enhance your hydration with herbs like mint, cucumber, or rosemary. This adds subtle flavors while providing detoxifying and digestive support.

3. Herbal Smoothies: Boost your morning smoothies with a handful of herbs such as parsley, turmeric, or spirulina for added nutrition and energy.

## COOKING WITH HERBS

1. Flavorful Cooking: Use fresh herbs like basil, cilantro, and thyme to enhance the flavor of your meals while gaining their health benefits.

2. Herbal Oils and Vinegars: Infuse oils and vinegars with herbs like rosemary or garlic to add depth to dishes and benefit from their anti-inflammatory properties.

3. Herbal Soups and Stews: Add medicinal herbs like astragalus or reishi mushrooms to soups and stews for immune-boosting properties.

# HERBAL SNACKS AND SUPPLEMENTS

1. Herbal Energy Balls: Make nutritious energy balls with herbs like maca, chia seeds, or cacao for a boost of energy and health.

2. Herbal Capsules and Tinctures: Take herbal capsules and tinctures for convenience. High-quality, organic supplements are best to ensure potency.

3. Herbal Spices: Use spices like turmeric, cinnamon, and cayenne in your daily meals for their anti-inflammatory and metabolic benefits.

# HERBAL SELF-CARE ROUTINES

1. Herbal Baths: Add lavender, chamomile, and rose petals to your bath for a relaxing experience that soothes the nervous system.

2. Herbal Skin Care: Use herbal-infused oils like calendula or chamomile for soothing irritated skin.

3. Aromatherapy: Diffuse essential oils like eucalyptus, peppermint, or lemon to purify the air and support respiratory health.

**Herbal Remedies for Common Ailments**

1. Digestive Support: Keep a stock of teas like peppermint, fennel, and ginger to soothe digestive discomforts such as bloating and indigestion.

2. Immune Boosting: Use echinacea, elderberry, and astragalus during flu season to enhance immune function.

3. Stress and Sleep: Use calming herbs like valerian, passionflower, and lemon balm for stress relief and better sleep.

# SAFETY AND PRECAUTIONS

1. Consulting with Professionals: Always consult with a healthcare provider before starting any new herbal regimen, particularly if you have existing health conditions or are on medication.

2. Understanding Contraindications: Be aware of potential interactions between herbs and medications. For instance, St. John's Wort can interfere with various prescription drugs.

3. Starting Slowly: Introduce herbs slowly into your routine and monitor how your body reacts, particularly when combining multiple herbs.

By integrating herbs into your daily life, you can improve digestion, boost immunity, reduce stress, and enhance your overall health and vitality. Inspired by Barbara O'Neill's holistic approach to health, these practices offer a natural way to support wellness through the consistent use of herbs.

# CHAPTER 08

# DETOXIFICATION AND CLEANSING

## UNDERSTANDING THE POWER OF DETOXIFICATION

In the world of holistic health, detoxification stands as a key pillar for maintaining balance and vitality. Rooted in Barbara O'Neill's extensive teachings, detoxification is not just a buzzword but a necessary practice for supporting the body's inherent ability to heal and cleanse itself from the toxic load of modern living.

Whether it's environmental pollutants, poor dietary choices, or stress, our bodies are continually exposed to substances that can compromise our health. Detoxification offers a reset, allowing the body to function at its best.

## HOW THE BODY NATURALLY DETOXIFIES

Your body is designed to detoxify itself every day, and several systems work in unison to eliminate toxins. These include the liver, kidneys, digestive system, lungs, and skin. The liver serves as the central detoxification hub, breaking down harmful substances so they can be safely eliminated.

The kidneys filter toxins from the blood, expelling them through urine, while the digestive system moves waste out of the body. Even your lungs and skin play critical roles, eliminating toxins through breathing and sweating.

While your body is fully equipped with these mechanisms, modern life can overwhelm them. Diets high in processed foods, exposure to chemicals, and chronic stress can lead to a buildup of toxins that your body struggles to clear. This is where intentional detoxification practices become essential, as they help restore balance and relieve the body of excess burden.

# RECOGNIZING THE NEED FOR DETOXIFICATION

Signs that your body may be struggling with detoxification are often subtle but significant. Persistent fatigue despite adequate sleep, digestive issues like bloating or constipation, recurring skin conditions such as acne or rashes, and even mental fog are all indicators that your body's detox pathways might need support. These are not symptoms to be ignored but signals that your body is asking for help.

# CORE DETOXIFICATION STRATEGIES

As a wellness coach and naturopath guided by Barbara O'Neill's principles, I emphasize a range of natural, practical approaches to detoxification that support the body's existing systems rather than overburden them.

1. Dietary Detoxification:

A plant-based, nutrient-dense diet is the foundation of any effective detox program. Incorporating foods like cruciferous vegetables (broccoli, cauliflower), leafy greens (spinach, kale), and citrus fruits (lemons, oranges) is essential for enhancing liver function and supporting digestion. These foods provide the vitamins, minerals, and antioxidants that drive detoxification.

2. Hydration:

Water is your body's essential detox tool. Staying hydrated flushes toxins through the kidneys and aids digestion. Make sure to drink clean, filtered water throughout the day and include hydrating foods like cucumbers and watermelon to boost your water intake.

3. Herbal Support:

Herbal remedies are a core part of detoxification. Milk thistle is particularly effective for protecting liver cells and promoting regeneration, while dandelion root and burdock root offer supportive roles in kidney function and blood purification. These herbs can be taken as teas or tinctures and are excellent adjuncts to a detox program.

4. Physical Activity:

Movement is vital for promoting circulation and lymphatic drainage, both of which are key to detoxification. Gentle exercises like yoga, walking, and even rebounding (small trampoline exercises) stimulate lymph flow and help the body eliminate waste.

## 5. Sweat Therapy:

Whether through vigorous exercise or sauna sessions, sweating is a natural way your body expels toxins. Infrared saunas, in particular, penetrate deeper into tissues, helping release stubborn toxins. I recommend combining sauna use with cold showers to boost circulation and support detox pathways.

## 6. Dry Brushing:

A simple but effective practice, dry brushing stimulates the lymphatic system and exfoliates the skin, which is another major detox organ. Using a natural bristle brush before your shower helps remove dead skin cells while enhancing blood flow.

## 7. Restorative Sleep:

Detoxification happens not just during the day but also while you sleep. Quality rest is critical for allowing the body to perform its deep cleaning functions. Establishing a consistent sleep routine is vital for optimal detoxification.

## 8. Stress Management:

Chronic stress can compromise your body's ability to detoxify effectively. Practices such as meditation, deep breathing, and spending time in nature help reduce stress and support detox processes. Remember that mental health is closely tied to physical well-being, and taking care of your mind is just as important as caring for your body.

# DETOX PROGRAMS AND FASTING

Barbara O'Neill advocates for periodic detox programs and fasting to give the body a break and reset its natural healing mechanisms. Here are some methods you can incorporate:

## 1. Juice Fasting:

A short juice fast, lasting one to three days, can deliver a concentrated dose of nutrients while giving your digestive system a rest. Fresh vegetable and fruit juices nourish your body and provide antioxidants to enhance detoxification.

## 2. Intermittent Fasting:

Alternating periods of eating and fasting, such as the popular 16/8 method, can give your body time to focus on repairing and detoxifying. This method can also improve metabolic health and support long-term vitality.

## 3. Detox Diets:

A detox diet can be as simple as eliminating processed foods, sugar, caffeine, and alcohol for a week or more, focusing on whole, plant-based foods instead. Supplementing this diet with herbs like milk thistle or turmeric can further support liver health.

## 4. Liver Cleanses:

A targeted liver cleanse involves consuming specific foods and supplements known to support liver function, such as beets, turmeric, and milk thistle. These ingredients boost the liver's ability to filter toxins and regenerate itself.

# SAFETY AND PRECAUTIONS

While detoxification is beneficial, it's important to approach it responsibly. Overdoing detox methods or fasting without proper guidance can be counterproductive. Always consult with a healthcare provider, especially if you have existing health conditions. Start slowly with any new detox practice, stay hydrated, and monitor your body's responses. Listen to your body and make adjustments as needed.

Detoxification is a vital practice for maintaining health in our toxin-laden world. Drawing from Barbara O'Neill's teachings, this chapter outlines practical and effective ways to integrate detoxification into your daily life.

By supporting your body's natural detox pathways through nutrition, hydration, herbal remedies, and lifestyle adjustments, you can experience the profound benefits of a cleaner, more vibrant body. Detoxification is not just about cleansing but empowering your body to thrive.

# NATURAL DETOX METHODS AND FOODS

Detoxification is an essential practice for maintaining long-term health and vitality. It's a process that involves supporting the body's natural mechanisms to eliminate toxins, reduce inflammation, and restore balance.

Barbara O'Neill, a well-respected voice in the field of natural health, consistently emphasizes the importance of integrating simple, natural detox methods and nourishing foods into everyday life. These strategies help promote the body's self-healing processes, enabling it to function at its peak.

## HYDRATION: THE FOUNDATION OF DETOXIFICATION

Water is the cornerstone of any detox regimen. It aids in flushing toxins out through urine and sweat, helping the body maintain proper function. Hydration is not just about drinking water; it's about making sure the water you consume is clean and pure.

- Water: Barbara recommends drinking at least 8-10 glasses of clean, filtered water daily to keep the kidneys functioning optimally. This supports the natural elimination of toxins through urine.

- Herbal Teas: Teas made from detoxifying herbs, like dandelion, nettle, and ginger, further enhance the body's ability to cleanse itself. These herbs not only support the liver and kidneys but also improve digestion and help reduce bloating.

## SWEATING: A KEY DETOX PATHWAY

The skin is one of the largest detoxification organs, and sweating is a powerful way to eliminate toxins, particularly heavy metals.

- Exercise: Engaging in regular physical activity, whether it's brisk walking, jogging, or yoga, promotes sweating and boosts circulation. Barbara suggests incorporating at least 30 minutes of movement daily to encourage toxin elimination.

- Saunas: For a more intensive detox, Barbara often recommends using saunas, especially infrared saunas, which can help the body release toxins stored deep within tissues. Alternating between sauna sessions and cold showers can improve circulation and enhance the detox effect.

## DRY BRUSHING: STIMULATING LYMPHATIC FLOW

Dry brushing is a simple, yet effective practice to exfoliate the skin and stimulate lymphatic drainage, which is critical for moving toxins out of the body.

- Skin Exfoliation: Using a natural bristle brush, dry brushing before a shower helps remove dead skin cells and encourages the release of toxins through the lymphatic system. Barbara advocates for this practice as part of a regular detox routine to promote smoother skin and better circulation.

# DEEP BREATHING EXERCISES: DETOXIFYING THROUGH OXYGENATION

Breathing is one of the most natural ways to detoxify. Deep breathing exercises help oxygenate the body and expel carbon dioxide, a metabolic waste product.

- Oxygenation: Barbara recommends techniques like diaphragmatic breathing or pranayama, as these methods not only increase oxygen levels but also support the body's detoxification process by clearing the lungs and improving circulation.

# COLON CLEANSING: SUPPORTING GUT HEALTH

A clean, well-functioning digestive system is essential for detoxification. Regular bowel movements help eliminate waste and prevent toxins from being reabsorbed into the bloodstream.

- Fiber-Rich Diet: A diet high in fiber from fruits, vegetables, and whole grains ensures regular bowel movements, which is key to colon health. Barbara emphasizes the importance of fiber for maintaining a clean and efficient digestive tract.

- Enemas and Colonics: While not always necessary, these methods can help remove built-up waste and improve gut function, especially for individuals dealing with chronic constipation or other digestive issues.

# DETOX FOODS: NOURISHING THE BODY FOR OPTIMAL CLEANSING

The right foods are as important as detox practices. A nutrient-dense diet provides the essential vitamins and minerals that support the body's detoxification systems, particularly the liver and kidneys.

1. Leafy Greens

- Kale, Spinach, Swiss Chard: These greens are packed with chlorophyll, which helps detoxify the liver and purify the blood. Barbara frequently advocates for adding leafy greens to every meal, noting their ability to support overall digestion and alkalize the body.

2. Cruciferous Vegetables

- Broccoli, Cauliflower, Brussels Sprouts: Cruciferous vegetables contain compounds that enhance the liver's detoxification process, enabling the body to neutralize and eliminate toxins more effectively. Regular consumption of these vegetables is a staple in Barbara's detox recommendations.

## 3. Berries

- Blueberries, Raspberries, Strawberries: These fruits are loaded with antioxidants that combat oxidative stress and inflammation—two conditions that often accompany toxin buildup. Barbara recommends a daily serving of berries to boost overall health and support detox pathways.

## 4. Citrus Fruits

- Lemons, Oranges, Grapefruits: Citrus fruits are rich in vitamin C and antioxidants that activate the body's detoxification enzymes. Starting the day with a glass of warm lemon water is one of Barbara's favorite tips for gently detoxifying the liver.

## 5. Herbs and Spices

- Turmeric, Ginger, Garlic: These potent herbs and spices have anti-inflammatory and antioxidant properties that support detoxification and strengthen the immune system. Barbara incorporates these ingredients into many of her detox recipes to enhance their effectiveness.

## 6. Green Tea

- Rich in Catechins: Green tea is known for its liver-supporting properties, thanks to its high concentration of catechins. Drinking several cups a day can help boost liver function and accelerate the elimination of toxins.

## 7. Probiotic-Rich Foods

- Yogurt, Sauerkraut, Kimchi: A healthy gut is critical for effective detoxification, and these probiotic-rich foods help maintain the balance of gut bacteria. Barbara emphasizes that a strong digestive system is key to any detox program.

## 8. Nuts and Seeds

- Flaxseeds, Chia Seeds, Almonds: These foods are excellent sources of fiber, healthy fats, and other essential nutrients that aid detoxification. Including a variety of nuts and seeds in your diet supports digestive health and promotes regular bowel movements, both of which are essential for toxin elimination.

By integrating natural detox methods and nourishing foods into your daily life, you can significantly enhance your body's ability to eliminate toxins and promote overall health.

Drawing from Barbara O'Neill's teachings, this holistic approach emphasizes supporting the body's natural processes through simple, sustainable practices like hydration, exercise, proper nutrition, and mindful breathing.

When practiced regularly, these detox strategies can help you achieve a cleaner, more balanced body, allowing you to feel your best every day.

## 14-DAYS SAFE AND EFFECTIVE DETOX PROGRAM

Detoxification is a natural and essential process that supports optimal health by eliminating toxins from the body. Inspired by Barbara O'Neill's holistic health principles, this 14-day detox program combines whole foods, hydration, exercise, and lifestyle practices to gently and effectively cleanse the body.

The goal is to enhance liver, kidney, and digestive health, improve energy levels, and support overall well-being.

## PROGRAM OVERVIEW:

- Duration: 14 Days

- Focus: Whole foods, hydration, exercise, and relaxation

- Goals: Support liver, kidney, and digestive health; enhance energy; and promote overall wellness

## GENERAL GUIDELINES FOR THE PROGRAM:

1. Whole Foods: Focus on a plant-based, nutrient-dense diet.

2. Hydration: Drink at least 8-10 glasses of filtered water daily, including herbal teas.

3. Exercise: Engage in light physical activities like yoga, walking, and stretching.

4. Rest and Recovery: Prioritize sleep and relaxation techniques to support the body's healing processes.

5. Herbs and Supplements: Use liver-supporting herbs such as milk thistle and dandelion root.

# DAILY MEAL PLAN BREAKDOWN:

**Morning Routine:**

- Start with Lemon Water: Begin each day with a glass of warm water with fresh lemon juice to stimulate digestion and detoxification.

- Herbal Tea: Sip on detox-supporting herbal teas such as ginger, dandelion root, or peppermint.

**Breakfast Options:**

- Green Smoothie: Blend spinach, kale, banana, flaxseeds, and a spoonful of spirulina for a nutrient-packed smoothie.

- Overnight Oats: Soak oats with chia seeds, almond milk, and berries for a fiber-rich breakfast that supports digestion.

**Mid-Morning Snack:**

- Fruit Salad: Include citrus fruits like oranges or grapefruit, along with antioxidant-rich berries.

- Handful of Nuts and Seeds: Almonds, sunflower seeds, or chia seeds to provide healthy fats and fiber.

**Lunch Options:**

- Quinoa and Vegetable Salad: Combine cooked quinoa with a variety of fresh vegetables like bell peppers, cucumbers, and leafy greens, topped with lemon-tahini dressing.

- Vegetable Soup: Enjoy a light, broth-based soup with vegetables such as carrots, celery, and broccoli, rich in detoxifying compounds.

**Afternoon Snack:**

- Herbal Tea: Drink a cup of green tea or turmeric-ginger tea for an antioxidant boost.

- Raw Veggies and Hummus: Carrot and cucumber sticks with hummus to support digestive health.

**Dinner Options:**

- Stir-Fried Vegetables: Lightly sauté broccoli, cauliflower, carrots, and tofu in coconut oil with garlic and ginger for added anti-inflammatory benefits.

- Baked Sweet Potatoes: Pair with a mixed greens salad and a simple olive oil and lemon dressing for a liver-supportive meal.

**Evening Routine:**

- Herbal Detox Tea: End the day with a soothing cup of chamomile or dandelion tea to relax and support liver function.

- Stretching and Meditation: Spend 10-15 minutes doing light stretches and deep breathing exercises to reduce stress and promote restful sleep.

## KEY DETOX FOODS TO INCLUDE:

1. Leafy Greens: Spinach, kale, Swiss chard – rich in chlorophyll, supporting liver function.

2. Cruciferous Vegetables: Broccoli, Brussels sprouts – contain compounds that enhance detoxification.

3. Berries: Blueberries, raspberries, strawberries – high in antioxidants to fight oxidative stress.

4. Citrus Fruits: Lemons, oranges, grapefruits – support liver enzymes and boost vitamin C intake.

5. Herbs and Spices: Ginger, turmeric, garlic – anti-inflammatory and immune-boosting properties.

6. Probiotic Foods: Sauerkraut, kimchi, yogurt – support gut health and digestion.

7. Hydrating Vegetables: Cucumbers, celery – keep the body hydrated and assist with kidney function.

## LIFESTYLE PRACTICES FOR OPTIMAL DETOXIFICATION

1. Dry Brushing: Stimulate lymphatic drainage and circulation by brushing the skin with a natural bristle brush before showering.

2. Sweat Therapy: Engage in light exercise or use an infrared sauna to promote toxin elimination through sweat.

3. Deep Breathing: Practice deep breathing exercises to enhance oxygen flow and eliminate toxins from the lungs.

4. Adequate Sleep: Ensure 7-8 hours of restful sleep each night to support the body's natural detoxification processes.

5. Stress Management: Incorporate meditation, mindfulness, and spending time in nature to reduce the effects of chronic stress on detoxification.

## HERBS AND SUPPLEMENTS FOR DETOX SUPPORT:

- Milk Thistle: Supports liver health and regeneration.

- Dandelion Root: Promotes bile production and kidney function.

- Burdock Root: Purifies the blood and supports liver and kidney detoxification.

- Spirulina: Provides powerful antioxidants that protect against free radicals.

## EXAMPLE DAY ON THE 14-DAY DETOX PROGRAM:

Morning:

- Start with a glass of lemon water

- Green smoothie with spinach, kale, banana, and spirulina

Mid-Morning:

- Herbal tea (ginger or peppermint)

- Handful of nuts and seeds

Lunch:

- Quinoa and vegetable salad with leafy greens, cucumbers, and a lemon-tahini dressing

Afternoon:

- Green tea or herbal detox tea

- Raw veggie sticks with hummus

Dinner:

- Stir-fried vegetables (broccoli, cauliflower, tofu) with garlic and ginger

- Baked sweet potato with mixed greens

Evening:

- Chamomile or dandelion tea

- Light stretching and deep breathing exercises

This 14-day detox program integrates Barbara O'Neill's holistic approach to natural detoxification, focusing on whole foods, hydration, exercise, and relaxation.

By following this plan, you will support your body's natural detox processes, enhance liver, kidney, and digestive health, and experience improved energy and overall well-being.

Always remember to listen to your body, adjust as needed, and consult with a healthcare provider if you have specific medical concerns. Detoxification is not just about cleansing the body, but also about nourishing it and fostering long-term health.

# 14-DAY DAILY DETOX ROUTINE

This detox routine is structured to gently cleanse and rejuvenate the body over two phases: the Preparation Phase (Days 1-7) and the Deep Cleanse Phase (Days 8-14). The plan focuses on whole foods, hydration, and lifestyle practices that support detoxification and overall well-being.

# DAYS 1-7: PREPARATION PHASE

Morning Routine

- Warm Lemon Water: Start the day with a glass of warm lemon water to stimulate digestion and liver function.

- Deep Breathing Exercises: Spend 5-10 minutes practicing deep breathing to oxygenate the body and reduce stress.

Breakfast

- Green Smoothie: Blend spinach, kale, banana, apple, chia seeds, and almond milk for a nutrient-dense smoothie, rich in fiber, vitamins, and minerals to start the day.

Mid-Morning Snack

- Fresh Fruit: Choose fresh fruit such as an apple, pear, or berries. These provide natural sugars for energy and fiber for digestion.

Lunch

- Quinoa Salad: Combine cooked quinoa with cucumber, tomatoes, bell peppers, and fresh herbs (parsley or cilantro), dressed with lemon juice and olive oil.

- Herbal Tea: Drink a cup of detoxifying herbal tea such as dandelion root or nettle.

## Afternoon Snack

- Nuts and Seeds: A small handful of raw almonds, walnuts, or sunflower seeds for healthy fats and protein.

## Dinner

- Vegetable Soup: A hearty vegetable soup made with carrots, celery, zucchini, and leafy greens. Add garlic and ginger for detox support.

- Mixed Green Salad: A simple salad with mixed greens, avocado, and a light vinaigrette.

## Evening Routine

- Detox Bath: Take a warm Epsom salt bath to relax muscles and draw out toxins.

- Herbal Tea: Drink chamomile tea to promote restful sleep.

# DAYS 8-14: DEEP CLEANSE PHASE

## Morning Routine

- Warm Lemon Water: Continue starting the day with warm lemon water.

- Dry Brushing: Before showering, spend a few minutes dry brushing to stimulate lymphatic drainage and exfoliate the skin.

## Breakfast

- Detox Juice: Make juice with beets, carrots, apple, ginger, and a bit of lemon to support liver detoxification.

## Mid-Morning Snack

- Raw Veggies: Snack on raw vegetables like carrot sticks, celery, and bell peppers with a small amount of hummus.

## Lunch

- Detox Salad: A large salad with mixed greens, shredded cabbage, grated beets, and carrots topped with sunflower seeds and dressed with tahini-lemon dressing.

- Herbal Tea: Drink a cup of milk thistle tea to support liver health.

Afternoon Snack

- Green Smoothie: Try a green smoothie with kale, pineapple, cucumber, and a spoonful of spirulina powder for added detox benefits.

Dinner

- Steamed Vegetables and Brown Rice: Steamed broccoli, cauliflower, and green beans with a side of brown rice and a drizzle of olive oil.

- Mixed Green Salad: Continue with a fresh green salad with a light vinaigrette.

Evening Routine

- Gentle Yoga or Stretching: Spend 15-20 minutes doing gentle yoga or stretching to relax the body.

- Herbal Tea: End the day with peppermint tea to aid digestion.

## ADDITIONAL DETOX PRACTICES

1. Hydration: Drink 8-10 glasses of water daily. Enhance with slices of cucumber, lemon, or fresh mint for added detox benefits.

2. Exercise: Incorporate 30 minutes of moderate exercise daily, such as brisk walking, yoga, or cycling to promote circulation and lymphatic drainage.

3. Sleep: Aim for 7-8 hours of quality sleep each night to support detoxification.

4. Avoid Toxins: Reduce exposure to environmental toxins by choosing organic foods, using natural cleaning products, and avoiding processed foods and alcohol.

This 14-day detox program, inspired by Barbara O'Neill's holistic approach, is designed to gently cleanse and rejuvenate the body.

It focuses on whole foods, hydration, and lifestyle practices that promote natural detoxification processes, leading to increased energy, a refreshed body, and long-term health benefits.

By following this structured daily routine, you will feel more balanced, energized, and in tune with your body's natural ability to heal and thrive.

# CHAPTER 09

## MANAGING STRESS AND ENHANCING EMOTIONAL WELLNESS

In our fast-paced world, stress is a constant part of daily life. While stress is a natural response to challenging situations, chronic stress can have serious effects on physical and emotional health.

Managing stress holistically is crucial for overall well-being, a principle deeply emphasized by Barbara O'Neill. This chapter delves into how stress affects the body and mind, and presents effective strategies to manage and reduce it.

## THE PHYSICAL IMPACT OF STRESS

Stress triggers a series of physiological reactions to help the body cope with perceived threats, known as the "fight or flight" response. This involves the release of hormones like adrenaline and cortisol. While helpful in short bursts, chronic stress can lead to various health problems:

1. Cardiovascular Health

Chronic stress can elevate blood pressure, heart rate, and cholesterol levels, increasing the risk of heart disease and stroke. Long-term strain on the cardiovascular system can also lead to inflammation and damage to blood vessels.

2. Immune Function

Stress weakens the immune system, making the body more susceptible to infections. Cortisol suppresses white blood cell production, reducing the body's ability to fight off pathogens.

3. Digestive Health

Stress can disrupt the digestive system, leading to conditions like irritable bowel syndrome (IBS), acid reflux, and ulcers. It also alters gut microbiota, affecting digestion and nutrient absorption.

4. Musculoskeletal System

Stress often manifests as muscle tension, particularly in the neck, shoulders, and back. Chronic tension can lead to headaches, migraines, and long-term discomfort.

5. Endocrine System

Stress disrupts hormone balance, leading to irregular menstrual cycles, reduced fertility, and the worsening of menopause symptoms or hormonal imbalances.

# THE EMOTIONAL AND MENTAL IMPACT OF STRESS

Stress affects not only physical health but also emotional well-being. Barbara O'Neill highlights the connection between the mind and body, emphasizing emotional wellness as an essential aspect of holistic health.

1. Anxiety and Depression

Chronic stress is a major contributor to anxiety and depression. Feelings of overwhelm and constant alertness can result in persistent worry, fear, or sadness.

2. Cognitive Function

Stress impairs cognitive abilities, such as memory, concentration, and decision-making. Prolonged stress can affect the brain's prefrontal cortex, hindering clear thinking and problem-solving.

3. Sleep Disturbances

Stress often causes insomnia or poor-quality sleep. Sleep deprivation further worsens stress, creating a cycle of fatigue and tension.

4. Emotional Regulation

Chronic stress can lead to mood swings, irritability, and difficulty managing emotions. This imbalance can strain relationships and affect daily functioning.

# HOLISTIC STRESS MANAGEMENT

Barbara O'Neill advocates for a holistic approach to stress management, focusing on the interconnectedness of the mind, body, and spirit. Effective stress management involves addressing all aspects of health:

## 1. Nutrition

A balanced diet rich in whole foods, vitamins, and minerals helps build resilience against stress. Antioxidant-rich foods, like fruits and vegetables, combat oxidative stress and inflammation.

## 2. Physical Activity

Regular exercise is a powerful tool for managing stress. It stimulates the release of endorphins, improving mood and sleep while reducing anxiety. Consistency is key, so choose exercises you enjoy.

## 3. Mindfulness and Relaxation

Practices like meditation, deep breathing, and yoga can calm the mind, reduce stress, and improve emotional regulation. Barbara O'Neill emphasizes taking time for mindfulness and self-care.

## 4. Social Support

Building and maintaining positive relationships can reduce feelings of isolation. Sharing stressors with trusted friends or family provides emotional relief and perspective.

## 5. Rest and Sleep

Quality sleep is essential for managing stress and restoring the body. Creating a restful environment and sticking to a sleep schedule can improve resilience to stress.

## 6. Herbal Remedies

Certain herbs, like chamomile, lavender, and ashwagandha, have calming properties. These can be incorporated into daily routines through teas, tinctures, or supplements to help manage stress.

# NATURAL STRESS RELIEF TECHNIQUES

Managing stress through natural methods is an effective way to promote emotional wellness. Barbara O'Neill often teaches natural techniques that support the body's ability to cope with stress.

## 1. MINDFULNESS AND MEDITATION

- Breathing Exercises: Focus on deep, slow breathing to calm the nervous system.

- Body Scan Meditation: Focus on different parts of the body, consciously relaxing tense areas.

- Mindful Walking: Pay attention to your steps and breath, transforming a simple walk into a meditative experience.

## 2. PHYSICAL ACTIVITY AND EXERCISE

Exercise releases endorphins and reduces stress. Barbara O'Neill promotes physical activity as a key stress-reliever.

- Aerobic Exercise: Activities like walking, jogging, and swimming reduce stress and improve cardiovascular health.

- Yoga: Combines physical postures, breathing, and meditation to reduce stress.

- Tai Chi: Slow, deliberate movements and deep breathing calm the mind.

- Strength Training: Builds physical strength and reduces stress.

Managing stress is essential for maintaining physical and emotional health. By adopting a holistic approach to stress management—incorporating nutrition, exercise, mindfulness, and social support—you can reduce the effects of stress and enhance overall well-being.

Inspired by Barbara O'Neill's teachings, this chapter offers a comprehensive guide to managing stress naturally, promoting a balanced, healthy, and emotionally resilient life.

Managing stress and nurturing emotional wellness are essential for maintaining overall health and quality of life. In this chapter, we explore holistic practices inspired by Barbara O'Neill's teachings, emphasizing natural remedies, lifestyle changes, and emotional support to reduce stress and enhance well-being.

# 3. HERBAL REMEDIES

Herbs have long been used to promote relaxation, reduce anxiety, and manage stress. Barbara O'Neill frequently recommends herbal remedies as a part of a holistic approach to emotional wellness.

Common Stress-Relieving Herbs

- Ashwagandha: An adaptogen that helps the body adapt to stress and supports adrenal health.

- Chamomile: Known for its calming properties, chamomile tea can help reduce anxiety and promote better sleep.

- Lavender: Lavender essential oil, used in aromatherapy, is known for its soothing effects, helping to calm the mind.

- Valerian Root: Often used as a natural remedy to relax the nervous system and improve sleep quality.

- Lemon Balm: A herb from the mint family that can help ease anxiety and enhance mood.

# 4. NUTRITION AND HYDRATION

Proper nutrition and hydration are crucial for managing stress and maintaining mental and emotional balance. Barbara O'Neill emphasizes that a nutrient-dense diet can directly affect emotional health.

## Nutritional Tips for Stress Relief

- Balanced Diet: Consuming whole foods, such as fruits, vegetables, lean proteins, and healthy fats, ensures your body gets the nutrients it needs to combat stress.

- Hydration: Staying hydrated with plenty of water supports both physical and mental health. Dehydration can lead to heightened anxiety and fatigue.

- Magnesium-Rich Foods: Magnesium helps regulate the nervous system. Leafy greens, nuts, seeds, and whole grains are excellent sources.

- Omega-3 Fatty Acids: Found in fatty fish, flaxseeds, and walnuts, omega-3s support brain health and reduce inflammation, which can impact emotional well-being.

- B Vitamins: B vitamins play a crucial role in energy production and stress management, found in whole grains, legumes, and leafy greens.

# 5. ADEQUATE SLEEP

Chronic sleep deprivation worsens stress and negatively affects mental clarity, mood, and emotional regulation. Prioritizing quality sleep can dramatically improve resilience to stress.

**Tips for Improving Sleep**

- Establish a Routine: Consistently going to bed and waking up at the same time helps regulate your circadian rhythm.

- Create a Relaxing Environment: Keep your bedroom cool, dark, and quiet to create an ideal sleep setting.

- Limit Screen Time: Reduce exposure to screens before bed, as blue light disrupts the production of melatonin, the sleep hormone.

- Practice Relaxation Techniques: Incorporate deep breathing exercises or calming music into your bedtime routine to promote relaxation.

# 6. SOCIAL SUPPORT AND CONNECTION

Building strong social connections is vital for emotional well-being. Barbara O'Neill emphasizes the importance of emotional support systems in managing stress and maintaining balance.

**Ways to Enhance Social Support**

- Connect with Loved Ones: Regularly spend time with family and friends, either in person or virtually.

- Join a Community: Engage in community groups, clubs, or activities that align with your interests.

- Seek Professional Support: Talking to a therapist or counselor can provide additional emotional support and coping strategies.

# 7. HOBBIES AND LEISURE ACTIVITIES

Engaging in hobbies and leisure activities provides a healthy distraction from stress, helping you relax and enjoy life.

Ideas for Hobbies and Leisure Activities

- Creative Arts: Painting, drawing, or writing can reduce stress while promoting self-expression.

- Gardening: Being outdoors and tending to plants is therapeutic and can boost mood.

- Reading: Enjoying books, especially those that inspire, can provide mental relaxation and a break from daily stressors.

- Puzzles and Games: Engaging in puzzles or board games can stimulate the mind and offer a fun way to unwind.

# 8. AROMATHERAPY

Aromatherapy, using essential oils, is a natural method to relieve stress and enhance emotional balance. Barbara O'Neill often recommends aromatherapy for emotional wellness.

### Popular Essential Oils for Stress Relief

- Lavender: Known for its calming and soothing properties.

- Bergamot: A citrus oil with uplifting and calming effects.

- Chamomile: Helps soothe nerves and promote relaxation.

- Frankincense: A grounding oil often used in meditation.

### Ways to Use Essential Oils

- Diffusion: Use an essential oil diffuser to fill your space with calming aromas.

- Topical Application: Dilute essential oils with a carrier oil (e.g., coconut or almond oil) and apply them to the skin for localized relaxation.

- Baths: Add a few drops of essential oil to your bath for a calming experience.

# 9. PRACTICES FOR EMOTIONAL BALANCE AND WELL-BEING

Achieving emotional balance is essential for overall well-being. Barbara O'Neill emphasizes the importance of mindfulness, physical activity, and spiritual practices in maintaining emotional stability.

### Mindfulness and Meditation

- Mindful Breathing: Focus on slow, deep breaths to calm the mind.

- Guided Meditation: Listening to guided meditation can help focus the mind and reduce anxiety.

- Loving-Kindness Meditation: Focus on cultivating compassion and empathy for yourself and others.

**Physical Activity**

- Yoga: Combining movement with deep breathing to reduce stress and enhance emotional resilience.

- Aerobic Exercise: Engaging in activities like walking, running, or swimming can boost mood by releasing endorphins.

**Herbal Remedies**

- Ashwagandha: Helps the body manage stress and supports emotional balance.

- Chamomile: Calming effects for emotional wellness and improved sleep.

# A HOLISTIC APPROACH TO EMOTIONAL WELLNESS

Incorporating these natural practices—herbal remedies, nutrition, exercise, mindfulness, and social connection—can enhance emotional well-being and manage stress effectively.

Inspired by Barbara O'Neill's holistic approach, you can create a life centered on balance, peace, and well-being. Embrace these practices to nurture your mind, body, and spirit, and lead a more harmonious, stress-free life.

# CHAPTER 10

## BOOSTING IMMUNITY NATURALLY

## HERBS AND FOODS FOR IMMUNE SUPPORT

Maintaining a resilient immune system is essential in today's fast-paced world, where stress, pollution, and an unhealthy diet can weaken our body's defenses. Boosting immunity naturally through the integration of herbs and nutrient-rich foods is a powerful way to protect against infections and promote overall well-being.

Inspired by Barbara O'Neill's holistic teachings, we explore herbs and foods that support immune health while also emphasizing the importance of adopting daily practices for optimal immune resilience.

1. Echinacea (Echinacea purpurea)

- Key Elements: Echinacea is renowned for its ability to stimulate the immune system, specifically by increasing the production of white blood cells, which are essential for fighting off infections.

- Uses Against Diseases: It is widely used for the prevention and treatment of colds, flu, and respiratory infections. It reduces both the duration and severity of symptoms when used at the onset of illness.

- Preparation Methods: Echinacea can be consumed as a tea, tincture, or in capsule form. For tea, steep 1-2 teaspoons of dried echinacea in hot water for 10-15 minutes.

- Dosage, Safety, and Precautions: A typical dosage is 300 mg of extract three times daily. While generally safe for short-term use, individuals with autoimmune disorders should seek professional advice before using echinacea.

2. Garlic (Allium sativum)

- Key Elements: Garlic is well-known for its potent antibacterial, antiviral, and antifungal properties, making it an excellent addition to an immune-boosting regimen.

- Uses Against Diseases: Garlic helps prevent and treat colds, flu, and respiratory infections. It also has cardiovascular benefits, such as lowering blood pressure and reducing cholesterol levels.

- Preparation Methods: Garlic can be consumed raw, cooked, or taken as a supplement. For maximum immune benefits, crush or chop garlic and let it sit for 10 minutes to activate the allicin.

- Dosage, Safety, and Precautions: The recommended dose is 1-2 cloves of raw garlic daily or 600-1200 mg of aged garlic extract. While garlic is generally safe, it may cause digestive issues or bad breath for some individuals.

3. Ginger (Zingiber officinale)

- Key Elements: Ginger's anti-inflammatory and antioxidant properties make it a valuable herb for reducing inflammation and supporting immune health.

- Uses Against Diseases: It is particularly effective in treating respiratory infections, sore throats, and digestive issues such as nausea.

- Preparation Methods: Ginger can be added to meals, consumed as a tea, or taken in supplement form. For ginger tea, steep 1-2 teaspoons of freshly grated ginger in hot water for 10-15 minutes.

- Dosage, Safety, and Precautions: A dose of 1-3 grams of ginger daily is recommended. While ginger is generally safe, excessive consumption may lead to heartburn or digestive discomfort.

4. Elderberry (Sambucus nigra)

- Key Elements: Elderberry is rich in antioxidants, particularly anthocyanins, which support immune function and help the body ward off infections.

- Uses Against Diseases: It is effective in preventing and treating colds, flu, and sinus infections, reducing the severity and duration of symptoms.

- Preparation Methods: Elderberry can be consumed as a syrup, tea, or supplement. To make elderberry syrup, simmer 1 cup of dried elderberries with 4 cups of water until reduced by half, then strain and add honey.

- Dosage, Safety, and Precautions: A typical dose is 1-2 tablespoons of syrup daily. However, raw elderberries are toxic and must not be consumed without proper preparation.

5. Turmeric (Curcuma longa)

- Key Elements: Turmeric is a powerful anti-inflammatory herb that supports the immune system by reducing inflammation and oxidative stress.

- Uses Against Diseases: It is highly effective in managing inflammatory conditions, enhancing immune function, and promoting overall health.

- Preparation Methods: Turmeric can be consumed in food, made into a tea, or taken as a supplement. For turmeric tea, simmer 1 teaspoon of turmeric powder in water for 10 minutes, then strain.

- Dosage, Safety, and Precautions: The recommended dosage is 500-2000 mg of turmeric extract daily. While generally safe, turmeric may cause digestive issues in high doses and should be avoided by individuals with gallbladder disease.

6. Astragalus (Astragalus membranaceus)

- Key Elements: Astragalus is a revered adaptogenic herb that boosts the immune system and helps the body resist physical, emotional, and environmental stress.

- Uses Against Diseases: It is especially effective in preventing colds and respiratory infections and supports overall vitality and longevity.

- Preparation Methods: Astragalus can be taken as a tea, tincture, or supplement. For tea, simmer 1-2 teaspoons of dried astragalus root in water for 20-30 minutes.

- Dosage, Safety, and Precautions: A typical dose is 250-500 mg of astragalus extract 2-3 times daily. It is generally safe but may interact with immune-suppressing medications.

## 7. Reishi Mushroom (Ganoderma lucidum)

- Key Elements: Reishi mushrooms are known for their ability to enhance immune function, reduce stress, and improve overall health due to their adaptogenic properties.

- Uses Against Diseases: Reishi helps prevent infections, reduce inflammation, and promote longevity.

- Preparation Methods: Reishi can be consumed as tea, tincture, or supplement. For tea, simmer 1-2 slices of dried reishi mushroom in water for 30-45 minutes.

- Dosage, Safety, and Precautions: A dose of 1-2 grams of reishi extract daily is recommended. While generally safe, it may cause mild digestive issues for some individuals.

# DAILY PRACTICES TO STRENGTHEN IMMUNITY

A strong immune system is built on consistent daily habits that support physical, mental, and emotional well-being. Integrating immune-boosting herbs and foods into your diet is essential, but adopting holistic daily practices can further reinforce your body's natural defenses.

## 1. Prioritize Quality Sleep

Importance: Sleep is crucial for immune health as the body repairs itself and produces immune cells during rest.

Daily Practice:

- Establish a routine: Go to bed and wake up at the same time daily, even on weekends.

- Create a sleep-conducive environment: Ensure your bedroom is dark, cool, and quiet.

- Limit screen time: Avoid screens an hour before bed to reduce blue light interference with melatonin production.

- Relaxation techniques: Incorporate activities like meditation, reading, or a warm bath to unwind before sleep.

## 2. Maintain a Balanced Diet

Importance: A nutrient-rich diet supports immune function by providing essential vitamins, minerals, and antioxidants.

Daily Practice:

- Eat a rainbow: Incorporate a variety of colorful fruits and vegetables to ensure a broad spectrum of nutrients.

- Focus on whole foods: Prioritize unprocessed foods like whole grains, lean proteins, and healthy fats.

- Stay hydrated: Drink plenty of water to support detoxification and cellular function.

## 3. Engage in Regular Physical Activity

Importance: Exercise improves circulation, helping immune cells move effectively throughout the body.

Daily Practice:

- Consistency: Aim for at least 30 minutes of moderate activity, such as brisk walking, yoga, or swimming.

- Variety: Incorporate both aerobic exercises and strength training to maximize immune benefits.

- Find joy in movement: Choose activities you enjoy to stay consistent and motivated.

## 4. Manage Stress Effectively

Importance: Chronic stress weakens the immune system, making the body more susceptible to illness.

Daily Practice:

- Mindfulness and meditation: Practice these techniques to reduce stress and improve mental clarity.

- Deep breathing exercises: Engage in deep breathing to activate the body's relaxation response.

- Prayer or reflection: Incorporate spiritual practices to foster peace and connection.

## 5. Foster Social Connections

Importance: Strong social ties and community involvement reduce stress and enhance emotional well-being, which directly impacts immune function.

Daily Practice:

- Stay connected: Make time for family and friends, even if it's just a phone call.

- Engage in community: Participate in activities, clubs, or support groups.

- Acts of kindness: Engaging in helping others can boost your mood and overall health.

## 6. Spend Time Outdoors

Importance: Exposure to sunlight is crucial for producing vitamin D, an essential nutrient for immune function. Spending time in nature also has a calming effect on both the mind and body, reducing stress and improving overall wellness. Barbara O'Neill advocates for regular outdoor activities to balance physical and mental health.

Daily Practice:

- Sunlight Exposure: Aim for 15-30 minutes of sunlight exposure daily, particularly in the morning. This helps regulate your circadian rhythm and provides natural vitamin D.

- Nature Walks: Incorporate regular walks in nature to benefit from fresh air, sunlight, and gentle physical activity.

- Outdoor Activities: Engage in hobbies like gardening, hiking, or outdoor sports to combine physical activity with the restorative power of nature.

## 7. Incorporate Herbal Supplements

Importance: Certain herbs and supplements provide additional immune support, working in tandem with the body's natural defenses. Barbara O'Neill frequently highlights the role of herbal teas and supplements in boosting immunity, particularly during times of increased stress or seasonal changes.

Daily Practice:

- Herbal Teas: Drink immune-boosting herbal teas, such as echinacea, ginger, and elderberry. These herbs help strengthen your body's defenses against infections.

- Dietary Supplements: Consider integrating supplements like vitamin C, vitamin D, zinc, and probiotics into your daily routine, particularly during flu season or times when your immune system may need extra support.

- Consistent Use: Make these herbs and supplements a regular part of your routine to ensure continuous immune support. Consistency is key in building long-term resilience.

By adopting these immune-boosting foods, herbs, and holistic lifestyle practices, you can significantly enhance your immune system's resilience. Barbara O'Neill's teachings emphasize the importance of a holistic approach, integrating both physical and emotional health, to achieve lasting wellness.

# LIFESTYLE CHANGES FOR A RESILIENT IMMUNE SYSTEM

Creating a strong and resilient immune system is about more than quick fixes; it requires adopting sustainable lifestyle habits that support long-term health. Drawing from Barbara O'Neill's holistic principles, these practices will help fortify your immune system and improve your overall wellness.

## 1. BALANCED NUTRITION

Importance: Nutrition forms the foundation of a robust immune system. Eating a balanced diet ensures that your body gets the essential nutrients it needs to function optimally and fight off illnesses.

Key Practices:

- Whole Foods: Focus on a variety of whole, unprocessed foods rich in vitamins, minerals, and antioxidants, including fruits, vegetables, whole grains, nuts, and lean proteins.

- Superfoods: Incorporate immune-boosting superfoods like garlic, ginger, turmeric, and leafy greens for their anti-inflammatory and antioxidant properties.

- Healthy Fats: Include sources of healthy fats like avocados, nuts, seeds, and olive oil, which support cellular health and reduce inflammation.

- Reduce Sugar and Processed Foods: Limit your intake of sugar and processed foods, as they can suppress immune function and contribute to inflammation.

## REGULAR EXERCISE

Importance: Regular exercise helps improve circulation, reduce stress, and increase the movement of immune cells throughout the body, enhancing your immune function.

Key Practices:

- Consistency: Aim for at least 150 minutes of moderate aerobic activity per week, or 75 minutes of vigorous activity, along with strength training exercises.

- Variety: Mix cardiovascular activities, strength training, flexibility exercises, and balance-promoting practices to build a comprehensive fitness routine.

- Enjoyable Activities: Choose activities that you enjoy, such as walking, dancing, or yoga, to stay motivated and consistent over the long term.

# 3. QUALITY SLEEP

Importance: Sleep is critical for immune health, allowing the body to repair, regenerate, and produce important immune cells and proteins.

Key Practices:

- Sleep Hygiene: Establish a relaxing bedtime routine and stick to a consistent sleep schedule to improve sleep quality.

- Sleep Environment: Optimize your bedroom for rest by keeping it dark, quiet, and cool. Use blackout curtains and white noise machines if needed.

- Limit Stimulants: Avoid caffeine, large meals, and electronic screens close to bedtime, as these can disrupt your sleep.

# 4. STRESS MANAGEMENT

Importance: Chronic stress weakens the immune system and leaves the body more vulnerable to illness. Managing stress effectively is crucial for long-term health.

Key Practices:

- Mindfulness and Meditation: Practice mindfulness or meditation to reduce stress and improve emotional resilience.

- Deep Breathing: Use deep breathing exercises to activate the parasympathetic nervous system, promoting relaxation and reducing stress.

- Prayer and Reflection: Incorporate moments of prayer or reflection into your routine to foster a sense of peace and connection.

# 5. HYDRATION

Importance: Proper hydration is essential for maintaining immune function and the health of every cell in the body.

Key Practices:

- Water Intake: Drink at least eight 8-ounce glasses of water a day, more if you are active or live in a warm climate.

- Hydrating Foods: Include hydrating foods such as cucumbers, watermelon, and oranges in your diet.

- Limit Dehydrating Beverages: Reduce consumption of caffeine and alcohol, as these can contribute to dehydration.

# 6. SOCIAL CONNECTIONS

Importance: A strong support system and positive social interactions are essential for emotional health and, by extension, immune health.

Key Practices:

- Stay Connected: Keep in touch with friends and family through calls, video chats, or visits.

- Community Involvement: Engage in community activities or groups that interest you and offer emotional support.

- Acts of Kindness: Performing acts of kindness can boost your mood and overall well-being, which indirectly strengthens your immune system.

# 7. EXPOSURE TO NATURE

Importance: Spending time outdoors in nature helps reduce stress, improve mood, and support immune health, especially through vitamin D production.

Key Practices:

- Outdoor Activities: Incorporate outdoor activities like hiking, gardening, or walking into your daily routine.

- Sunlight Exposure: Aim for 15-30 minutes of direct sunlight daily to help maintain healthy vitamin D levels.

# 8. PERSONAL HYGIENE

Importance: Good hygiene habits are essential to prevent infections and maintain a strong immune system.

Key Practices:

- Hand Washing: Wash your hands regularly, especially before eating and after being in public spaces.

- Oral Hygiene: Brush and floss daily to prevent oral infections that could affect your immune system.

- Clean Environment: Keep your living space clean to minimize exposure to harmful pathogens.

## 9. HERBAL SUPPORT

Importance: Herbal teas and supplements provide additional support to the immune system, helping to fortify the body's defenses.

Key Practices:

- Herbal Teas: Drink immune-boosting herbal teas like echinacea, elderberry, and astragalus regularly.

- Dietary Supplements: Take vitamin C, vitamin D, zinc, and probiotics, especially during times of stress or illness.

- Consistent Use: Make these herbs and supplements part of your daily routine for long-term immune support.

By incorporating these lifestyle changes inspired by Barbara O'Neill's holistic approach, you can strengthen your immune system and improve your overall well-being.

Consistency in these practices will help build a resilient body, mind, and spirit, promoting health and longevity.

# CHAPTER 11

## DIGESTIVE HEALTH AND HERBAL REMEDIES

Digestive health is central to overall well-being, influencing everything from energy levels to immune function. Understanding common digestive issues and their symptoms is critical for maintaining gut health.

In this chapter, we explore some prevalent digestive disorders, the symptoms they present, and how to manage them using both lifestyle changes and herbal remedies.

## THE IMPORTANCE OF ACID-ALKALINE BALANCE

A proper acid-alkaline balance in the body is essential for optimal health. The pH level, which measures how acidic or alkaline a substance is, affects multiple bodily functions, including digestion, immunity, and energy metabolism. Achieving the right balance is crucial for maintaining your health and preventing disease.

## UNDERSTANDING PH BALANCE

The pH scale ranges from 0 (most acidic) to 14 (most alkaline), with 7 being neutral. The body functions best at a slightly alkaline level, around 7.4. While our bodies have mechanisms to maintain this balance, diet and lifestyle can either support or hinder these processes.

## WHY PH BALANCE MATTERS

1. Enzyme Function: Many enzymes that drive essential biochemical reactions work best within specific pH ranges.

2. Metabolism: Balanced pH ensures efficient energy production and nutrient absorption.

3. Immune System: An alkaline environment supports immune function, helping the body fend off infections.

4. Bone Health: Maintaining alkalinity prevents the body from leaching calcium from bones to neutralize excess acid, thus protecting against osteoporosis.

# CONSEQUENCES OF IMBALANCE

An imbalanced pH can lead to several health issues:

- Acidosis: Excessive acidity can cause fatigue, confusion, headaches, and increase the risk of chronic conditions like diabetes and cancer.

- Alkalosis: Though less common, excess alkalinity can lead to nausea, muscle twitching, and confusion.

# FACTORS AFFECTING PH BALANCE

Several factors, including diet, stress, and lifestyle, can impact your body's pH. Processed foods, sugar, and high stress promote acidity, while a diet rich in vegetables, fruits, and water promotes alkalinity.

# PRACTICAL TIPS FOR MAINTAINING ACID-ALKALINE BALANCE

1. Dietary Changes:

- Increase Alkaline Foods: Focus on vegetables (especially leafy greens), fruits, nuts, and seeds.

- Reduce Acidic Foods: Limit processed foods, sugar, red meats, and dairy products.

- Balance Your Plate: Make sure your meals contain a higher proportion of alkaline-forming foods to balance out acidic ones.

2. Hydration:

- Drink Water: Stay hydrated throughout the day to help flush out toxins.

- Alkaline Water: Consider incorporating alkaline water to help balance your body's pH.

3. Natural Supplements:

- Lemon Water: Although acidic, lemon has an alkalizing effect when metabolized, making it a great addition to your morning routine.

- Apple Cider Vinegar: Diluted in water, apple cider vinegar can aid digestion and promote pH balance.

4. Lifestyle Adjustments:

- Exercise: Regular physical activity supports metabolism and helps maintain pH balance.

- Stress Management: Practices like yoga, meditation, and deep breathing reduce stress, which can contribute to acidity.

5. Monitoring pH:

- pH Testing: Use strips to test your saliva or urine pH and monitor how diet and lifestyle choices impact your acid-alkaline balance.

Maintaining an acid-alkaline balance is key for optimal health. By incorporating mindful dietary choices, hydration, and lifestyle changes, you can promote a balanced internal environment that supports both physical and emotional well-being.

# COMMON DIGESTIVE DISORDERS AND HERBAL REMEDIES

## 1. GASTROESOPHAGEAL REFLUX DISEASE (GERD)

GERD is a chronic condition where stomach acid flows back into the esophagus, causing irritation. This happens when the lower esophageal sphincter (LES) does not close properly, allowing acid to escape.

Symptoms:

- Heartburn, especially after meals or at night

- Regurgitation of sour or bitter-tasting acid

- Difficulty swallowing

- Chronic cough or throat irritation

- Hoarseness or sore throat

Herbal Remedies:

- Peppermint Tea: Peppermint helps soothe digestive discomfort, but it should be avoided in severe cases of GERD as it can relax the LES.

- Instructions: Steep 1-2 tsp. of peppermint leaves in boiling water for 10 minutes. Drink 1-2 cups daily, especially after meals.

- Precaution: Avoid if you have a hiatal hernia or severe GERD.

- Chamomile Tea: Chamomile is anti-inflammatory and can soothe the digestive tract.

- Instructions: Steep 2-3 tsp. of dried chamomile flowers in boiling water for 5-10 minutes. Drink 2-3 cups daily.

- Precaution: Avoid if allergic to ragweed or related plants.

- Slippery Elm Lozenges: Slippery elm forms a soothing coating in the throat and esophagus.

- Instructions: Mix 1 tsp. of slippery elm powder with water or honey to form lozenges. Suck on these as needed.

- Precaution: Ensure adequate water intake to prevent choking.

## 2. IRRITABLE BOWEL SYNDROME (IBS)

IBS affects the large intestine, causing abdominal pain, bloating, and changes in bowel habits. The cause is believed to be a combination of abnormal gut movements, heightened pain sensitivity, and brain-gut communication issues.

Symptoms:

- Abdominal pain and cramping

- Bloating and gas

- Diarrhea, constipation, or alternating between the two

- Mucus in stool

- Incomplete bowel movements

Herbal Remedies:

- Peppermint Oil Capsules: Enteric-coated capsules can ease IBS symptoms by relaxing muscles in the digestive tract.

- Dosage: Take 1-2 capsules, 2-3 times daily before meals.

- Precaution: Only use enteric-coated capsules to avoid heartburn.

- Ginger Tea: Ginger reduces nausea and aids digestion.

- Instructions: Boil 1-2 inches of fresh ginger in water for 10 minutes. Drink 1-2 cups daily.

- Precaution: Avoid excessive consumption if you have gallstones.

- Chamomile and Fennel Tea: This blend helps alleviate bloating and cramping.

- Instructions: Steep 1 tsp. of dried chamomile and fennel seeds in boiling water for 10 minutes. Drink 2-3 cups daily.

- Precaution: Avoid if allergic to any of the ingredients.

## 3. CONSTIPATION

Constipation involves difficulty passing stools or infrequent bowel movements. It can be caused by dehydration, lack of fiber, and inactivity.

Symptoms:

- Fewer than three bowel movements per week

- Hard, dry, or lumpy stools

- Straining during bowel movements

- Feeling of blockage or incomplete evacuation

Herbal Remedies:

- Flaxseed Water: Flaxseeds add fiber and help ease bowel movements.

- Instructions: Soak 1 tbsp. of flaxseeds in a cup of water overnight. Drink the mixture in the morning.

- Precaution: Drink plenty of water to avoid blockage.

- Dandelion Root Tea: Dandelion stimulates digestion and acts as a mild laxative.

- Instructions: Steep 1-2 tsp. of dried dandelion root in boiling water for 10-15 minutes. Drink 2-3 cups daily.

- Precaution: Avoid if allergic to dandelion.

- Senna Tea: Senna is a natural laxative for short-term constipation relief.

- Instructions: Steep 1-2 grams of dried senna leaves in boiling water for 5-10 minutes. Drink 1 cup before bed.

- Precaution: Do not use for more than 7 days to prevent dependency.

These herbal remedies, alongside proper diet and lifestyle adjustments, offer effective and natural solutions for managing common digestive issues.

Emphasizing the importance of a balanced pH and incorporating these practices into daily life can improve digestive health and overall wellness.

## 4. DIARRHEA

Overview:

Diarrhea is a digestive condition that involves loose, watery stools and frequent bowel movements. It can arise from infections, dietary intolerances, medications, or other underlying health issues. Managing diarrhea effectively is important to avoid dehydration and other complications.

Symptoms:

- Frequent, loose, or watery stools

- Abdominal cramps and pain

- Urgent need to use the bathroom

- Nausea or vomiting

- Signs of dehydration (dry mouth, dizziness, reduced urine output)

Herbal Remedies:

Chamomile and Peppermint Tea:

- Ingredients: 1 tsp dried chamomile flowers, 1 tsp dried peppermint leaves, 1 cup boiling water.

- Instructions:

1. Combine chamomile and peppermint in a teapot or cup.

2. Pour boiling water over the herbs.

3. Cover and steep for 10 minutes.

4. Strain and drink warm.

- Dosage: Drink 2-3 cups daily.

- Precautions: Avoid if allergic to any of the ingredients.


Slippery Elm Gruel:

- Ingredients: 1 tbsp slippery elm powder, 1 cup warm water or milk.

- Instructions:

1. Mix slippery elm powder with warm water or milk to make a smooth paste.

2. Consume immediately.

- Dosage: Take 1-2 times daily.

- Precautions: Drink plenty of water to prevent choking.


Blackberry Leaf Tea:

- Ingredients: 1-2 tsp dried blackberry leaves, 1 cup boiling water.

- Instructions:

1. Place blackberry leaves in a teapot or cup.

2. Pour boiling water over the leaves.

3. Cover and steep for 10 minutes.

4. Strain and drink warm.

- Dosage: Drink 2-3 cups daily.

- Precautions: Generally safe, but consult a healthcare provider if pregnant or breastfeeding.

# 5. PEPTIC ULCERS

Overview:

Peptic ulcers are painful sores that develop on the stomach lining, small intestine, or esophagus. They are frequently caused by Helicobacter pylori infections or long-term use of NSAIDs. Without proper treatment, ulcers can lead to serious complications such as internal bleeding.

Symptoms:

- Burning stomach pain

- Bloating and belching

- Fatty food intolerance

- Heartburn

- Nausea

- Severe cases may cause vomiting blood or black, tarry stools

Herbal Remedies:

Licorice Root Tea:

- Ingredients: 1 tsp dried licorice root, 1 cup boiling water.

- Instructions:

1. Place licorice root in a teapot or cup.

2. Pour boiling water over the root.

3. Cover and steep for 10-15 minutes.

4. Strain and drink warm.

- Dosage: Drink 2-3 cups daily.

- Precautions: Use deglycyrrhizinated licorice (DGL) to avoid side effects such as high blood pressure or low potassium levels.

Marshmallow Root Tea:

- Ingredients: 1-2 tsp dried marshmallow root, 1 cup cold water.

- Instructions:

1. Place marshmallow root in a teapot or cup.

2. Pour cold water over the root and let it steep overnight.

3. Strain and drink cold.

- Dosage: Drink 2-3 cups daily.

- Precautions: Generally safe, but drink plenty of water to stay hydrated.

Cabbage Juice:

- Ingredients: Fresh cabbage.

- Instructions:

1. Wash and chop fresh cabbage.

2. Juice the cabbage using a juicer.

3. Drink the juice immediately.

- Dosage: Drink 1/2 cup 2-3 times daily.

- Precautions: Start with a small amount to ensure your body tolerates it, as cabbage can sometimes cause bloating.

These natural remedies, in combination with proper diet and medical advice, can help manage digestive conditions like diarrhea and peptic ulcers. Always consult with a healthcare provider if symptoms persist or worsen.

## 6. INFLAMMATORY BOWEL DISEASE (IBD)

Overview: IBD refers to chronic inflammation of the digestive tract, primarily affecting people with Crohn's disease and ulcerative colitis.

While Crohn's disease can affect any part of the gastrointestinal tract, ulcerative colitis is limited to the colon and rectum. The exact cause is unknown, but it is believed to involve a combination of genetic predisposition, immune system malfunction, and environmental factors.

Symptoms:

- Persistent diarrhea.

- Abdominal pain and cramping.

- Blood in the stool.

- Reduced appetite and weight loss.

- Fatigue and general malaise.

- Fever, in some cases.

# 7. HERBAL REMEDIES FOR IBD

Turmeric (Curcuma longa) Tea

- Ingredients: 1 teaspoon turmeric powder, 1 cup hot water, pinch of black pepper.

- Instructions:

1. Mix turmeric powder and black pepper into the hot water.

2. Stir well and let steep for 5-10 minutes.

3. Drink warm.

- Dosage: Drink 1-2 cups daily to reduce inflammation.

- Precautions: Consult with a healthcare provider before using turmeric if you have gallbladder issues or are taking blood thinners.

Slippery Elm Bark Tea

- Ingredients: 1 tablespoon slippery elm powder, 1 cup warm water or milk.

- Instructions:

1. Mix slippery elm powder with warm water or milk to create a smooth consistency.

2. Drink immediately.

- Dosage: Drink 1-2 times daily to soothe the digestive tract.

- Precautions: Slippery elm is generally safe but should be consumed with plenty of water to avoid choking.

Aloe Vera Juice

- Ingredients: 1/4 cup pure aloe vera juice.

- Instructions:

1. Drink aloe vera juice in the morning before meals.

- Dosage: Start with 1/4 cup daily, gradually increasing to 1/2 cup.

- Precautions: Avoid aloe vera juice with added sugars or chemicals. Excessive intake may cause diarrhea.

Marshmallow Root Tea

- Ingredients: 1-2 teaspoons dried marshmallow root, 1 cup cold water.

- Instructions:

1. Place marshmallow root in water and let it sit overnight.

2. Strain and drink cold.

- Dosage: Drink 2-3 cups daily to soothe inflammation.

- Precautions: Generally safe, but ensure adequate hydration.

# 8. GALLSTONES

Overview:

Gallstones are hardened deposits of bile that can form in the gallbladder, potentially leading to blocked bile ducts, pain, and inflammation. If untreated, gallstones can result in serious complications such as infections or jaundice.

Symptoms:

- Sudden, intense pain in the upper right abdomen

- Pain between the shoulder blades

- Nausea or vomiting

- Indigestion or gas

- Jaundice (yellowing of the skin and eyes) if bile ducts are blocked

Herbal Remedies:

Dandelion Root Tea:

- Ingredients: 1-2 tsp dried dandelion root, 1 cup boiling water.

- Instructions:

1. Place the dandelion root in a teapot or cup.

2. Pour boiling water over the root.

3. Cover and steep for 10-15 minutes.

4. Strain and drink warm.

- Dosage: Drink 2-3 cups daily.

- Precautions: Avoid if allergic to dandelion or related plants.


Milk Thistle Tea:

- Ingredients: 1-2 tsp crushed milk thistle seeds, 1 cup boiling water.

- Instructions:

1. Place the crushed seeds in a teapot or cup.

2. Pour boiling water over the seeds.

3. Cover and steep for 10-15 minutes.

4. Strain and drink warm.

- Dosage: Drink 2-3 cups daily.

- Precautions: Generally safe, but consult a healthcare provider if pregnant or breastfeeding.


Peppermint Oil Capsules:

- Ingredients: Enteric-coated peppermint oil capsules.

- Instructions:

1. Purchase enteric-coated peppermint oil capsules from a reputable supplier.

2. Follow the dosage instructions on the packaging.

- Dosage: Typically, 1-2 capsules, 2-3 times daily before meals.

- Precautions: Ensure the capsules are enteric-coated to avoid heartburn.

# 9. LACTOSE INTOLERANCE

Overview:

Lactose intolerance occurs when the body lacks the enzyme lactase, making it difficult to digest lactose, a sugar found in dairy products. This results in uncomfortable digestive symptoms.

Symptoms:

- Diarrhea

- Bloating

- Gas

- Abdominal cramps

- Nausea

Herbal Remedies:

Ginger Tea:

- Ingredients: 1-2 inches fresh ginger root, 2 cups water.

- Instructions:

1. Peel and slice the ginger root.

2. Boil the ginger slices in water for 10 minutes.

3. Strain and drink warm.

- Dosage: Drink 1-2 cups daily.

- Precautions: Avoid excessive consumption if you have gallstones.

Chamomile Tea:

- Ingredients: 2-3 tsp dried chamomile flowers, 1 cup boiling water.

- Instructions:

1. Place chamomile flowers in a teapot or cup.

2. Pour boiling water over the flowers.

3. Cover and steep for 5-10 minutes.

4. Strain and drink warm.

- Dosage: Drink 2-3 cups daily.

- Precautions: Avoid if allergic to ragweed, daisies, marigolds, or chrysanthemums.

# 10. DIVERTICULITIS

Overview:

Diverticulitis is the inflammation or infection of small pouches, known as diverticula, which can form along the digestive tract, particularly in the colon. This condition can cause significant discomfort and, in severe cases, may lead to complications.

Symptoms:

- Severe abdominal pain, usually on the left side

- Fever

- Nausea and vomiting

- Constipation or diarrhea

- Bloating

Herbal Remedies:

Slippery Elm Gruel:

- Ingredients: 1 tbsp slippery elm powder, 1 cup warm water or milk.

- Instructions:

1. Mix slippery elm powder with warm water or milk to create a smooth paste.

2. Consume immediately.

- Dosage: Take 1-2 times daily.

- Precautions: Drink plenty of water to avoid choking, as the gruel can become thick when ingested.

Incorporating these herbal remedies into your daily routine can help manage symptoms and support overall digestive health. As always, consult with a healthcare provider, especially if you have ongoing or severe symptoms.

# MANAGING DIGESTIVE HEALTH HOLISTICALLY

Digestive health impacts more than just the gastrointestinal system—it influences immune function, mental clarity, and even emotional well-being. A holistic approach that balances herbal remedies, dietary changes, and lifestyle adjustments can improve overall digestive health and relieve common conditions such as GERD, IBS, and IBD.

Here's how to approach digestive health from a comprehensive, natural perspective:

1. Eat a Balanced Diet

A nutrient-dense, fiber-rich diet is fundamental to optimal digestion and overall health.

- Incorporate fiber: Whole grains, fruits, vegetables, nuts, and seeds aid bowel regularity and promote a healthy gut microbiome.

- Limit processed foods: Processed foods and added sugars can cause inflammation and disrupt the gut.

- Probiotic-rich foods: Yogurt, kefir, sauerkraut, and kombucha introduce beneficial bacteria into the gut, supporting digestion and immunity.

2. Manage Stress

Stress negatively impacts digestion, leading to issues like acid reflux, IBS, and even IBD flare-ups.

- Meditation and mindfulness: Daily mindfulness practices can reduce stress and improve digestion.

- Yoga and exercise: Regular physical activity stimulates the digestive system and promotes overall well-being.

3. Hydration

Drinking enough water is essential for healthy digestion. Water helps break down food, absorb nutrients, and ease waste elimination.

- Water intake: Aim for at least eight glasses of water per day.

- Herbal teas: Chamomile, ginger, and peppermint teas are soothing and can alleviate digestive discomfort.

## 4. Regular Movement

Physical activity stimulates bowel movements, improves digestion, and prevents constipation.

- Daily exercise: Walking, swimming, and yoga are excellent choices for promoting healthy digestion.

## 5. Adequate Sleep

Good quality sleep is crucial for digestive health. Sleep deprivation can disrupt the gut microbiome and contribute to digestive disorders.

- Sleep hygiene: Aim for 7-9 hours of sleep per night, and establish a bedtime routine that promotes relaxation.

By focusing on a comprehensive approach to digestive health, incorporating herbal remedies, and making lifestyle changes, you can achieve better gut function and overall well-being.

Addressing digestive disorders holistically not only improves physical health but also contributes to emotional and mental balance. These insights, inspired by Barbara O'Neill's teachings, empower you to take charge of your digestive health naturally and effectively.

# LIFESTYLE TIPS FOR OPTIMAL GUT HEALTH - CHRONIC FATIGUE AND IBS

Gut health is integral to overall well-being, influencing not only digestion but also immune function, mental health, and energy levels.

This section explores the connection between gut health, chronic fatigue, and Irritable Bowel Syndrome (IBS) and provides practical solutions for improving digestive wellness through diet, natural remedies, and lifestyle changes.

# THE IMPORTANCE OF GUT HEALTH

The gut is home to trillions of bacteria that form the microbiome, a crucial ecosystem that supports digestion, nutrient absorption, and immune function. When this microbiome is disrupted, it can lead to chronic conditions like fatigue and IBS.

- Microbiome Balance: Maintaining a healthy balance of beneficial bacteria is essential for digestive health. Probiotic-rich foods and prebiotics (fibers that feed beneficial bacteria) are critical for preserving this balance.

- Gut-Brain Connection: The gut communicates with the brain through the vagus nerve, influencing mood, stress, and mental health. An imbalanced gut microbiome can contribute to mood disorders, anxiety, and chronic fatigue.

## CHRONIC FATIGUE AND GUT HEALTH

Chronic Fatigue Syndrome (CFS) is marked by long-lasting fatigue that doesn't improve with rest. Gut health plays a significant role in this condition, particularly through nutrient absorption and systemic inflammation.

- Nutrient Absorption: Poor gut health can impair the absorption of essential nutrients, leading to deficiencies that contribute to fatigue. Ensuring sufficient intake of vitamins (especially B vitamins and magnesium) is critical.

- Inflammation: Chronic gut inflammation can cause fatigue. Incorporating anti-inflammatory foods like turmeric, ginger, and omega-3 fatty acids (found in fish, flaxseeds, and walnuts) can help reduce systemic inflammation.

## MANAGING IBS

Irritable Bowel Syndrome (IBS) affects the large intestine and is often triggered by certain foods and stress. Managing IBS typically involves making dietary adjustments, increasing fiber, and reducing gut irritation.

- Identify Dietary Triggers: IBS symptoms can worsen with foods high in FODMAPs (fermentable carbohydrates), gluten, or dairy. Keeping a food diary and eliminating these triggers may help manage symptoms.

- Increase Soluble Fiber: Soluble fiber helps regulate bowel movements. Foods like oats, flaxseeds, and psyllium husk are excellent sources of fiber that can ease IBS symptoms, especially constipation.

# PEPPERMINT OIL CAPSULES

- Ingredients: Enteric-coated peppermint oil capsules.

- Dosage: Take 1-2 capsules, 2-3 times daily before meals to help relieve IBS symptoms.

- Precautions: Use enteric-coated capsules to avoid heartburn.

# NATURAL REMEDIES FOR GUT HEALTH, CHRONIC FATIGUE, AND IBS

Probiotics

- Sources: Yogurt, kefir, sauerkraut, kimchi, and kombucha.

- Benefits: Probiotics help restore the balance of beneficial bacteria in the gut, improving digestion, reducing inflammation, and supporting immune health.

Ginger Tea

- Ingredients: Fresh ginger root (1-2 inches), 2 cups of water.

- Instructions: Boil the ginger in water for 10 minutes, then strain and drink warm.

- Dosage: Drink 1-2 cups daily to reduce inflammation and improve digestion.

Slippery Elm Gruel

- Ingredients: 1 tablespoon slippery elm powder, 1 cup warm water or milk.

- Instructions: Mix the powder with warm water to form a paste and consume immediately.

- Dosage: Consume 1-2 times daily to soothe digestive discomfort.

- Precautions: Drink plenty of water to prevent choking.

Aloe Vera Juice

- Ingredients: Fresh aloe vera gel (2 tablespoons), 1 cup of water or juice.

- Instructions: Blend and drink immediately.

- Dosage: Drink 1/2 cup, 2-3 times daily to promote gut healing and reduce inflammation.

# LIFESTYLE ADJUSTMENTS FOR GUT HEALTH

Stress Management

- Impact on Gut: Stress can worsen gut symptoms, particularly in IBS. Managing stress through mindfulness, yoga, and breathing exercises is crucial for maintaining gut health.

- Mindfulness Practices: Incorporating daily mindfulness practices, such as deep breathing or meditation, can reduce gut discomfort triggered by stress.

Exercise

- Benefits: Regular physical activity promotes healthy digestion and reduces stress, which can relieve IBS symptoms and improve overall gut function.

- Recommendation: Aim for at least 30 minutes of moderate exercise (such as walking or yoga) most days of the week.

Sleep

- Impact on Gut: Poor sleep can disrupt the gut microbiome and impair digestion.

- Tips for Better Sleep: Establish a regular sleep routine, avoid screens before bedtime, and create a restful environment. Aim for 7-9 hours of sleep per night.

# ACHIEVING OPTIMAL GUT HEALTH

Maintaining a healthy gut is essential for overall well-being, affecting everything from energy levels to immune function. For those struggling with conditions like chronic fatigue or IBS, a holistic approach combining dietary changes, natural remedies, and lifestyle adjustments can significantly improve digestive health and reduce symptoms.

By incorporating Barbara O'Neill's natural health teachings—focusing on stress reduction, proper nutrition, and herbal remedies—you can support your gut and enjoy better physical and emotional health.

Maintaining gut health is crucial for preventing and managing chronic conditions like Chronic Fatigue Syndrome (CFS) and Irritable Bowel Syndrome (IBS). A holistic approach, incorporating a balanced diet, natural remedies, and healthy lifestyle practices, can significantly improve digestive health and overall quality of life.

This chapter provides practical guidance on how to achieve optimal gut health through manageable and sustainable lifestyle changes.

## 1. Balanced Diet Rich in Fiber

A diet high in fiber is essential for digestive health, as it promotes regular bowel movements, prevents constipation, and nourishes beneficial gut bacteria.

- Whole Grains: Incorporate fiber-rich whole grains like brown rice, quinoa, oats, and barley. These foods provide essential nutrients and support digestive regularity.

- Fruits and Vegetables: Include a wide variety of colorful fruits and vegetables daily, such as berries, apples, carrots, broccoli, and leafy greens. These foods provide fiber, vitamins, and minerals that are crucial for gut health.

- Legumes: Beans, lentils, and chickpeas are excellent sources of plant-based protein and fiber, which help maintain a healthy digestive system.

## 2. Stay Hydrated

Proper hydration is vital for the digestive process, as it helps break down food, absorb nutrients, and eliminate waste.

- Daily Water Intake: Aim for at least 8 glasses of water per day, adjusting for individual needs, climate, and activity levels.

- Hydrating Foods: Include water-rich foods like cucumbers, watermelon, oranges, and lettuce to help meet hydration needs.

## 3. Regular Physical Activity

Exercise stimulates the digestive system, helping to prevent constipation and promote regular bowel movements.

- Daily Exercise: Engage in at least 30 minutes of moderate physical activity daily. Activities such as walking, cycling, swimming, or yoga can boost digestion and improve gut function.

- Core Strengthening: Strengthening core muscles can support digestive organs and aid in maintaining healthy gut function.

## 4. Probiotics and Fermented Foods

Probiotics are beneficial bacteria that support the gut microbiome. Consuming fermented foods rich in probiotics helps maintain gut balance.

- Yogurt and Kefir: Opt for plain, unsweetened yogurt and kefir that contain live and active cultures.

- Sauerkraut and Kimchi: Fermented vegetables like sauerkraut and kimchi are excellent sources of probiotics and fiber.

- Miso and Tempeh: These fermented soy products provide probiotics and plant-based protein to promote digestive health.

## 5. Adequate Sleep

Quality sleep is essential for overall health, including gut health. Poor sleep can disrupt the gut microbiome, leading to digestive issues.

- Sleep Hygiene: Maintain a consistent sleep schedule, create a calming bedtime routine, and ensure your sleep environment is conducive to rest.

- Avoid Stimulants: Limit caffeine and avoid electronic devices before bedtime to improve sleep quality and duration.

## 6. Stress Management

Chronic stress can negatively affect gut health, contributing to conditions like IBS, acid reflux, and ulcers.

- Relaxation Techniques: Practice deep breathing, meditation, or progressive muscle relaxation to manage stress effectively.

- Physical Activity: Engage in calming exercises like yoga, tai chi, or walking to reduce stress and improve gut health.

- Hobbies and Interests: Participate in activities that bring joy and relaxation, such as reading, painting, or spending time in nature.

## 7. Mindful Eating

Mindful eating improves digestion and prevents overeating by allowing you to focus on the experience of eating and recognize hunger and fullness cues.

- Chew Thoroughly: Chewing food thoroughly aids digestion and helps your body absorb nutrients more efficiently.

- Eat Slowly: Eating slowly helps prevent indigestion, bloating, and overeating.

- Avoid Distractions: Focus on your meal without distractions such as television or smartphones to enhance the eating experience.

## 8. Limit Processed Foods and Sugars

Processed foods and excessive sugar can disrupt the gut microbiome, contributing to digestive issues and inflammation.

- Whole Foods: Prioritize whole, unprocessed foods like fresh fruits, vegetables, whole grains, and lean proteins.

- Read Labels: Check ingredient lists to avoid added sugars, artificial sweeteners, and preservatives, which can harm the gut.

- Healthy Alternatives: Replace sugary snacks with nutrient-dense options such as fresh fruit, nuts, and seeds.

## 9. Regular Meal Times

Eating meals at regular intervals can help regulate your digestive system and reduce issues like acid reflux and indigestion.

- Consistent Schedule: Try to eat your meals at the same times each day to establish a routine for your digestive system.

- Small, Frequent Meals: If you experience digestive discomfort after large meals, consider smaller, more frequent meals throughout the day.

## 10. Avoid Smoking and Excessive Alcohol

Both smoking and excessive alcohol intake can damage the digestive system, leading to various gastrointestinal issues.

- Quit Smoking: If you smoke, seek resources and support to quit, as smoking can contribute to acid reflux, ulcers, and other digestive problems.

- Moderate Alcohol: Limit alcohol consumption to moderate levels, or eliminate it entirely for optimal gut health.

By adopting these lifestyle tips, you can significantly improve your digestive health and overall well-being. Focusing on a fiber-rich, whole-food diet, staying hydrated, exercising regularly, and managing stress are essential steps in supporting a healthy gut.

Following Barbara O'Neill's emphasis on holistic health, these practices will help you achieve and maintain optimal gut health, leading to a healthier and more balanced life.

# CHAPTER 12

## HEART HEALTH

## NUTRITIONAL STRATEGIES FOR CARDIOVASCULAR SUPPORT

Maintaining heart health is essential for overall well-being, and adopting the right nutritional strategies can significantly support cardiovascular function. In this chapter, we delve into several approaches inspired by Barbara O'Neill's teachings to optimize heart health through diet, lifestyle adjustments, and natural remedies.

1. Embrace a Plant-Based Diet

A plant-based diet provides essential nutrients, fiber, and antioxidants that help maintain cardiovascular health.

- Fruits and Vegetables: Ensure half your plate is filled with a variety of fruits and vegetables. Leafy greens, berries, and cruciferous vegetables are particularly beneficial due to their high antioxidant content.

- Whole Grains: Incorporate whole grains like oats, brown rice, quinoa, and barley, which are rich in fiber and help lower cholesterol.

- Nuts and Seeds: Almonds, walnuts, flaxseeds, and chia seeds offer healthy fats, fiber, and protein, contributing to better cholesterol management.

2. Healthy Fats for Heart Health

Choosing the right types of fats can promote heart health while lowering the risk of cardiovascular disease.

- Omega-3 Fatty Acids: Found in fatty fish like salmon and mackerel, as well as flaxseeds and walnuts, omega-3s help reduce inflammation and lower triglycerides.

- Monounsaturated Fats: Avocados, olive oil, and nuts are rich in these heart-friendly fats, which lower bad cholesterol (LDL) and raise good cholesterol (HDL).

- Limit Saturated Fats and Trans Fats: These fats, commonly found in red meat and processed foods, should be minimized as they increase the risk of heart disease.

3. Increase Fiber Intake

Fiber, especially soluble fiber, helps reduce cholesterol levels and supports heart health.

- Soluble Fiber: Found in oats, beans, lentils, apples, and citrus fruits, soluble fiber can lower LDL cholesterol.

- Insoluble Fiber: Found in whole grains, vegetables, and seeds, this fiber type promotes healthy digestion, which indirectly benefits the heart.

## 4. Antioxidant-Rich Foods

Antioxidants protect the heart by neutralizing harmful free radicals and reducing inflammation.

- Berries: Blueberries, strawberries, and raspberries contain anthocyanins, which reduce oxidative stress and inflammation in the cardiovascular system.

- Dark Chocolate: With at least 70% cocoa, dark chocolate contains flavonoids that lower blood pressure and improve blood flow.

- Green Tea: Rich in catechins and flavonoids, green tea improves blood vessel function and lowers cholesterol.

## 5. Herbs and Spices for Heart Health

Certain herbs and spices provide cardiovascular benefits and can be easily incorporated into your diet.

- Garlic: Known for lowering blood pressure and cholesterol, garlic can be added raw or cooked to enhance heart health.

- Turmeric: Containing curcumin, turmeric has anti-inflammatory properties that benefit the cardiovascular system.

- Ginger: Ginger promotes better blood circulation and reduces inflammation.

## 6. Reduce Sodium Intake

Excess sodium contributes to high blood pressure, which increases the risk of heart disease.

- Limit Processed Foods: Processed and packaged foods are often high in sodium. Opt for fresh, whole foods whenever possible.

- Herbal Seasonings: Use herbs and spices like basil, thyme, and oregano instead of salt to flavor your food and reduce sodium intake.

## 7. Moderate Alcohol Consumption

While moderate alcohol consumption, particularly red wine, may offer heart benefits, excessive drinking increases the risk of heart disease.

- Moderation: If you choose to drink, do so in moderation—up to one drink per day for women and two drinks per day for men.

- Red Wine: Contains resveratrol, an antioxidant linked to improved heart health, but the benefits should be weighed against potential risks.

## 8. Stay Hydrated

Proper hydration supports cardiovascular function by maintaining optimal blood volume and blood pressure.

- Water: Aim to drink at least eight glasses of water a day to stay hydrated, with adjustments based on activity level and climate.

- Hydrating Foods: Foods like cucumbers, melons, and oranges are high in water content and contribute to hydration.

## 9. Balanced Diet with Adequate Protein

Protein is necessary for muscle maintenance, including the heart, and choosing the right sources is important.

- Plant-Based Proteins: Beans, lentils, and tofu are excellent sources of heart-healthy protein.

- Lean Animal Proteins: Opt for lean cuts of meat like chicken and fish, and avoid processed meats that are high in unhealthy fats and sodium.

## 10. Regular Monitoring and Adjustments

Track your health markers to ensure your diet and lifestyle are supporting optimal heart health.

- Cholesterol Levels: Regularly check your cholesterol levels and adjust your diet to maintain healthy ranges.

- Blood Pressure: Keep an eye on your blood pressure, and make dietary changes if needed to reduce hypertension.

# CARDIOVASCULAR AILMENTS AND HERBAL REMEDIES

In addition to the nutritional strategies, certain herbal remedies can support heart health and manage specific cardiovascular conditions. Below are common ailments and their corresponding herbal treatments:

1. Hypertension (High Blood Pressure)

Herbal Remedy: Hawthorn Berry Tea

- Ingredients: 1 tablespoon dried hawthorn berries, 2 cups water

- Instructions: Boil water and add hawthorn berries. Simmer for 10 minutes, strain, and drink twice daily.

- Benefits: Hawthorn dilates blood vessels and lowers blood pressure.

2. Atherosclerosis

Herbal Remedy: Garlic and Lemon Infusion

- Ingredients: 4 cloves garlic, 1 lemon, 1 liter water

- Instructions: Boil water and add garlic and lemon. Simmer for 20 minutes, strain, and store in the fridge. Drink 50 ml daily before breakfast.

- Benefits: Garlic reduces cholesterol and prevents plaque buildup in arteries, while lemon provides antioxidant support.

3. Angina

Herbal Remedy: Ginger and Turmeric Tea

- Ingredients: 1-inch ginger piece, 1 teaspoon turmeric powder, 2 cups water

- Instructions: Boil water, add ginger and turmeric, simmer for 10 minutes, strain, and drink twice daily.

- Benefits: Ginger improves blood circulation, and turmeric reduces inflammation, which can alleviate angina symptoms.

Adopting these nutritional strategies and herbal remedies will help support cardiovascular health, reduce the risk of heart disease, and promote overall well-being.

Barbara O'Neill's emphasis on holistic approaches—focusing on diet, lifestyle changes, and natural remedies—empowers individuals to take charge of their heart health and live longer, healthier lives.

Maintaining heart health requires a multifaceted approach that includes regular exercise, a balanced diet, and lifestyle modifications.

Drawing from Barbara O'Neill's holistic teachings, this chapter explores the importance of integrating natural remedies and practical lifestyle changes to promote cardiovascular well-being.

4. Heart Failure

Heart failure occurs when the heart is unable to pump blood efficiently, leading to symptoms like fatigue, shortness of breath, and fluid retention.

Herbal Remedy: Dandelion Leaf Tea

- Ingredients: 1 tablespoon dried dandelion leaves, 2 cups water, lemon juice (optional)

- Instructions:

1. Rinse the dried dandelion leaves under cold water.

2. Bring 2 cups of water to a boil.

3. Add the leaves to the boiling water.

4. Simmer for 10 minutes.

5. Strain and drink once daily, with a splash of lemon if desired.

- Benefits: Dandelion leaves act as a natural diuretic, helping reduce fluid retention and supporting heart function by reducing the workload on the heart.

5. Arrhythmia

Arrhythmia refers to an irregular heartbeat, which can be too fast, too slow, or erratic. It can result from stress, electrolyte imbalances, or underlying heart conditions.

Herbal Remedy: Motherwort Tincture

- Ingredients: 1 cup dried motherwort, 2 cups vodka or brandy, glass jar with lid

- Instructions:

1. Place the dried motherwort in a glass jar and cover with vodka or brandy.

2. Seal and store in a cool, dark place for 4-6 weeks, shaking daily.

3. Strain the mixture and store in a clean glass bottle.

4. Take 1 teaspoon diluted in water, up to three times daily.

- Benefits: Motherwort has calming properties that help regulate heart rhythm and reduce palpitations.

Exercise and Lifestyle Changes for a Healthy Heart

Barbara O'Neill emphasizes that physical activity, alongside natural remedies and a heart-healthy diet, is critical for promoting cardiovascular health. Below are key exercise routines and lifestyle adjustments that can help keep your heart strong.

Importance of Regular Exercise

Exercise strengthens the heart muscle, improves circulation, lowers blood pressure, and helps manage cholesterol. It also reduces stress and improves overall mood.

# TYPES OF EXERCISE FOR HEART HEALTH

1. Aerobic Exercise (Cardio)

- Description: Aerobic exercises increase heart rate and improve the efficiency of the cardiovascular system.

- Examples: Walking, jogging, swimming, cycling, and dancing.

- Benefits: Enhances heart function, reduces blood pressure, and lowers the risk of heart disease.

- Recommended Frequency: Aim for at least 150 minutes of moderate-intensity or 75 minutes of vigorous-intensity aerobic exercise per week.

- Tips: Start with a 30-minute walk five times a week and gradually increase intensity.

2. Strength Training

- Description: Strength training involves exercises that increase muscle mass using resistance.

- Examples: Weightlifting, body-weight exercises like push-ups and squats, and resistance band workouts.

- Benefits: Increases muscle strength, helps manage weight, and supports metabolism.

- Recommended Frequency: Incorporate strength training exercises twice per week.

- Tips: Begin with two 20-minute sessions per week, focusing on all major muscle groups.

3. Flexibility and Balance Exercises

- Description: These exercises improve flexibility and balance, reducing the risk of injury.

- Examples: Yoga, Pilates, and stretching routines.

- Benefits: Enhances range of motion, reduces muscle stiffness, and supports overall physical performance.

- Recommended Frequency: Perform flexibility exercises daily or at least three times per week.

- Tips: Incorporate a 10-minute stretching routine or try yoga classes.

Incorporating Exercise into Daily Life

- Set Realistic Goals: Start small and increase your activity gradually.

- Tip: Use a fitness tracker to set and monitor goals like walking 5,000 steps daily, then gradually aim for 10,000.

- Find Enjoyable Activities: Choose activities you enjoy to stay motivated.

- Tip: Experiment with dancing, swimming, or group fitness classes until you find one that excites you.

- Make It a Habit: Schedule workouts at the same time each day for consistency.

- Tip: Set reminders or use apps to help create a routine.

- Stay Active Throughout the Day: Opt for physical activity throughout your routine, like taking the stairs or walking during breaks.

# LIFESTYLE CHANGES FOR HEART HEALTH

1. Healthy Diet

- Whole Foods Focus: Prioritize fruits, vegetables, whole grains, lean proteins, and healthy fats.

- Tip: Plan meals ahead to ensure a balance of nutrients and reduce reliance on processed foods.

- Limit Processed Foods: Reduce consumption of refined sugars, trans fats, and sodium.

- Tip: Check food labels and prepare meals at home to control ingredients.

- Herbal Supplements: Integrate heart-healthy herbs like garlic, turmeric, and hawthorn into your diet.

- Tip: Add fresh garlic to meals, brew hawthorn tea, and include turmeric in stews or smoothies.


## 2. Manage Stress

- Relaxation Techniques: Practice meditation, deep breathing, and yoga to manage stress.

- Tip: Dedicate 10-15 minutes a day to relaxation or mindfulness practices.

- Prayer and Spiritual Practices: Barbara O'Neill advocates for spiritual practices to promote inner peace.

- Tip: Set aside time daily for quiet reflection or prayer.

- Adequate Sleep: Aim for 7-9 hours of sleep each night to support cardiovascular health.

- Tip: Create a calming bedtime routine, avoid screens before bed, and maintain a consistent sleep schedule.


## 3. Avoid Harmful Habits

- Quit Smoking: Smoking is a major risk factor for heart disease.

- Tip: Seek support groups or counseling, and consider nicotine replacement therapies.

- Limit Alcohol: Drink alcohol in moderation or avoid it entirely.

- Tip: Substitute alcohol with herbal teas or flavored water for a healthier option.


## 4. Regular Health Check-ups

- Monitor Blood Pressure: Keep track of your blood pressure and address any concerns early.

- Tip: Use a home monitor to track blood pressure levels regularly.

- Check Cholesterol Levels: Ensure cholesterol levels are in a healthy range through diet and exercise.

- Tip: Schedule annual check-ups and maintain a fiber-rich diet to help manage cholesterol.

# HOLISTIC APPROACHES TO HEART HEALTH

1. Herbal Remedies

- Garlic: Known for its blood-thinning and cholesterol-lowering properties.

- Tip: Consume 1-2 raw cloves daily or take garlic supplements after consulting a doctor.

- Hawthorn: Improves blood circulation and strengthens the heart muscle.

- Tip: Brew hawthorn tea and drink it 2-3 times daily.

- Turmeric: Reduces inflammation and oxidative stress, supporting heart health.

- Tip: Add turmeric powder to smoothies or meals, or consider supplements.


2. Emotional and Social Well-being

- Maintain Social Connections: Relationships with family and friends contribute to emotional and mental well-being.

- Tip: Schedule regular gatherings or virtual meetings with loved ones.

- Cultivate a Positive Mindset: Practicing gratitude and positivity can enhance emotional resilience.

- Tip: Keep a gratitude journal and reflect on the positive aspects of your life daily.


By adopting a comprehensive approach that integrates exercise, a heart-healthy diet, and lifestyle changes, you can significantly improve your cardiovascular health.


Inspired by Barbara O'Neill's holistic principles, these strategies aim to empower individuals to live a balanced, heart-healthy life with vitality and joy.

# CHAPTER 13

## MANAGING DIABETES

### UNDERSTANDING BLOOD SUGAR CONTROL

Diabetes is a chronic condition requiring diligent management of blood sugar levels to prevent complications. Drawing from Barbara O'Neill's teachings, understanding how the body controls blood sugar and implementing natural strategies can empower individuals to take control of their health.

### THE BASICS OF BLOOD SUGAR

Blood sugar (glucose) is the body's primary energy source, derived from the carbohydrates we eat. After meals, carbohydrates are broken down into glucose, which is transported through the bloodstream to cells. Insulin, a hormone produced by the pancreas, allows cells to absorb glucose for energy. In people with diabetes, this process is impaired, leading to elevated blood sugar levels.

### KEY FACTORS AFFECTING BLOOD SUGAR CONTROL

1. Diet

- Carbohydrate Intake: Simple carbs (sugars) cause rapid blood sugar spikes, while complex carbs (whole grains, vegetables) lead to a slower rise.

- Glycemic Index (GI): Choose low-GI foods, like whole grains and vegetables, to help stabilize blood sugar.

2. Physical Activity

- Exercise: Increases insulin sensitivity and helps cells use glucose effectively. Both aerobic (walking, swimming) and resistance exercises (strength training) can lower blood sugar.

3. Stress

- Impact on Blood Sugar: Stress hormones like cortisol raise blood sugar levels. Techniques like deep breathing, yoga, and mindfulness can help manage stress.

4. Sleep

- Sleep Quality: Lack of sleep can affect hormone levels, including insulin, making blood sugar harder to control. Aim for 7-9 hours of sleep.

## 5. Hydration

- Water Intake: Staying hydrated helps kidneys flush out excess sugar, supporting better blood sugar management.

# NATURAL STRATEGIES FOR BLOOD SUGAR CONTROL

Barbara O'Neill emphasizes the importance of natural methods to manage blood sugar. Here are key strategies to incorporate:

## 1. Dietary Adjustments

- Balanced Meals: Include carbohydrates, proteins, and healthy fats in every meal to prevent blood sugar spikes.

- Fiber-Rich Foods: Foods like vegetables, fruits, and whole grains slow the digestion of carbohydrates, helping to maintain stable blood sugar.

- Healthy Fats: Incorporate sources like avocados, nuts, seeds, and olive oil to improve insulin sensitivity.

## 2. Herbal Remedies

- Bitter Melon (Momordica charantia): Known for its ability to lower blood sugar, it can be consumed as a juice or in meals.

- Fenugreek (Trigonella foenum-graecum): Soaked fenugreek seeds can help regulate blood sugar when consumed on an empty stomach.

- Cinnamon (Cinnamomum verum): Cinnamon improves insulin sensitivity and can be added to teas or meals.

## 3. Physical Activity

- Exercise Regularly: Engage in 30 minutes of moderate exercise (walking, cycling) most days. Incorporate strength training to build muscle, which uses glucose efficiently.

- Daily Movement: Integrate movement throughout the day by walking during breaks, taking the stairs, or engaging in active hobbies.

## 4. Stress Management

- Mindfulness and Meditation: Reducing stress through mindfulness and relaxation techniques like yoga or tai chi can help control blood sugar.

- Deep Breathing: Practicing deep breathing exercises can lower cortisol levels and reduce stress-induced blood sugar spikes.

## 5. Regular Monitoring

- Track Blood Sugar: Monitor your levels to identify how different foods, activities, or stressors affect blood sugar. This can help in tailoring diet and exercise plans to individual needs.

# NATURAL SUPPLEMENTS AND HERBS FOR DIABETES

In addition to lifestyle changes, certain herbs and natural supplements can support blood sugar management. Below are some remedies endorsed by Barbara O'Neill.

## 1. Bitter Melon (Momordica charantia)

- Properties: Contains compounds like charantin and polypeptide-p that mimic insulin, helping lower blood sugar levels.

- Preparation: Drink 50-100 ml of bitter melon juice daily or include cooked bitter melon in meals.

- Dosage: Consume 50-100 ml juice daily, or 1-2 servings of bitter melon.

## 2. Fenugreek (Trigonella foenum-graecum)

- Properties: Rich in soluble fiber, fenugreek helps slow down carbohydrate absorption and regulate blood sugar.

- Preparation: Soak 2 tbsp of fenugreek seeds in water overnight and consume in the morning on an empty stomach.

- Dosage: 2 tbsp of seeds daily or 1-2 cups of fenugreek tea.

## 3. Cinnamon (Cinnamomum verum)

- Properties: Improves insulin sensitivity and reduces fasting blood sugar levels.

- Preparation: Add 1 tsp ground cinnamon to boiling water for a tea, or mix into smoothies and meals.

- Dosage: 1-2 tsp of cinnamon daily.

## 4. Ginseng (Panax ginseng)

- Properties: Contains ginsenosides that improve insulin production and enhance glucose uptake.

- Preparation: Drink ginseng tea daily, made by steeping 1 g of dried ginseng root in boiling water.

- Dosage: 1-2 g of dried root daily.

## 5. Gymnema Sylvestre

- Properties: Gymnemic acids block sugar absorption in the intestines, reducing sugar cravings and improving blood sugar control.

- Preparation: Brew gymnema tea or add powdered leaves to smoothies or juices.

- Dosage: 1 tsp of dried leaves daily.

Managing diabetes involves more than just medication—it requires a comprehensive approach that includes diet, exercise, stress management, and natural remedies. Barbara O'Neill's holistic teachings emphasize the power of nature in supporting blood sugar control.

By incorporating these strategies, individuals with diabetes can enhance their quality of life and improve overall health naturally. Always consult a healthcare provider before making significant changes to your treatment plan.

# ADDITIONAL HERBAL REMEDIES FOR DIABETES

In addition to the dietary strategies discussed, incorporating natural supplements and herbs into your routine can support blood sugar control.

Here are some effective herbs and supplements, along with their preparation and dosages, that can help manage diabetes, based on Barbara O'Neill's holistic approach:

## 6. Bilberry (Vaccinium myrtillus)

- Key Constituents and Properties: Contains anthocyanins, which improve blood sugar control and protect against oxidative stress.

- Preparation: Use dried bilberries to make tea or take them as a supplement. To make tea, add 1-2 teaspoons of dried bilberries to boiling water, steep for 10 minutes, and strain. Drink once daily.

- Dosage, Safety, and Precautions: 1-2 teaspoons of dried bilberries daily. Generally safe but consult a healthcare provider if on anticoagulant medication.

## 7. Aloe Vera (Aloe barbadensis)

- Key Constituents and Properties: Contains glucomannan and aloin, which help lower blood sugar levels and improve insulin sensitivity.

- Preparation: Extract fresh aloe vera gel and blend it with water or juice. Consume 1-2 tablespoons daily.

- Dosage, Safety, and Precautions: 1-2 tablespoons of aloe vera gel daily. May cause gastrointestinal upset in some individuals. Consult a healthcare provider if pregnant or breastfeeding.

## 8. Holy Basil (Ocimum sanctum)

- Key Constituents and Properties: Contains eugenol, caryophyllene, and triterpenoids, which improve insulin sensitivity and lower blood sugar levels.

- Preparation: Use fresh or dried leaves to make tea. Add 1-2 teaspoons of leaves to boiling water, steep for 5-10 minutes, and strain. Drink once or twice daily.

- Dosage, Safety, and Precautions: 1-2 cups of tea daily. Generally safe but may cause mild side effects in some individuals.

## 9. Neem (Azadirachta indica)

- Key Constituents and Properties: Contains nimbin, nimbidin, and quercetin, which help lower blood sugar levels and improve insulin sensitivity.

- Preparation: Use fresh or dried neem leaves to make tea. Add 1 teaspoon of leaves to boiling water, steep for 5-10 minutes, and strain. Drink once daily.

- Dosage, Safety, and Precautions: 1 cup of tea daily. Consult a healthcare provider if pregnant or breastfeeding.

## 10. Prickly Pear (Opuntia ficus-indica)

- Key Constituents and Properties: Contains pectin and fiber, which help lower blood sugar levels and improve insulin sensitivity.

- Preparation: Consume fresh prickly pear pads or juice. For juice, blend the pads and strain the mixture.

- Dosage, Safety, and Precautions: 1 cup of juice or 1 pad daily. Generally safe but may cause mild gastrointestinal upset in some individuals.

# DIETARY AND LIFESTYLE CHANGES FOR DIABETES MANAGEMENT

In addition to incorporating these herbs, adopting key dietary and lifestyle changes can enhance blood sugar control and improve overall health. Here are some essential strategies:

1. Embrace a Low Glycemic Index (GI) Diet

Foods with a low glycemic index (GI) cause slower, more stable increases in blood sugar levels. Incorporate low-GI foods into your diet:

- Non-Starchy Vegetables: Leafy greens, broccoli, cauliflower, zucchini, and bell peppers.

- Whole Grains: Quinoa, barley, steel-cut oats, and brown rice.

- Legumes: Lentils, chickpeas, black beans, and kidney beans.

- Fruits: Berries, cherries, apples, and pears (in moderation).

2. Increase Fiber Intake

Dietary fiber helps slow down the absorption of sugar and improves blood sugar control. Aim for 25-30 grams of fiber daily:

- Vegetables: Brussels sprouts, carrots, and artichokes.

- Fruits: Avocados, raspberries, and oranges.

- Whole Grains: Oats, flaxseeds, and chia seeds.

- Legumes: Lentils, black beans, and split peas.

3. Choose Healthy Fats

Healthy fats improve insulin sensitivity and reduce inflammation. Incorporate these sources of healthy fats:

- Nuts and Seeds: Almonds, walnuts, chia seeds, and flaxseeds.

- Oils: Extra virgin olive oil, coconut oil, and avocado oil.

- Fish: Salmon, mackerel, sardines, and other fatty fish high in omega-3 fatty acids.

4. Opt for Lean Protein Sources

Lean protein can help stabilize blood sugar levels. Choose these sources:

- Poultry: Skinless chicken and turkey.

- Fish: Salmon, tuna, and trout.

- Plant-Based Proteins: Tofu, tempeh, edamame, and lentils.

5. Avoid Processed and Sugary Foods

Processed foods and sugary items can cause rapid blood sugar spikes. Limit or eliminate:

- Sugary Beverages: Sodas, fruit juices, and energy drinks.

- Refined Carbohydrates: White bread, pastries, and pasta.

- Processed Snacks: Chips, cookies, and candies.

# LIFESTYLE CHANGES FOR EFFECTIVE DIABETES MANAGEMENT

In addition to dietary changes, making sustainable lifestyle modifications can have a profound impact on blood sugar control.

1. Regular Physical Activity

- Exercise Benefits: Physical activity increases insulin sensitivity and helps the body use glucose more efficiently.

- Types of Exercise: Include a mix of aerobic exercises (walking, swimming) and resistance training (weights, bodyweight exercises) for optimal benefits.

- Frequency: Aim for at least 30 minutes of moderate exercise five days a week.

2. Stress Management

- Stress Impact on Blood Sugar: Chronic stress can raise blood sugar levels due to the release of cortisol.

- Stress-Relieving Practices: Incorporate deep breathing, yoga, and mindfulness practices to manage stress effectively.

3. Adequate Sleep

- Sleep's Role in Blood Sugar Control: Poor sleep can disrupt hormones, including insulin, leading to higher blood sugar levels.

- Sleep Hygiene: Maintain a regular sleep schedule and create a calming bedtime routine for better rest.


4. Hydration

- Water's Role in Blood Sugar Control: Proper hydration helps the kidneys flush excess sugar through urine, aiding in blood sugar regulation.

- Recommendation: Drink 8-10 glasses of water daily to stay hydrated.


By incorporating these dietary and lifestyle changes, along with herbal remedies, individuals can take a holistic approach to managing diabetes.


This aligns with Barbara O'Neill's teachings, which emphasize the importance of natural and balanced methods for maintaining optimal blood sugar control and overall well-being. Always consult with a healthcare provider before making significant changes to your regimen.


# LIFESTYLE CHANGES FOR MANAGING DIABETES


Managing diabetes effectively involves a combination of lifestyle modifications, including regular physical activity, maintaining a healthy weight, stress management, and proper hydration.


These steps, inspired by holistic approaches like those advocated by Barbara O'Neill, can help individuals achieve better blood sugar control and enhance overall well-being.


1. Regular Physical Activity

Exercise is essential for improving insulin sensitivity and lowering blood sugar levels. Aim for a balanced routine that includes both aerobic exercises and strength training:

- Aerobic Exercise: Aim for at least 150 minutes of moderate-intensity aerobic activity per week.

- Walking: A brisk 30-minute walk five times a week.

- Cycling: Biking in your neighborhood or using a stationary bike.

- Swimming: Engaging in lap swimming or water aerobics for cardiovascular health.

- Strength Training: Incorporate strength training exercises, such as weightlifting or resistance band exercises, two to three times a week to build muscle mass and improve insulin sensitivity.

## 2. Maintain a Healthy Weight

Maintaining a healthy weight can significantly enhance blood sugar control and reduce the risk of complications associated with diabetes:

- Balanced Diet: Focus on a diet rich in whole foods, such as vegetables, lean proteins, whole grains, and healthy fats.

- Regular Exercise: Combine aerobic activities with strength training to help achieve weight loss goals and maintain muscle mass.

- Mindful Eating: Practice mindful eating by paying attention to hunger and fullness cues, and avoid emotional eating. This can prevent overeating and promote healthy food choices.

## 3. Stress Management

Chronic stress can lead to elevated blood sugar levels. Managing stress is crucial for maintaining healthy glucose levels:

- Mindfulness and Meditation: Practice mindfulness meditation or deep breathing exercises daily to calm the mind and body.

- Yoga: Yoga promotes relaxation, improves flexibility, and can help alleviate stress while improving physical health.

- Adequate Sleep: Ensure you get 7-9 hours of quality sleep each night. Sleep is vital for stress reduction and overall well-being.

## 4. Regular Monitoring

Regularly monitoring blood sugar levels provides insight into how your body reacts to different foods, exercises, and stressors. This can help in adjusting your lifestyle choices and medications for optimal management:

- Glucose Monitoring: Use a glucose meter to check your blood sugar levels regularly, especially after meals and physical activities.

- Adjust Lifestyle: Based on your glucose readings, make necessary adjustments to your diet, exercise routine, and stress management techniques.

## 5. Hydration

Staying hydrated is essential for blood sugar regulation. Drinking enough water supports kidney function and helps in flushing out excess glucose through urine:

- Water Intake: Aim to drink at least eight 8-ounce glasses of water daily. Adjust water intake based on physical activity, weather, and individual needs.

Managing diabetes effectively requires a multifaceted approach, including physical activity, healthy eating, stress management, regular monitoring, and proper hydration.

By incorporating these strategies into your daily routine, you can achieve better blood sugar control, reduce the risk of complications, and improve your overall quality of life. Always consult a healthcare provider before making significant changes to your regimen, especially when adding herbal remedies or adjusting medications.

# CHAPTER 14

## WOMEN'S HEALTH

### NATURAL APPROACHES TO HORMONAL BALANCE

Maintaining hormonal balance is essential for women's overall health and well-being, influencing everything from mood and metabolism to reproductive health.

Hormonal imbalances can lead to various issues, including irregular menstrual cycles, infertility, and menopausal symptoms. Below are natural approaches for achieving and maintaining hormonal balance, based on the holistic principles of Barbara O'Neill.

1. Nutrient-Rich Diet

A balanced diet plays a key role in regulating hormone production. Here are some foods that can help:

- Healthy Fats: Incorporate avocados, nuts, seeds, and olive oil. These fats provide the essential fatty acids necessary for hormone production.

- Leafy Greens: Vegetables like spinach, kale, and broccoli are rich in vitamins and minerals that support the endocrine system.

- Whole Grains: Brown rice, quinoa, and oats help stabilize blood sugar, a critical factor in hormonal health.

- Lean Proteins: Choose fish, chicken, and plant-based proteins to support tissue repair and hormone regulation.

2. Herbal Remedies

Herbs have long been used to balance hormones naturally. Consider these herbal options:

- Maca Root (Lepidium meyenii): Known for balancing hormones and improving fertility, it can be consumed as a powder in smoothies or oatmeal.

- Chaste Tree Berry (Vitex agnus-castus): Helps regulate menstrual cycles and alleviate PMS symptoms. It is often taken in capsule or tincture form.

- Black Cohosh (Actaea racemosa): Known for easing menopausal symptoms like hot flashes and mood swings. Available as tea or supplement.

- Evening Primrose Oil (Oenothera biennis): Rich in gamma-linolenic acid (GLA), which helps balance hormones and alleviate PMS symptoms. Usually taken in capsule form.

## 3. Stress Management

Chronic stress elevates cortisol levels, which can disrupt hormonal balance. To combat stress, integrate these practices:

- Mindfulness and Meditation: Daily mindfulness exercises or deep-breathing practices reduce cortisol levels and promote relaxation.

- Yoga: Yoga combines physical exercise with mental calm, reducing stress while improving flexibility and balance.

- Adequate Sleep: Ensuring 7-9 hours of restful sleep every night supports overall health and hormone regulation.

## 4. Regular Physical Activity

Exercise helps regulate hormones and improves insulin sensitivity. Aim for a combination of:

- Aerobic Exercise: Activities like walking, swimming, or running boost metabolism and improve heart health.

- Strength Training: Exercises such as weightlifting build muscle and enhance metabolic function.

- Flexibility Exercises: Yoga and stretching routines help maintain flexibility and reduce stress.

## 5. Avoid Endocrine Disruptors

Endocrine-disrupting chemicals can interfere with hormonal balance. Reduce your exposure by:

- Using Natural Products: Opt for skincare and cleaning products free from parabens, phthalates, and other harmful chemicals.

- Avoiding Plastic: Store food and drinks in glass or stainless steel containers instead of plastic.

- Choosing Organic: Select organic produce to avoid pesticides and herbicides that can disrupt hormones.

## 6. Hydration

Staying hydrated is vital for supporting overall health and ensuring hormones function properly. Aim to drink at least eight 8-ounce glasses of water daily.

## 7. Supplementation

Certain supplements can help balance hormones naturally:

- Vitamin D: Crucial for immune function and hormonal balance. Get adequate sunlight or supplement if needed.

- Magnesium: Reduces stress and supports sleep, both of which are essential for hormone health.

- Omega-3 Fatty Acids: Found in fish oil and flaxseed oil, omega-3s reduce inflammation and support hormonal balance.

## HERBS FOR REPRODUCTIVE HEALTH

Reproductive health is essential to overall well-being, especially for women. Below are key herbs that support hormonal balance, regulate menstrual cycles, and enhance fertility, inspired by Barbara O'Neill's holistic teachings.

1. Chaste Tree (Vitex agnus-castus)

- Uses: Regulates menstrual cycles, reduces PMS symptoms, and supports fertility.

- Preparation: Commonly taken as a tincture or capsule. Recommended dose is 400-500 mg per day.

- Safety: Generally safe, but may interact with hormone therapies. Avoid during pregnancy unless advised by a healthcare provider.

2. Red Raspberry Leaf (Rubus idaeus)

- Uses: Strengthens the uterus, eases menstrual cramps, and supports pregnancy.

- Preparation: Steep 1-2 tsp of dried leaves in hot water for 10-15 minutes. Drink 2-3 cups daily.

- Safety: Safe for most women, but consult a healthcare provider during pregnancy.

3. Dong Quai (Angelica sinensis)

- Uses: Balances hormones, improves blood flow, and reduces menstrual cramps.

- Preparation: Available as a tincture or capsule. For a decoction, simmer 1-2 tsp of dried root for 20-30 minutes. Drink 1-2 cups daily.

- Safety: Avoid during pregnancy and while breastfeeding. May interact with blood-thinning medications.

4. Black Cohosh (Actaea racemosa)

- Uses: Alleviates menopausal symptoms and menstrual discomfort.

- Preparation: Steep 1 tsp of dried root in hot water for 10-15 minutes. Drink 1-2 cups daily.

- Safety: Safe for short-term use, but consult a healthcare provider if on hormone replacement therapy.

5. Maca Root (Lepidium meyenii)

- Uses: Balances hormones, improves fertility, and boosts energy.

- Preparation: Commonly available as a powder or capsule. Add 1-2 tsp to smoothies or yogurt.

- Safety: Generally safe, but avoid during pregnancy or breastfeeding without consulting a healthcare provider.

By incorporating these natural approaches—nutrient-rich diets, herbal remedies, stress management, regular physical activity, and avoiding endocrine disruptors—women can support hormonal health and reproductive wellness. Always consult a healthcare provider before making significant changes to your health routine or starting any new supplements.

## MANAGING MENSTRUAL AND MENOPAUSAL SYMPTOMS

Menstrual and menopausal symptoms can have a significant impact on a woman's daily life. Natural remedies, along with dietary and lifestyle changes, offer effective ways to manage these symptoms, as emphasized by Barbara O'Neill.

This chapter covers common menstrual and menopausal symptoms and provides holistic strategies to help alleviate discomfort and improve overall well-being.

### Common Menstrual Symptoms

- Dysmenorrhea (Menstrual Cramps): Painful cramps that occur before or during menstruation.

- Premenstrual Syndrome (PMS): A group of symptoms including mood swings, bloating, and breast tenderness.

- Heavy Menstrual Bleeding (Menorrhagia): Excessive bleeding during menstruation.

- Mood Swings and Irritability: Emotional fluctuations that may occur before or during the menstrual cycle.

- Bloating and Water Retention: Swelling and discomfort due to fluid retention.

# HERBAL REMEDIES FOR MENSTRUAL SYMPTOMS

1. Ginger (Zingiber officinale)

- Overview: Ginger is a powerful anti-inflammatory herb known for its ability to alleviate menstrual cramps.

- Uses: Reduces inflammation and relieves pain associated with menstrual cramps.

- Preparation:

- Ginger Tea: Slice fresh ginger and steep in hot water for 10-15 minutes. Drink 2-3 cups daily during your cycle.

- Safety: Generally safe. Consult a healthcare provider if pregnant or on blood-thinning medications.


2. Chamomile (Matricaria recutita)

- Overview: Chamomile is calming and can help reduce menstrual pain and improve mood.

- Uses: Alleviates menstrual cramps and reduces anxiety.

- Preparation:

- Chamomile Tea: Steep 1-2 teaspoons of dried chamomile flowers in hot water for 10 minutes. Drink 2-3 cups daily.

- Safety: Avoid if allergic to ragweed or related plants.


3. Chaste Tree (Vitex agnus-castus)

- Overview: Helps balance hormones and reduce symptoms of PMS.

- Uses: Alleviates breast tenderness, mood swings, and bloating.

- Preparation:

- Vitex Tincture: Follow the instructions on the tincture bottle. Generally, 20-40 drops daily in water or juice.

- Safety: Avoid during pregnancy. Consult with a healthcare provider if on hormone therapies.


4. Evening Primrose Oil (Oenothera biennis)

- Overview: Rich in gamma-linolenic acid (GLA), which helps alleviate PMS symptoms.

- Uses: Reduces breast tenderness and mood swings.

- Preparation:

- Capsules: Typically, 500 mg taken 2-3 times daily.

- Safety: Consult a healthcare provider if taking blood-thinning medications.

# DIETARY AND LIFESTYLE TIPS FOR MENSTRUAL HEALTH

1. Maintain a Balanced Diet

- Focus on consuming whole foods rich in fruits, vegetables, whole grains, and lean proteins.

- Reduce processed and sugary foods that may exacerbate PMS symptoms.

2. Stay Hydrated

- Drink plenty of water to reduce bloating and support overall health.

3. Regular Exercise

- Engage in moderate physical activity such as walking, yoga, or swimming to help reduce the severity of cramps and improve mood.

4. Stress Management

- Practice relaxation techniques like meditation, yoga, or deep breathing to help alleviate PMS-related stress and mood swings.

# MANAGING MENOPAUSAL SYMPTOMS

Menopause brings a range of symptoms due to hormonal changes, including hot flashes, night sweats, mood swings, and sleep disturbances. Below are natural remedies and lifestyle changes that can help manage menopausal symptoms.

**Common Menopausal Symptoms**

- Hot Flashes and Night Sweats: Sudden feelings of heat, often accompanied by sweating.

- Mood Swings and Irritability: Emotional fluctuations due to hormonal changes.

- Vaginal Dryness: A common symptom that can cause discomfort during menopause.

- Sleep Disturbances: Difficulty falling or staying asleep.

- Weight Gain: Often due to changes in metabolism.

## HERBAL REMEDIES FOR MENOPAUSAL SYMPTOMS

1. Black Cohosh (Actaea racemosa)

- Overview: Commonly used to reduce hot flashes and night sweats.

- Uses: Eases hot flashes, night sweats, and mood swings.

- Preparation:

- Black Cohosh Tea: Steep 1 teaspoon of dried root in hot water for 10-15 minutes. Drink 1-2 cups daily.

- Safety: Avoid during pregnancy. Consult with a healthcare provider if on hormone replacement therapy or with liver conditions.


2. Red Clover (Trifolium pratense)

- Overview: Contains phytoestrogens, which help balance hormones.

- Uses: Reduces hot flashes and improves bone health.

- Preparation:

- Red Clover Tea: Steep 1-2 teaspoons of dried flowers in hot water for 10-15 minutes. Drink 2-3 cups daily.

- Safety: Generally safe. Consult with a healthcare provider if on blood-thinning medications.


3. Sage (Salvia officinalis)

- Overview: Effective in reducing hot flashes and night sweats.

- Uses: Reduces hot flashes and night sweats.

- Preparation:

- Sage Tea: Steep 1-2 teaspoons of dried leaves in hot water for 10 minutes. Drink 1-2 cups daily.

- Safety: Avoid during pregnancy and breastfeeding. Consult a healthcare provider if on medications.

4. Maca (Lepidium meyenii)

- Overview: An adaptogen that helps balance hormones and improve energy levels.

- Uses: Reduces menopausal symptoms and increases stamina.

- Preparation:

- Maca Powder: Add 1-2 teaspoons to smoothies, yogurt, or oatmeal daily.

- Safety: Generally safe. Start with a small dose to assess tolerance.

Dietary and Lifestyle Tips for Menopausal Health

1. Adopt a Healthy Diet

- Nutrient-Dense Foods: Include plenty of fruits, vegetables, whole grains, and lean proteins in your diet.

- Phytoestrogens: Incorporate foods like soy, flaxseed, and legumes to help balance hormones.

2. Stay Hydrated

- Drink water throughout the day to help manage hot flashes and maintain overall health.

3. Exercise Regularly

- Engage in physical activities such as walking, yoga, or weight training to help manage weight, improve mood, and reduce symptoms.

4. Stress Management

- Practice relaxation techniques, including yoga, meditation, and deep breathing exercises, to reduce stress and ease symptoms.

5. Ensure Adequate Sleep

- Create a calming bedtime routine and aim for 7-8 hours of sleep to manage sleep disturbances and mood swings.

6. Maintain Social Connections

- Stay connected with friends, family, and community support groups to help manage emotional changes during menopause.

By incorporating these natural remedies and lifestyle adjustments, women can effectively manage menstrual and menopausal symptoms, improving their quality of life.

Inspired by Barbara O'Neill's teachings, these holistic approaches provide a safe and effective way to support women's health. Always consult a healthcare professional before starting any new herbal regimen, especially if you are pregnant, breastfeeding, or on medication.

# CHAPTER 15

## SKIN HEALTH AND BEAUTY

## NATURAL TREATMENTS FOR COMMON SKIN CONDITIONS

Our skin, the largest organ of the body, reflects our internal health. Conditions such as acne, eczema, psoriasis, and dry skin can be managed effectively using natural treatments and holistic practices.

Drawing inspiration from Barbara O'Neill's teachings, this chapter explores remedies and lifestyle adjustments to support skin health.

1. Acne

Overview: Acne is a common condition involving pimples, blackheads, and whiteheads, often caused by hormonal imbalances, poor diet, or improper skincare.

Natural Treatments:

1. Tea Tree Oil (Melaleuca alternifolia)

- Active Compounds: Terpinen-4-ol

- Uses: Antibacterial and anti-inflammatory properties reduce acne.

- Application: Dilute tea tree oil in a 1:10 ratio with a carrier oil (coconut oil). Apply with a cotton swab twice daily.

- Precautions: Always dilute and conduct a patch test.

2. Aloe Vera (Aloe barbadensis)

- Active Compounds: Polysaccharides, gibberellins

- Uses: Soothes inflammation and reduces acne scars.

- Application: Apply fresh aloe vera gel for 20 minutes, then rinse with lukewarm water. Use twice daily.

- Precautions: Safe for most skin types. Patch test recommended.

3. Honey and Cinnamon Mask

- Active Compounds: Honey (antibacterial), cinnamon (anti-inflammatory)

- Uses: Reduces bacteria and inflammation.

- Application: Mix 2 tbsp honey and 1 tsp cinnamon into a paste. Apply for 10-15 minutes, then rinse. Use 1-2 times a week.

- Precautions: Patch test for allergies.


2. Eczema

Overview: Eczema causes dry, itchy, inflamed skin. It can be triggered by allergens, stress, and environmental factors.


Natural Treatments:

1. Oatmeal Baths

- Active Compounds: Beta-glucans, saponins

- Uses: Soothes and moisturizes dry skin.

- Application: Blend 1 cup oatmeal into a powder and add to a lukewarm bath. Soak for 15-20 minutes.

- Precautions: Ensure water is lukewarm, not hot.


2. Coconut Oil (Cocos nucifera)

- Active Compounds: Lauric acid, caprylic acid

- Uses: Moisturizes and reduces inflammation.

- Application: Apply virgin coconut oil to affected areas 2-3 times daily.

- Precautions: Avoid if allergic to coconut.


3. Chamomile Compress (Matricaria recutita)

- Active Compounds: Bisabolol, flavonoids

- Uses: Soothes inflamed skin.

- Application: Soak a cloth in chamomile tea and apply for 15-20 minutes.

- Precautions: Patch test for allergies.

3. Psoriasis

Overview: Psoriasis is an autoimmune condition that causes scaling and inflammation of the skin.

Natural Treatments:

1. Turmeric (Curcuma longa)

- Active Compounds: Curcumin

- Uses: Anti-inflammatory properties reduce symptoms.

- Application: Apply a turmeric paste for 15 minutes, then rinse.

- Precautions: May stain the skin temporarily.

2. Aloe Vera (Aloe barbadensis)

- Active Compounds: Polysaccharides, gibberellins

- Uses: Moisturizes and reduces inflammation.

- Application: Apply aloe vera gel for 30 minutes. Use 2-3 times daily.

- Precautions: Safe for most skin types.

3. Apple Cider Vinegar (Acetic acid)

- Active Compounds: Acetic acid

- Uses: Restores skin's pH balance and reduces itching.

- Application: Dilute with water and apply with a cotton ball for 10 minutes.

- Precautions: Avoid on broken skin.

4. Dry Skin

Overview: Dry skin can be caused by environmental factors, dehydration, or aging, leading to rough, flaky, and itchy patches.

Natural Treatments:

1. Honey (Apis mellifera)

- Active Compounds: Glucose, fructose, amino acids

- Uses: Moisturizes and soothes dry skin.

- Application: Apply raw honey for 15-20 minutes, then rinse. Use 2-3 times a week.


2. Olive Oil (Olea europaea)

- Active Compounds: Oleic acid, squalene

- Uses: Deeply nourishes and moisturizes skin.

- Application: Apply extra virgin olive oil for 30 minutes, then rinse.

- Precautions: Patch test for sensitivity.


3. Shea Butter (Vitellaria paradoxa)

- Active Compounds: Stearic acid, oleic acid

- Uses: Deeply moisturizes and repairs dry skin.

- Application: Apply shea butter after bathing, 2-3 times daily.

- Precautions: Generally safe. Patch test if using for the first time.


## HOLISTIC PRACTICES FOR SKIN HEALTH


In addition to natural treatments, holistic practices can improve overall skin health by addressing both internal and external factors. Barbara O'Neill advocates for nourishing the body through proper nutrition, hydration, and stress management.


1. Healthy Diet

- Focus on whole foods, including fruits, vegetables, whole grains, and lean proteins.

- Hydrate by drinking plenty of water to keep the skin nourished and flush out toxins.


2. Regular Exercise

- Enhances blood circulation, delivering nutrients to the skin and promoting a healthy glow.

- Exercise also helps manage stress, which can exacerbate skin conditions.

3. Adequate Sleep

- Aim for 7-8 hours of sleep per night to support the skin's natural repair processes.

4. Stress Management

- Incorporate yoga, meditation, and deep breathing exercises to manage stress and improve skin conditions like acne and eczema.

5. Proper Skincare Routine

- Cleanse gently: Use a mild cleanser to remove impurities without stripping the skin of its natural oils.

- Moisturize regularly: Apply a suitable moisturizer to maintain hydration.

- Protect from sun damage: Use sunscreen with at least SPF 30 daily.

By integrating these natural treatments and holistic practices into your routine, you can significantly improve your skin health.

Always consult with a healthcare professional before starting any new regimen, especially if you have underlying conditions or are on medication. Inspired by Barbara O'Neill, these strategies will help you achieve radiant, healthy skin while promoting overall wellness.

# SKINCARE ROUTINES WITH HERBAL REMEDIES

Incorporating herbal remedies into your skincare routine offers natural nourishment and healing for your skin, addressing different skin types and concerns.

Inspired by Barbara O'Neill's holistic approach, here is a detailed guide to creating effective morning and evening skincare routines, along with weekly treatments that incorporate herbal remedies.

1. Morning Skincare Routine

Step 1: Cleansing

Herbal Remedy: Chamomile and Green Tea Cleanser

- Ingredients:

- 1 cup of brewed chamomile tea

- 1 cup of brewed green tea

- 2 tablespoons of raw honey

- 1 tablespoon of apple cider vinegar

- Preparation and Use:

1. Brew chamomile and green tea and allow them to cool.

2. Mix the teas with honey and apple cider vinegar.

3. Store in a bottle and use as a gentle morning cleanser. Apply, massage gently, and rinse with lukewarm water.

- Benefits: Chamomile soothes inflammation, green tea provides antioxidants, honey moisturizes, and apple cider vinegar balances pH.


Step 2: Toning

Herbal Remedy: Rose and Witch Hazel Toner

- Ingredients:

- 1 cup of rose water

- ½ cup of witch hazel

- 5 drops of lavender essential oil

- Preparation and Use:

1. Mix rose water and witch hazel in a bottle.

2. Add lavender oil and shake well.

3. Apply with a cotton pad after cleansing.

- Benefits: Rose water hydrates, witch hazel tightens pores, and lavender oil soothes the skin.


Step 3: Moisturizing

Herbal Remedy: Aloe Vera and Jojoba Oil Moisturizer

- Ingredients:

- 2 tablespoons of fresh aloe vera gel

- 1 tablespoon of jojoba oil

- 5 drops of tea tree oil (optional for acne-prone skin)

- Preparation and Use:

1. Mix aloe vera gel and jojoba oil, adding tea tree oil if needed.

2. Massage a small amount into the face and neck.

- Benefits: Aloe vera hydrates, jojoba oil mimics skin's natural oils, and tea tree oil prevents acne.

Step 4: Sun Protection

Herbal Remedy: Natural Sunscreen with Carrot Seed Oil

- Ingredients:

- ¼ cup of coconut oil

- ¼ cup of shea butter

- 2 tablespoons of zinc oxide

- 10 drops of carrot seed oil

- Preparation and Use:

1. Melt coconut oil and shea butter in a double boiler.

2. Remove from heat, add zinc oxide and carrot seed oil, and mix.

3. Apply a thin layer before sun exposure.

- Benefits: Carrot seed oil provides natural SPF, while coconut oil and shea butter moisturize and protect.

2. Evening Skincare Routine

Step 1: Makeup Removal

Herbal Remedy: Calendula and Coconut Oil Makeup Remover

- Ingredients:

- ¼ cup calendula-infused oil

- ¼ cup coconut oil

- Preparation and Use:

1. Combine calendula-infused oil and coconut oil.

2. Apply with a cotton pad to remove makeup.

- Benefits: Calendula soothes skin, and coconut oil removes impurities.


Step 2: Cleansing

Use Chamomile and Green Tea Cleanser from the morning routine.


Step 3: Exfoliation (2-3 times per week)

Herbal Remedy: Oatmeal and Honey Scrub

- Ingredients:

- 2 tablespoons ground oatmeal

- 1 tablespoon honey

- 1 tablespoon yogurt

- Preparation and Use:

1. Mix oatmeal, honey, and yogurt to form a paste.

2. Apply in circular motions, avoiding the eye area, and rinse off.

- Benefits: Oatmeal exfoliates, honey moisturizes, and yogurt offers lactic acid for gentle exfoliation.


Step 4: Toning

Use Rose and Witch Hazel Toner from the morning routine.


Step 5: Night Serum

Herbal Remedy: Rosehip and Frankincense Night Serum

- Ingredients:

- 1 tablespoon rosehip oil

- 1 tablespoon jojoba oil

- 5 drops frankincense essential oil

- Preparation and Use:

1. Mix oils in a dropper bottle.

2. Apply 3-4 drops to your face and neck, gently massaging.

- Benefits: Rosehip oil regenerates skin, jojoba oil nourishes, and frankincense reduces fine lines.

Step 6: Moisturizing

Herbal Remedy: Shea Butter and Lavender Night Cream

- Ingredients:

- ¼ cup shea butter

- 1 tablespoon almond oil

- 5 drops lavender essential oil

- Preparation and Use:

1. Melt shea butter, then mix in almond oil and lavender oil.

2. Apply to face and neck before bed.

- Benefits: Shea butter deeply moisturizes, almond oil nourishes, and lavender promotes relaxation and healing.

3. Weekly Skincare Treatments

Herbal Remedy: Detoxifying Clay Mask

- Ingredients:

- 2 tablespoons bentonite clay

- 1 tablespoon apple cider vinegar

- 1 tablespoon water

- 5 drops tea tree oil

- Preparation and Use:

1. Mix all ingredients into a paste.

2. Apply to the face, avoiding the eyes. Leave for 10-15 minutes, then rinse.

- Benefits: Bentonite clay detoxifies, and tea tree oil fights acne.

Herbal Remedy: Hydrating Herbal Facial Steam

- Ingredients:

- 1 tablespoon dried chamomile

- 1 tablespoon dried calendula

- 1 tablespoon dried lavender

- 4 cups boiling water

- Preparation and Use:

1. Place dried herbs in a bowl, pour boiling water, and steep for 5 minutes.

2. Lean over the bowl, drape a towel over your head, and steam for 10-15 minutes.

- Benefits: The steam opens pores, and the herbs soothe and hydrate the skin.

## DIET AND LIFESTYLE FOR RADIANT SKIN

Skin health is not only about topical treatments but also influenced by diet and lifestyle. Barbara O'Neill emphasizes a holistic approach, nourishing your body from the inside out.

1. Nutrient-Rich Diet for Radiant Skin

- Antioxidant-Rich Foods: Berries, leafy greens, and nuts protect against aging.

- Healthy Fats: Avocados, fatty fish, and olive oil maintain skin elasticity.

- Hydrating Foods: Cucumbers and watermelon keep skin hydrated.

- Collagen-Boosting Foods: Bone broth, citrus fruits, and bell peppers promote skin firmness.

- Detoxifying Foods: Beets, garlic, and green tea cleanse the body and support liver function.

2. Lifestyle Tips for Radiant Skin

- Exercise: Regular cardio and strength training improve circulation and skin health.

- Stress Management: Practices like meditation and yoga reduce stress-induced skin issues.

- Adequate Sleep: Aim for 7-8 hours of rest to allow the skin to repair and rejuvenate.

- Hydration: Drink at least 8 glasses of water daily and limit caffeine and alcohol.

- Skincare Routine: Use gentle, herbal-based products that nourish and protect the skin.

By incorporating these routines and lifestyle adjustments inspired by Barbara O'Neill's teachings, you can maintain healthy, radiant skin. Always consult with a healthcare professional before using new ingredients or remedies, especially if you have skin conditions or allergies.

# CHAPTER 16

## MENTAL HEALTH AND COGNITIVE FUNCTION

### HERBS FOR MOOD AND MENTAL CLARITY

Mental health and cognitive function are essential to overall well-being, and natural approaches, including herbal remedies, offer a gentle yet effective way to enhance these aspects.

Barbara O'Neill advocates for a holistic approach, emphasizing the power of herbs in boosting mood and improving mental clarity. Below are key herbs that support cognitive function and emotional balance, along with their preparation methods, dosages, and safety considerations.

1. Ashwagandha (Withania somnifera)

- Key Elements: Adaptogen, stress relief, anxiety reduction

- Active Compounds: Withanolides, alkaloids

- Uses: Helps the body manage stress, reduce anxiety and depression, improve mood, and enhance cognitive function by lowering cortisol levels.

- Preparation and Dosage:

- Preparation: Can be consumed as powder, capsule, or tincture, often mixed with warm milk or water.

- Dosage: 300-500 mg standardized extract, twice daily.

- Safety: Safe for most, but avoid during pregnancy and with hyperthyroidism.

2. Rhodiola (Rhodiola rosea)

- Key Elements: Adaptogen, reduces fatigue, cognitive enhancer

- Active Compounds: Rosavins, salidroside

- Uses: Improves mental performance, reduces fatigue, and enhances concentration while managing stress.

- Preparation and Dosage:

- Preparation: Available in capsules, tablets, tinctures, or brewed as tea.

- Dosage: 200-400 mg of standardized extract daily.

- Safety: Generally well-tolerated; take earlier in the day to avoid sleep disturbances.


3. Bacopa (Bacopa monnieri)

- Key Elements: Memory enhancement, cognitive support, anxiety reduction

- Active Compounds: Bacosides

- Uses: Improves memory, reduces anxiety, enhances brain function, and promotes clarity.

- Preparation and Dosage:

- Preparation: Powder, capsule, or tincture, often taken with ghee or milk.

- Dosage: 300-450 mg standardized extract daily.

- Safety: May cause digestive issues. Use with caution if you have a slow heart rate.


4. St. John's Wort (Hypericum perforatum)

- Key Elements: Mood enhancement, antidepressant, anxiety relief

- Active Compounds: Hypericin, hyperforin

- Uses: Treats mild to moderate depression and reduces anxiety by stabilizing mood.

- Preparation and Dosage:

- Preparation: Capsules, tablets, teas, and tinctures.

- Dosage: 300 mg standardized extract, three times daily.

- Safety: Can interact with medications like antidepressants and birth control. Consult a healthcare provider.


5. Ginkgo Biloba (Ginkgo biloba)

- Key Elements: Cognitive enhancement, memory support, improves circulation

- Active Compounds: Flavonoids, terpenoids

- Uses: Improves blood flow to the brain, sharpens focus, and enhances memory.

- Preparation and Dosage:

- Preparation: Available as capsules, teas, or tinctures.

- Dosage: 120-240 mg standardized extract daily.

- Safety: May cause headaches or interact with blood-thinning medications.

6. Holy Basil (Ocimum sanctum)

- Key Elements: Adaptogen, stress relief, cognitive function enhancement

- Active Compounds: Eugenol, rosmarinic acid

- Uses: Reduces stress, enhances cognitive function, and supports overall brain health.

- Preparation and Dosage:

- Preparation: Tea, capsule, or tincture.

- Dosage: 300-500 mg extract daily or 2-3 cups of tea.

- Safety: Consult with a healthcare provider if pregnant.


7. Lemon Balm (Melissa officinalis)

- Key Elements: Anxiety relief, cognitive enhancement, mood stabilizer

- Active Compounds: Rosmarinic acid, flavonoids

- Uses: Reduces anxiety, improves mood, and promotes relaxation.

- Preparation and Dosage:

- Preparation: Tea, capsules, or tinctures.

- Dosage: 300-500 mg extract daily or 2-3 cups of tea.

- Safety: May cause nausea or headaches in some individuals.


8. Valerian (Valeriana officinalis)

- Key Elements: Anxiety reduction, sleep aid, mood enhancer

- Active Compounds: Valerenic acid, isovaleric acid

- Uses: Promotes relaxation, improves sleep quality, and reduces anxiety.

- Preparation and Dosage:

- Preparation: Capsules, tablets, teas, or tinctures.

- Dosage: 400-900 mg extract before bedtime.

- Safety: May cause drowsiness; avoid driving after use.

9. Passionflower (Passiflora incarnata)

- Key Elements: Anxiety relief, sleep aid, mood stabilizer

- Active Compounds: Flavonoids, alkaloids

- Uses: Calms the mind, reduces anxiety, and improves sleep.

- Preparation and Dosage:

- Preparation: Tea, capsules, or tinctures.

- Dosage: 200-400 mg extract or 2-3 cups of tea daily.

- Safety: Can cause drowsiness; avoid activities requiring alertness.


10. Lavender (Lavandula angustifolia)

- Key Elements: Stress relief, cognitive enhancement, anxiety reduction

- Active Compounds: Linalool, linalyl acetate

- Uses: Reduces anxiety, promotes relaxation, and sharpens mental clarity.

- Preparation and Dosage:

- Preparation: Essential oil, tea, capsules, or tinctures.

- Dosage: 80-160 mg extract or 2-3 cups of tea daily.

- Safety: Dilute essential oil before topical use to avoid irritation.


# NATURAL APPROACHES TO OVERCOMING INSOMNIA

Insomnia affects millions and can impact overall health and well-being. Natural remedies, as recommended by Barbara O'Neill, provide effective alternatives to pharmaceutical treatments.


Diet and Nutrition

- Magnesium and Calcium: Support muscle relaxation and nervous system function. Foods include leafy greens, nuts, seeds, and dairy.

- Sleep-Promoting Foods: Almonds, bananas, and leafy greens contain tryptophan, magnesium, and potassium, promoting relaxation and sleep.

- Avoid Stimulants: Reduce caffeine, sugar, and alcohol intake.

Herbal Remedies for Sleep

- Valerian Root Tea: Steep 1 teaspoon in boiling water, drink 30-60 minutes before bed.

- Chamomile Tea: Steep chamomile flowers in hot water, drink before bedtime for calming effects.

- Passionflower Tea: A calming tea to ease into sleep, drink 30 minutes before bed.

- Lavender Tea: Soothing lavender tea promotes sleep and reduces stress.

Lifestyle Adjustments

- Consistent Sleep Schedule: Keep regular sleep and wake times.

- Evening Relaxation: Engage in calming activities like reading, yoga, or deep breathing.

- Comfortable Sleep Environment: Ensure your bedroom is dark, cool, and quiet for optimal rest.

## REDUCING ANXIETY AND STRESS NATURALLY

Managing stress and anxiety through holistic approaches is vital for mental clarity and emotional balance. Incorporating mindfulness, stress management techniques, and herbal remedies like lavender and passionflower can significantly reduce anxiety.

By adopting these natural remedies, you can enhance mental health, cognitive clarity, and overall well-being, providing long-term support for a balanced life. Always consult with a healthcare provider before starting a new herbal regimen, especially if you have pre-existing conditions or take medication.

## NUTRITIONAL SUPPORT FOR MENTAL WELLNESS

Barbara O'Neill emphasizes that nutrition is foundational in managing stress and anxiety. The food we consume has a direct impact on our mood, brain function, and ability to handle stress. A diet rich in essential nutrients can provide the building blocks for mental clarity, emotional stability, and a sense of calm.

- Magnesium-Rich Foods: Magnesium is known as nature's tranquilizer due to its calming effect on the nervous system. It aids in muscle relaxation, stress reduction, and sleep improvement.

- Incorporate: Spinach, almonds, cashews, pumpkin seeds, and black beans into your meals.

- Tip: Snack on a handful of nuts or enjoy a spinach salad daily to boost magnesium intake.

- Omega-3 Fatty Acids: These essential fats play a crucial role in brain health, reducing inflammation, and improving cognitive function. Omega-3s also support emotional balance, making them vital for stress and anxiety reduction.

- Incorporate: Salmon, chia seeds, flaxseeds, and walnuts.

- Tip: Eat fatty fish like salmon twice a week or add ground flaxseeds to smoothies or oatmeal for a daily boost.

- Hydration: Dehydration can worsen anxiety and irritability. Staying hydrated supports cognitive function and keeps stress at bay.

- Tip: Drink at least 8 cups of water daily. Keep a water bottle with you to remind yourself to hydrate.

# HERBAL REMEDIES FOR NATURAL STRESS RELIEF

Herbal remedies are time-tested natural solutions for calming the mind, improving mood, and reducing anxiety. These herbs offer gentle yet powerful effects on mental well-being.

- Passionflower: Passionflower is well-known for its calming properties, easing anxiety, and improving sleep quality.

- Preparation: Steep 1 teaspoon of dried passionflower in 1 cup of boiling water for 10 minutes. Strain and drink before bedtime to induce restful sleep and calm the mind.

- Ashwagandha: A powerful adaptogen, Ashwagandha helps the body adapt to stress, lowers cortisol levels, and supports mental clarity.

- Instructions: Take 500 mg of Ashwagandha supplement daily or add 1 teaspoon of Ashwagandha powder to a smoothie for daily stress resilience.

- Lemon Balm: Known for its mood-enhancing and calming effects, lemon balm can help reduce anxiety and promote relaxation.

- Preparation: Steep 1-2 teaspoons of dried lemon balm leaves in boiling water for 5-10 minutes. Enjoy as a soothing tea in the evening.

Aromatherapy harnesses the power of essential oils to promote relaxation, reduce stress, and enhance emotional well-being. Scents like lavender and chamomile have been shown to calm the mind and ease anxiety.

- Lavender Oil: Lavender is the go-to oil for relaxation, helping to calm the nervous system and reduce feelings of stress.

- Instructions: Add a few drops of lavender oil to a diffuser or mix it with a carrier oil and apply to your temples and wrists.

- Bergamot Oil: This citrusy essential oil is known for its uplifting properties that can soothe anxiety and reduce stress.

- Instructions: Add 3-4 drops to a warm bath or diffuse in your living space for a refreshing, calming atmosphere.

- Chamomile Oil: Chamomile has long been used to promote relaxation and reduce anxiety. Its gentle, soothing scent can calm the mind and encourage restful sleep.

- Instructions: Use in a diffuser or add a few drops to a bath for a peaceful, calming effect.

## PHYSICAL ACTIVITY FOR MENTAL RESILIENCE

Exercise is a powerful tool for managing stress and anxiety. It stimulates the production of endorphins, the body's natural mood elevators, and helps improve sleep quality. Physical activity also reduces the stress hormone cortisol, allowing the body to reset and recover.

- Yoga: Yoga combines physical postures with breathwork, helping to calm the mind, reduce tension, and promote emotional balance.

- Instructions: Practice yoga for at least 30 minutes, three times a week. Follow online classes or join a local studio to improve both mental and physical flexibility.

- Tai Chi: This gentle, flowing practice promotes relaxation and mindfulness, making it an excellent option for stress reduction.

- Instructions: Engage in tai chi sessions for 20-30 minutes daily to cultivate a sense of balance and inner calm.

- Nature Walks: Spending time in nature has been shown to lower cortisol levels and increase feelings of calm and well-being.

- Instructions: Take a 20-minute walk in nature each day to reconnect with the natural world and reduce stress levels.

## MINDFULNESS AND MEDITATION FOR INNER PEACE

Mindfulness and meditation are powerful tools for reducing anxiety and stress. They help you focus on the present moment, quiet the mind, and cultivate a sense of peace and centeredness.

- Mindfulness Meditation: This practice encourages you to focus on the present moment, helping to quiet anxious thoughts and reduce stress.

- Instructions: Spend 10-15 minutes each morning focusing on your breath. Sit quietly, close your eyes, and bring your attention to your breathing. When your mind wanders, gently bring it back to your breath.

- Guided Imagery: This visualization technique allows you to mentally transport yourself to a calm, peaceful setting.

- Instructions: Use guided imagery recordings or apps to help you visualize relaxing settings, alleviating stress and anxiety.

- Gratitude Practice: Cultivating gratitude shifts your focus from stress and worry to appreciation and positivity.

- Instructions: Keep a gratitude journal and write down three things you are thankful for each day to help refocus your mind on the positive aspects of your life.

## STRESS MANAGEMENT TECHNIQUES

Incorporating stress-reducing techniques into your daily routine can significantly improve mental well-being and resilience to anxiety.

- Deep Breathing Exercises: Focused breathing can quickly calm the nervous system and reduce anxiety.

- Instructions: Practice the 4-7-8 breathing technique: Inhale for 4 seconds, hold for 7 seconds, and exhale for 8 seconds. Repeat 4-5 cycles to restore calm.

- Progressive Muscle Relaxation: This technique helps to release physical tension, promoting relaxation throughout the body.

- Instructions: Starting from your toes, tense each muscle group for 5 seconds, then slowly release. Move upward through your body, finishing with your shoulders and face.

- Journaling: Writing down your thoughts allows you to process emotions, relieve mental tension, and gain perspective on stressful situations.

- Instructions: Set aside 10 minutes each day to write freely about your thoughts and feelings. This simple act can help you clarify emotions and reduce anxiety.

## CREATING A RELAXING ENVIRONMENT

Your environment plays a crucial role in your mental state. By designing a space that fosters relaxation and calm, you can create a sanctuary for mental well-being.

- Declutter: A clean, organized space promotes mental clarity and reduces stress.

- Instructions: Spend 15 minutes a day decluttering and organizing your space to create a peaceful, stress-free environment.

- Natural Light: Exposure to natural light helps regulate mood and energy levels.

- Instructions: Open curtains and blinds during the day to let in natural light, and spend time outdoors when possible.

- Comfort Items: Surround yourself with items that make you feel comfortable and at ease.

- Instructions: Incorporate soft blankets, scented candles, or plants into your space to foster a soothing, cozy atmosphere.

# SPIRITUAL PRACTICES AND PRAYER FOR INNER STRENGTH

Spirituality can be a source of strength and comfort during times of stress and anxiety. Whether through prayer, meditation, or connection to a higher power, spiritual practices can help center the mind and provide emotional resilience.

- Daily Prayer: Prayer can offer solace and emotional support, helping you feel connected and guided during stressful times.

- Instructions: Set aside time each day for prayer or spiritual reflection. Find a quiet space where you can connect with your faith or inner wisdom.

- Spiritual Community: Being part of a supportive spiritual or religious community can help you feel grounded and less isolated.

- Instructions: Engage in group activities, such as study groups or service projects, within your spiritual community.

- Meditative Prayer: Combining prayer with meditation can deepen your spiritual practice and promote inner peace.

- Instructions: Focus on a sacred word or phrase during meditation. Repeat the word or phrase, allowing it to center and calm your mind.

Incorporating these holistic strategies into your daily routine will create a comprehensive approach to reducing stress and anxiety.

By supporting your body with proper nutrition, engaging in calming activities, and fostering a peaceful environment, you can enhance your mental health and cultivate long-term resilience.

Through these natural remedies and lifestyle changes, you can take charge of your well-being, living a more balanced and fulfilling life.

# CHAPTER 17

## NATURAL SOLUTIONS FOR DIVERSE RESPIRATORY CONDITIONS

Respiratory health is a cornerstone of overall well-being, as it ensures the body receives the oxygen it needs while expelling carbon dioxide. Many respiratory conditions—such as asthma, bronchitis, sinusitis, and chronic obstructive pulmonary disease (COPD)—can severely affect quality of life.

In alignment with the teachings of Barbara O'Neill, this chapter explores how natural remedies can be incorporated into a holistic approach to support respiratory health.

Asthma

Understanding Asthma: Asthma is a chronic condition where inflammation causes the airways to narrow, making breathing difficult. Common symptoms include wheezing, chest tightness, coughing, and shortness of breath.

Herbal Remedies for Asthma:

1. Licorice Root (Glycyrrhiza glabra):

- Active Compounds: Glycyrrhizin, flavonoids

- Benefits: Anti-inflammatory properties help soothe inflamed airways and reduce asthma symptoms.

- Preparation and Use:

- Tea: Steep 1 teaspoon of dried licorice root in a cup of boiling water for 10 minutes. Drink up to three times a day.

- Precautions: Long-term use may lead to high blood pressure. Avoid if pregnant or if you have heart conditions.

2. Mullein (Verbascum thapsus):

- Active Compounds: Saponins, mucilage

- Benefits: Clears mucus and soothes the respiratory tract.

- Preparation and Use:

- Tea: Steep 1-2 teaspoons of dried mullein leaves in hot water for 10-15 minutes. Drink twice daily.

- Precautions: Ensure leaves are well-strained to avoid throat irritation.


Bronchitis


Understanding Bronchitis: Bronchitis is inflammation of the bronchial tubes, often triggered by infection. It leads to coughing, mucus production, and shortness of breath.


Herbal Remedies for Bronchitis:

1. Thyme (Thymus vulgaris):

- Active Compounds: Thymol, carvacrol

- Benefits: Antimicrobial properties help fight infection while acting as an expectorant to clear mucus.

- Preparation and Use:

- Tea: Steep 1 teaspoon of dried thyme in boiling water for 10 minutes. Drink three times daily.

- Steam Inhalation: Add a few drops of thyme essential oil to hot water and inhale the steam.

- Precautions: Avoid during pregnancy.


2. Eucalyptus (Eucalyptus globulus):

- Active Compounds: Eucalyptol, cineole

- Benefits: Reduces inflammation and clears respiratory congestion.

- Preparation and Use:

- Steam Inhalation: Add a few drops of eucalyptus oil to a bowl of hot water. Inhale the steam for 10 minutes.

- Chest Rub: Mix eucalyptus oil with a carrier oil like coconut oil and rub onto the chest.

- Precautions: Avoid using essential oil undiluted directly on the skin.


Sinusitis


Understanding Sinusitis: Sinusitis is an inflammation of the sinus cavities, often caused by infection or allergies. Symptoms include nasal congestion, facial pain, and a thick nasal discharge.

Herbal Remedies for Sinusitis:

1. Peppermint (Mentha piperita):

- Active Compounds: Menthol, menthone

- Benefits: Acts as a decongestant, easing sinus pressure.

- Preparation and Use:

- Steam Inhalation: Add peppermint oil to hot water and inhale.

- Tea: Steep 1 teaspoon of dried peppermint leaves in hot water for 10 minutes. Drink up to three times daily.

- Precautions: May cause allergic reactions in some individuals.


2. Goldenseal (Hydrastis canadensis):

- Active Compounds: Berberine, hydrastine

- Benefits: Helps fight sinus infections and reduce inflammation.

- Preparation and Use:

- Tea: Steep 1 teaspoon of dried goldenseal root in hot water for 10 minutes. Drink twice daily.

- Nasal Rinse: Mix a saline solution with a few drops of goldenseal tincture for nasal irrigation.

- Precautions: Avoid prolonged use or during pregnancy.

# CHRONIC OBSTRUCTIVE PULMONARY DISEASE (COPD)

Understanding COPD: COPD is a progressive condition that includes emphysema and chronic bronchitis. Symptoms include a chronic cough, shortness of breath, and frequent respiratory infections.


Herbal Remedies for COPD:

1. Ginseng (Panax ginseng):

- Active Compounds: Ginsenosides, polysaccharides

- Benefits: Improves lung function and boosts energy.

- Preparation and Use:

- Tea: Steep 1 teaspoon of dried ginseng root in hot water for 15 minutes. Drink daily.

- Precautions: Consult a healthcare provider, especially if you take medication for diabetes or blood pressure.

2. Ginger (Zingiber officinale):

- Active Compounds: Gingerol, shogaol

- Benefits: Helps reduce inflammation and clears mucus from the lungs.

- Preparation and Use:

- Tea: Steep 1 teaspoon of grated ginger in hot water for 10 minutes. Drink up to three times daily.

- Syrup: Combine ginger juice with honey and take 1 teaspoon twice daily.

- Precautions: May cause mild heartburn or gastrointestinal discomfort.

## PRACTICAL TIPS FOR RESPIRATORY HEALTH

1. Maintain a Healthy Diet: Incorporate antioxidant-rich foods such as berries, citrus fruits, and leafy greens to support lung health and reduce inflammation.

2. Stay Hydrated: Drink plenty of water to help thin mucus and keep respiratory tracts moist.

3. Avoid Irritants: Reduce exposure to pollutants, cigarette smoke, and allergens by using air purifiers and maintaining a clean home environment.

4. Breathing Exercises: Practice diaphragmatic and pursed-lip breathing to improve lung function.

5. Stay Active: Engage in regular physical activity to strengthen respiratory muscles and enhance lung capacity.

6. Use a Humidifier: Adding moisture to dry indoor air can ease breathing and reduce nasal congestion.

Natural remedies, combined with lifestyle adjustments, can help manage respiratory conditions effectively. Before starting any new herbal treatment, consult with a healthcare provider, especially if you have pre-existing conditions or are taking medications. By following Barbara O'Neill's holistic approach, you can support your respiratory health and breathe easier naturally.

# CHAPTER 18

# NATURAL REMEDIES FOR RESPIRATORY ALLERGIES

Respiratory allergies, such as allergic rhinitis and asthma, result from the immune system's overreaction to allergens like pollen, pet dander, and dust. Symptoms include sneezing, runny nose, itchy eyes, and difficulty breathing.

Barbara O'Neill recommends natural methods to manage and heal respiratory allergies by addressing their root causes and strengthening the immune system.

## STRENGTHENING THE IMMUNE SYSTEM

A robust immune system can minimize the severity of allergic reactions. Here are practical steps to boost immunity:

- Diet: Focus on fruits, vegetables, nuts, seeds, and whole grains for their vitamins and antioxidants.

- Hydration: Drink enough water to maintain moisture in the respiratory tract.

- Sleep: Ensure restful sleep to support immune function.

- Exercise: Regular physical activity keeps the immune system strong.

Reducing Exposure to Allergens

Minimizing exposure to allergens helps prevent allergic reactions. Here's how to reduce allergen exposure:

- Keep Windows Closed: During high pollen seasons, close windows to prevent allergens from entering your home.

- Air Purifiers: Use HEPA filters to reduce indoor allergens.

- Regular Cleaning: Clean your home frequently, and use a vacuum cleaner with a HEPA filter.

- Wash Bedding: Wash bedding regularly in hot water to eliminate dust mites.

Herbal Remedies for Respiratory Allergies

Herbal remedies provide natural relief from allergy symptoms:

1. Nettle (Urtica dioica):

- Active Compounds: Antihistamines, anti-inflammatory agents.

- Uses: Reduces histamine production.

- Preparation: Steep 1-2 teaspoons of dried nettle in hot water for 10-15 minutes. Drink up to three times a day.

2. Butterbur (Petasites hybridus):

- Active Compounds: Petasin, isopetasin.

- Uses: Helps with hay fever and allergic reactions.

- Preparation: Use PA-free butterbur capsules as directed.

3. Quercetin:

- Active Compounds: Antioxidant and antihistamine properties.

- Uses: Reduces histamine release.

- Preparation: Take 500 mg supplements twice daily or consume quercetin-rich foods like onions, apples, and berries.

## LIFESTYLE ADJUSTMENTS FOR RESPIRATORY HEALTH

1. Dietary Changes:

- Anti-inflammatory Foods: Include turmeric, garlic, and leafy greens.

- Probiotics: Yogurt, kefir,

and fermented foods support gut health and immune function.

2. Exercise:

- Outdoor Activities: Engage in outdoor activities when pollen counts are low.

- Breathing Exercises: Practice deep breathing to enhance lung capacity.

3. Stress Management:

- Mindfulness and Meditation: Practice mindfulness to reduce stress, which can exacerbate allergy symptoms.

- Adequate Sleep: Get sufficient sleep to support overall health.

## PRACTICAL TIPS FOR DAILY LIFE

- Nasal Rinse: Use saline nasal rinses to clear allergens from nasal passages.

- Essential Oils: Eucalyptus and lavender oils can reduce congestion and promote relaxation.

- Humidifier: Use a humidifier to keep your home's air moist, reducing respiratory irritation.

By incorporating these natural solutions and lifestyle adjustments into your daily routine, you can manage respiratory allergies effectively.

With a strengthened immune system and reduced allergen exposure, you can enjoy improved respiratory health and an overall better quality of life.

# CHAPTER 19

# NATURAL SOLUTIONS AGAINST CHRONIC INFLAMMATION

Chronic inflammation is a prolonged, low-grade inflammatory response that can persist for months or years. This type of inflammation is associated with a wide range of health issues, including arthritis, cardiovascular disease, diabetes, and autoimmune disorders.

Barbara O'Neill advocates a holistic approach to managing chronic inflammation through natural remedies, dietary changes, and lifestyle adjustments.

## UNDERSTANDING CHRONIC INFLAMMATION

Chronic inflammation differs from acute inflammation in that it is less visible but far more damaging over time. Unlike acute inflammation, which helps the body heal from injuries and infections, chronic inflammation is a sustained response that can slowly destroy tissues and organs.

## DIETARY STRATEGIES FOR REDUCING INFLAMMATION

1. Anti-Inflammatory Foods

Incorporating anti-inflammatory foods into your diet can significantly reduce inflammation and improve overall health.

- Fatty Fish: Rich in omega-3 fatty acids, which are known for their potent anti-inflammatory effects.

- Practical Tip: Include fatty fish like salmon, mackerel, and sardines in your diet at least twice a week. Opt for grilled or baked preparations to preserve the omega-3 content.

- Leafy Greens: Vegetables like spinach, kale, and Swiss chard are loaded with antioxidants and vitamins.

- Practical Tip: Add a handful of leafy greens to your daily smoothies, salads, or soups for an antioxidant boost.

- Berries: Blueberries, strawberries, and raspberries are packed with antioxidants, which help fight inflammation.

- Practical Tip: Use berries as a topping for breakfast cereal, yogurt, or snack on them throughout the day.

- Nuts and Seeds: Almonds, walnuts, flaxseeds, and chia seeds are excellent sources of essential fatty acids and antioxidants.

- Practical Tip: Sprinkle seeds over salads, oatmeal, or blend them into smoothies. Carry a small bag of nuts for a quick snack.

- Turmeric: Contains curcumin, a powerful anti-inflammatory compound that also offers antioxidant benefits.

- Practical Tip: Incorporate turmeric into curries, soups, and teas. Combine it with black pepper to enhance curcumin absorption.

2. Avoiding Inflammatory Foods

Certain foods can exacerbate inflammation and should be minimized or eliminated from your diet.

- Refined Sugars and Carbohydrates: These can trigger inflammatory responses and contribute to chronic conditions.

- Practical Tip: Reduce the consumption of sugary drinks, processed snacks, and pastries. Opt for whole grains such as quinoa, brown rice, and oats.

- Trans Fats: Found in fried and processed foods, these fats promote inflammation and increase the risk of heart disease.

- Practical Tip: Avoid fast food, fried snacks, and read food labels to ensure no hydrogenated oils are included.

- Excessive Alcohol: Can contribute to inflammation and damage the liver over time.

- Practical Tip: Limit alcohol intake to moderate levels, and if consuming, prefer red wine in small amounts as it contains resveratrol, which has anti-inflammatory properties.

# HERBAL REMEDIES FOR CHRONIC INFLAMMATION

1. Turmeric (Curcuma longa)

- Active Compounds: Curcumin

- Benefits: Curcumin reduces inflammation, protects cells from oxidative damage, and helps manage joint pain.

- Preparation and Use:

- Golden Milk: Mix 1 teaspoon of turmeric powder with a pinch of black pepper and 1 cup of warm almond milk. Sweeten with honey if desired. Drink daily.

- Turmeric Paste: Combine turmeric powder with coconut oil to make a paste. Apply to inflamed joints or muscles for localized relief.

2. Ginger (Zingiber officinale)

- Active Compounds: Gingerol, shogaol

- Benefits: Anti-inflammatory and analgesic properties make ginger useful for reducing inflammation and easing pain.

- Preparation and Use:

- Ginger Tea: Grate 1-2 teaspoons of fresh ginger into boiling water. Steep for 10 minutes. Drink 2-3 times daily.

- Ginger Compress: Mix grated ginger with hot water, soak a cloth, and apply it to the inflamed area.

3. Boswellia (Boswellia serrata)

- Active Compounds: Boswellic acids

- Benefits: Boswellia is effective at reducing inflammation, especially in cases of joint-related disorders such as arthritis.

- Preparation and Use:

- Boswellia Capsules: Take 300-500 mg of Boswellia extract up to three times daily.

- Boswellia Cream: Apply topically to inflamed areas for relief.

4. Green Tea (Camellia sinensis)

- Active Compounds: Epigallocatechin gallate (EGCG)

- Benefits: The antioxidant properties of green tea reduce inflammation and oxidative stress.

- Preparation and Use:

- Green Tea: Brew 1 teaspoon of green tea leaves in hot water for 3-5 minutes. Drink 2-3 cups daily.

- Green Tea Compress: Use cooled green tea bags as compresses for inflamed skin or joints.

5. Pineapple (Ananas comosus)

- Active Compounds: Bromelain

- Benefits: Bromelain, found in pineapple, helps reduce inflammation and aids in digestion.

- Preparation and Use:

- Fresh Pineapple: Incorporate fresh pineapple into your diet by consuming half a cup daily.

- Bromelain Supplement: Take 200-400 mg of bromelain supplements three times daily, as directed.

# LIFESTYLE CHANGES FOR MANAGING INFLAMMATION

1. Regular Physical Activity

- Benefits: Exercise reduces inflammation, boosts circulation, and supports overall health.

- Practical Tips:

- Engage in moderate exercise like walking, swimming, or cycling for at least 30 minutes a day.

- Incorporate strength training twice a week to support muscle and joint health.

2. Stress Management

- Benefits: Chronic stress increases inflammation, while stress reduction helps lower inflammatory markers in the body.

- Practical Tips:

- Practice mindfulness, meditation, and deep breathing exercises.

- Establish a regular sleep routine to ensure 7-8 hours of quality rest.

3. Maintaining a Healthy Weight

- Benefits: Excess weight contributes to inflammation and joint strain.

- Practical Tips:

- Adopt a balanced diet rich in whole foods while monitoring portion sizes.

- Avoid overeating and focus on nutrient-dense meals.

4. Hydration

- Benefits: Staying hydrated helps flush out toxins and reduces inflammation.

- Practical Tips:

- Drink at least 8 cups (64 ounces) of water daily.

- Include hydrating foods like cucumbers, watermelons, and oranges.

# PRACTICAL SOLUTIONS AND INSTRUCTIONS

1. Anti-Inflammatory Smoothie Recipe

- Ingredients:

- 1 cup almond milk

- 1 cup fresh pineapple chunks

- 1 banana

- 1 teaspoon turmeric powder

- 1 teaspoon grated ginger

- 1 handful of spinach

- Instructions: Combine all ingredients in a blender and blend until smooth. Drink once daily to support inflammation reduction.

2. Turmeric-Ginger Anti-Inflammatory Tea

- Ingredients:

- 1 teaspoon turmeric powder

- 1 teaspoon grated ginger

- 1 teaspoon honey

- 2 cups water

- Instructions:

- Bring water to a boil and add turmeric and ginger.

- Simmer for 10 minutes, strain, and add honey. Drink twice daily.

3. Boswellia and Ginger Joint Rub

- Ingredients:

- 2 tablespoons Boswellia powder

- 1 tablespoon grated ginger

- 2 tablespoons coconut oil

- Instructions:

- Mix all ingredients to form a paste.

- Apply to inflamed joints for 30 minutes and rinse with warm water. Use daily as needed.

Managing chronic inflammation naturally involves a multifaceted approach that includes anti-inflammatory foods, herbal remedies, regular exercise, and stress management techniques.

By incorporating these strategies into your daily routine, you can reduce inflammation, support overall health, and prevent the long-term consequences of chronic inflammation.

# CHAPTER 20

# NATURAL SOLUTIONS FOR CANCER PREVENTION AND HEALING

Cancer is one of the most significant health challenges of our time. While conventional treatments like chemotherapy and radiation play a central role, many holistic practitioners, including Barbara O'Neill, advocate for natural and integrative approaches to prevent and support cancer healing.

This chapter explores holistic strategies, focusing on nutrition, detoxification, immune support, and lifestyle changes that can help prevent cancer and support the body in healing from it.

## UNDERSTANDING CANCER FROM A HOLISTIC PERSPECTIVE

Cancer occurs when abnormal cells in the body grow uncontrollably, often forming tumors that can spread to other parts of the body. Barbara O'Neill emphasizes that cancer thrives in an environment of toxicity, inflammation, and poor immune function.

A holistic approach addresses these factors by nourishing the body, detoxifying harmful substances, and supporting emotional and mental well-being.

## NUTRITIONAL STRATEGIES FOR CANCER PREVENTION

1. Anti-Cancer Foods

Certain foods have powerful cancer-fighting properties and should be included in the diet regularly.

- Cruciferous Vegetables: Broccoli, cauliflower, Brussels sprouts, and kale are high in sulforaphane, which detoxifies carcinogens and supports liver health.

- Practical Tip: Eat a serving of cruciferous vegetables daily. Steaming or lightly sautéing preserves their nutrients while making them easier to digest.

- Berries: Blueberries, strawberries, and raspberries are rich in antioxidants that help protect cells from free radical damage.

- Practical Tip: Add a handful of berries to your breakfast or smoothies. Aim for at least one serving per day.

- Garlic and Onions: These sulfur-rich vegetables enhance the immune system's ability to fight cancer and reduce inflammation.

- Practical Tip: Incorporate fresh garlic and onions into your meals. Aim for at least one clove of garlic per day for optimal benefits.

- Green Tea: Packed with catechins, which have been shown to inhibit cancer growth.

- Practical Tip: Drink 2-3 cups of green tea daily. For variety, you can also take green tea supplements containing EGCG (epigallocatechin gallate).

- Turmeric: Contains curcumin, a potent anti-inflammatory compound that has shown anti-cancer effects in numerous studies.

- Practical Tip: Add turmeric to your meals or make golden milk (see recipe below). Combining it with black pepper enhances curcumin's absorption.

2. Alkaline Diet

Cancer cells tend to thrive in acidic environments. An alkaline diet, rich in plant-based foods, helps create conditions less favorable for cancer growth.

- Practical Tip: Focus on alkaline-forming foods such as leafy greens, fruits, nuts, seeds, and root vegetables. Limit or avoid acidic foods like processed meats, dairy, and refined sugar.

3. Plant-Based Diet

A predominantly plant-based diet provides essential nutrients, fiber, and antioxidants that help lower cancer risk.

- Practical Tip: Fill your plate with vegetables, fruits, legumes, nuts, seeds, and whole grains. Aim for at least five servings of vegetables and two servings of fruit daily.

# DETOXIFICATION AND CANCER PREVENTION

Detoxifying the body is crucial to preventing cancer and supporting recovery. A buildup of toxins can contribute to cellular damage and inflammation.

1. Liver Detox

The liver plays a critical role in detoxifying harmful substances from the body. Supporting liver function is essential for overall detoxification.

- Practical Tip: Incorporate liver-supporting herbs like milk thistle, dandelion root, and turmeric into your daily routine.

- Milk Thistle Tea: Steep 1 teaspoon of milk thistle seeds in hot water for 10 minutes. Drink twice daily.

- Dandelion Root Tea: Steep 1-2 teaspoons of dried dandelion root in hot water for 10 minutes. Drink twice daily.

2. Regular Detox Programs

Engaging in periodic detox programs helps cleanse the body of accumulated toxins.

- 14-Day Detox Program: A gentle detox involving raw fruits, vegetables, herbal teas, and green juices in the first week, followed by the gradual reintroduction of whole grains and legumes in the second week.

3. Avoiding Environmental Toxins

Reducing exposure to environmental toxins can significantly lower your risk of cancer.

- Practical Tip: Use natural cleaning products, avoid plastics for food storage, and choose organic produce when possible to reduce pesticide exposure.

# HERBAL REMEDIES FOR CANCER SUPPORT

Herbs have been used for centuries to support the body's ability to heal and fight diseases, including cancer.

1. Essiac Tea

Essiac tea is a traditional herbal blend that supports the body's natural healing processes.

- Ingredients: Burdock root, sheep sorrel, slippery elm bark, and Indian rhubarb root.
- Preparation:
- Combine equal parts of the herbs.
- Boil 1 tablespoon of the herb mixture in 1 quart of water for 10 minutes.
- Let it steep for 12 hours, then reheat and strain.
- Drink 1-2 ounces daily on an empty stomach.

2. Turmeric and Black Pepper

Turmeric's anti-cancer properties are well-documented, and combining it with black pepper enhances curcumin absorption.

- Preparation: Mix 1 teaspoon of turmeric with a pinch of black pepper in warm water or add to food daily.

3. Green Tea Extract

Green tea extract provides concentrated doses of antioxidants that can help inhibit cancer growth.

- Dosage: Take 300-400 mg of green tea extract daily, preferably with at least 50% EGCG.

# LIFESTYLE CHANGES FOR CANCER PREVENTION AND HEALING

1. Regular Exercise

Physical activity improves immune function, reduces inflammation, and helps maintain a healthy weight.

- Practical Tip: Engage in at least 30 minutes of moderate exercise, such as walking, swimming, or cycling, five days a week.

## 2. Stress Management

Chronic stress weakens the immune system, making it harder for the body to fight disease.

- Practical Tip: Incorporate relaxation techniques such as yoga, meditation, or deep breathing into your daily routine. Aim for 10-15 minutes of mindfulness meditation each day.

## 3. Adequate Sleep

Restorative sleep is crucial for immune health and overall well-being.

- Practical Tip: Prioritize 7-8 hours of sleep per night. Create a calming pre-sleep routine by avoiding screens before bed, practicing relaxation techniques, and keeping your bedroom cool and dark.

## 4. Avoiding Carcinogens

Limiting exposure to known carcinogens can significantly reduce your cancer risk.

- Practical Tip: Quit smoking, limit alcohol intake, and choose fresh, whole foods over processed or smoked meats.

## GOLDEN MILK RECIPE

Ingredients:

- 1 cup almond milk (or another plant-based milk)

- 1 teaspoon turmeric

- 1/4 teaspoon cinnamon

- A pinch of black pepper

- 1/2 teaspoon coconut oil

- Honey (optional)

Instructions:

1. Heat the almond milk in a small pot.

2. Whisk in the turmeric, cinnamon, black pepper, and coconut oil.

3. Simmer for 5-10 minutes.

4. Sweeten with honey if desired and drink warm.

Preventing and supporting the healing of cancer involves a multifaceted approach that includes proper nutrition, regular detoxification, stress management, and exercise.

By incorporating anti-cancer foods, avoiding toxins, and utilizing powerful herbal remedies, you can create a holistic strategy that supports your body's natural defenses. Always consult with a healthcare professional before beginning any new treatments, especially if you're undergoing cancer treatment.

## PRACTICAL SOLUTIONS AND INSTRUCTIONS FOR HOLISTIC CANCER PREVENTION AND HEALING

### Golden Milk Recipe

Golden milk is a powerful anti-inflammatory drink rich in turmeric, which supports immune function and fights cancer cells.

- Ingredients:

- 1 cup almond milk (or other plant-based milk)

- 1 teaspoon turmeric powder

- 1/4 teaspoon black pepper

- 1/2 teaspoon cinnamon

- 1 teaspoon honey (optional)

- Instructions:

1. Combine all ingredients in a small saucepan.

2. Heat gently over medium heat, stirring continuously until the mixture is warm (avoid boiling).

3. Pour into a cup and enjoy.

4. Drink once daily, especially in the evening, for optimal benefits.

Berry Antioxidant Smoothie

This smoothie is packed with antioxidants that protect against cancer by neutralizing free radicals.

- Ingredients:

- 1 cup mixed berries (blueberries, strawberries, raspberries)

- 1 banana

- 1 cup spinach

- 1 tablespoon ground flaxseed

- 1 cup almond milk

- Instructions:

1. Place all ingredients in a blender.

2. Blend until smooth.

3. Drink once daily to boost your intake of cancer-fighting nutrients.

Green Detox Juice

This juice is rich in chlorophyll, antioxidants, and detoxifying agents that help cleanse the body and support liver function.

- Ingredients:

- 1 cucumber

- 2 celery stalks

- 1 handful of spinach

- 1 apple (for sweetness)

- 1 lemon

- 1-inch piece of fresh ginger

- Instructions:

1. Juice all the ingredients using a juicer or blend and strain the mixture.

2. Stir well and drink immediately for maximum freshness.

3. Consume once daily to support detoxification and immune health.

## HOLISTIC CANCER PREVENTION AND HEALING

By incorporating these practical recipes into your daily routine, along with Barbara O'Neill's holistic principles, you can nourish your body with cancer-fighting nutrients, detoxify effectively, and support overall well-being. Always work with healthcare professionals to tailor your regimen, especially if undergoing conventional cancer treatments.

This integrative approach ensures your body, mind, and spirit are aligned toward optimal healing.

# CHAPTER 21

## THE 9 WORST FOODS THAT FEED CANCER CELLS

Cancer cells thrive in an acidic environment, and certain foods contribute to this imbalance, fostering conditions that support their growth. Understanding which foods to limit or avoid is a key step in maintaining a healthier internal environment.

Barbara O'Neill teaches that by reducing acid-forming foods and embracing an alkaline-rich diet, you can create a less hospitable space for cancer to develop.

1. Meat

- Impact on Health:

- Phosphorus and Sulfur: Red and processed meats are rich in acid-forming minerals such as phosphorus and sulfur.

- Cancer Connection: Research, including findings from Dr. Colin Campbell, suggests that consuming large amounts of meat can promote cancer cell growth due to its acidic nature.

- Recommendations:

- Moderation: Limit consumption of red and processed meats.

- Alternatives: Opt for plant-based proteins like lentils, beans, tofu, and tempeh.

2. Wheat

- Impact on Health:

- Hybridization: Modern wheat varieties are harder to digest and contribute to acidity.

- Acidic Nature: Wheat products, particularly processed versions, create an acidic internal environment.

- Recommendations:

- Ancient Grains: Use ancient grains like spelt, einkorn, or emmer wheat, which are less processed and easier to digest.

- Gluten-Free Options: Consider gluten-free alternatives like quinoa, millet, and buckwheat.

3. Caffeine

- Impact on Health:

- Acidity: Caffeine consumption increases the acid load in the body, which can lead to the depletion of essential minerals such as calcium and magnesium.

- Sugar Combination: Caffeinated drinks are often paired with sugar, amplifying the acidic effect.

- Recommendations:

- Limit Intake: Reduce the consumption of coffee, black tea, energy drinks, and sodas.

- Healthier Alternatives: Drink herbal teas or water infused with a pinch of natural salt to maintain hydration.


4. Refined Sugar

- Impact on Health:

- Acidic Byproducts: The metabolism of sugar produces lactic and acetic acids, leading to an acidic environment.

- Mineral Depletion: Refined sugars drain essential minerals, reducing the body's ability to neutralize acidity.

- Recommendations:

- Reduce Sugar: Limit sugary snacks, soft drinks, and processed foods.

- Natural Sweeteners: Opt for natural sweeteners like honey, stevia, or maple syrup.


5. Aged Cheese

- Impact on Health:

- Mold Content: Aged cheeses like blue cheese contain molds that can be acid-forming.

- High in Protein: Cheese is rich in protein and phosphorus, contributing to acidity.

- Recommendations:

- Fresh Cheeses: Use fresh cheeses like cottage cheese or ricotta, which have a less acidic profile.

- Dairy Alternatives: Explore plant-based cheese options made from nuts or soy.


6. Alcohol

- Impact on Health:

- Acidic Breakdown: Alcohol is metabolized into acetic acid, contributing to the body's acid load.

- Neurotoxicity: Acetaldehyde, a toxic byproduct of alcohol, negatively affects the brain.

- Recommendations:

- Moderation: Limit alcohol consumption to reduce acidity.

- Healthier Options: Choose beverages with lower alcohol content and avoid sugary mixers.


7. Tobacco

- Impact on Health:

- Acidity: Tobacco use creates an acidic environment within the body.

- Toxic Compounds: Smoking introduces numerous toxins that exacerbate acidity.

- Recommendations:

- Avoid Tobacco: Eliminate smoking and avoid secondhand smoke to reduce acidity and improve overall health.


8. Processed Foods

- Impact on Health:

- High in Additives: Processed foods are loaded with preservatives and artificial ingredients that increase the body's acid load.

- Low in Nutrients: These foods lack the nutrients needed to maintain pH balance.

- Recommendations:

- Whole Foods: Focus on whole, unprocessed foods rich in essential nutrients.

- Home-Cooked Meals: Preparing your own meals allows you to control what goes into your body.


9. Artificial Sweeteners

- Impact on Health:

- Acid Production: Artificial sweeteners can lead to acid production during digestion.

- Gut Health: They can negatively affect the gut microbiome, promoting the growth of acid-forming bacteria.

- Recommendations:

- Natural Sweeteners: Use natural alternatives like honey, fruit, or stevia.

- Moderation: Limit the use of sweeteners in your diet overall.


By limiting or avoiding these nine acid-forming foods and incorporating more alkaline-forming foods into your diet, you can maintain a balanced pH and create a healthier internal environment.

Following Barbara O'Neill's teachings on the impact of diet on cancer, you can take significant steps toward improving your overall health and reducing cancer risks.

# CHAPTER 22

## 30-DAY DISEASE PREVENTION PROGRAM

Welcome to your 30-day journey toward optimal health. Over the next month, you'll be guided through a comprehensive program designed to prevent disease and promote healing by nourishing your body, supporting detoxification, and cultivating a balanced lifestyle.

Barbara O'Neill's approach emphasizes the body's inherent ability to heal when given the right conditions—through nutrition, exercise, hydration, and mental well-being.

## WEEK 1: DETOX AND NOURISH

- Day 1-3: Start with a gentle detox.

- Focus: Raw fruits, vegetables, and green juices to cleanse the digestive system.

- Hydration: Drink 8-10 glasses of water daily, incorporating lemon for an alkalizing effect.

- Day 4-7: Introduce light, steamed vegetables and whole grains.

- Foods: Continue with green juices and herbal teas (e.g., dandelion root, milk thistle).

- Physical Activity: Gentle yoga or walking for 30 minutes daily to support lymphatic drainage.

## WEEK 2: REBUILD AND STRENGTHEN

- Day 8-10: Focus on strengthening the immune system.

- Foods: Increase intake of plant-based proteins like lentils, beans, and quinoa.

- Hydration: Continue with 8-10 glasses of water and herbal teas.

- Exercise: Incorporate strength training twice a week to support muscle mass.

- Day 11-14: Add in healthy fats.

- Foods: Avocados, nuts, seeds, and olive oil to provide essential nutrients.

- Mental Wellness: Introduce 10-15 minutes of mindfulness or meditation practice daily.

# WEEK 3: BALANCE AND ENERGIZE

- Day 15-17: Focus on balancing blood sugar levels.

- Foods: Eliminate refined sugars and opt for low-glycemic foods like sweet potatoes, berries, and leafy greens.

- Hydration: Incorporate coconut water for electrolytes.

- Physical Activity: Add moderate-intensity cardio exercises, such as brisk walking or swimming, 3-4 times a week.

- Day 18-21: Support energy and reduce inflammation.

- Foods: Add anti-inflammatory foods like turmeric, ginger, and green leafy vegetables.

- Self-Care: Focus on restorative sleep, aiming for 7-8 hours a night.

# WEEK 4: SUSTAIN AND MAINTAIN

- Day 22-24: Incorporate immune-boosting strategies.

- Foods: Include garlic, onions, mushrooms, and citrus fruits.

- Physical Activity: Continue with regular exercise, adding more variety such as cycling or dancing.

- Stress Management: Engage in stress-relieving activities such as nature walks, journaling, or creative hobbies.

- Day 25-30: Focus on long-term habits.

- Foods: Continue with a balanced, plant-based diet rich in whole foods.

- Hydration: Maintain adequate water intake and herbal teas.

- Mental Health: Solidify mindfulness practices and maintain a balanced routine of physical activity and rest.

By the end of this 30-day program, you will have established a solid foundation of health, incorporating Barbara O'Neill's principles of holistic wellness.

This program is not just a temporary cleanse—it is a pathway to a sustained, healthy lifestyle that prioritizes disease prevention and natural healing.

# CHAPTER 23

## BARBARA O'NEILL'S GUIDE TO NUTRIENT-POWERED HEALING

In your journey toward self-healing, understanding the nutrients that support your body in combating common ailments is essential. Drawing from Barbara O'Neill's extensive teachings on natural health and healing, this chapter explores specific nutrients that target key health concerns.

Let's dive into how you can harness the power of nutrition to enhance your wellness naturally.

## 1. VITAMIN C: IMMUNE BOOSTER EXTRAORDINAIRE

Why It Matters: Vitamin C is critical for tissue repair, immune defense, and antioxidant protection. Whether it's warding off colds or helping your body recover faster, this nutrient should be a staple in your diet.

Top Sources:

- Citrus fruits like oranges, lemons, and grapefruits

- Berries such as strawberries and blueberries

- Kiwi

- Bell peppers

- Broccoli and Brussels sprouts

How to Incorporate:

- Start your day with warm water and lemon.

- Add fresh berries to oatmeal or yogurt.

- Munch on bell peppers with hummus or dip.

- Include broccoli and Brussels sprouts in your lunch or dinner.

## 2. OMEGA-3 FATTY ACIDS: PROTECTING YOUR HEART

Why It Matters: Omega-3s reduce inflammation, lower blood pressure, and protect the heart. These healthy fats are essential for cardiovascular health and overall longevity.

Top Sources:

- Fatty fish like salmon, mackerel, and sardines

- Flaxseeds and chia seeds

- Walnuts

- Algal oil (for vegetarians and vegans)

How to Incorporate:

- Enjoy a serving of fatty fish at least twice a week.

- Sprinkle chia seeds or flaxseeds on your smoothie or oatmeal.

- Snack on walnuts.

- Consider algal oil supplements if you don't consume fish.

## 3. MAGNESIUM: FOR MUSCLES, NERVES, AND A CALM MIND

Why It Matters: Magnesium is vital for muscle relaxation, nerve function, and keeping stress in check. It also helps regulate blood sugar levels.

Top Sources:

- Leafy greens like spinach and kale

- Nuts such as almonds and seeds like pumpkin seeds

- Legumes like chickpeas and black beans

- Whole grains such as quinoa and brown rice

- Dark chocolate

How to Incorporate:

- Blend leafy greens into smoothies or add them to your meals.

- Snack on nuts and seeds or add them to salads.

- Make whole grains a part of your main dishes.

- Indulge in a small piece of dark chocolate after meals.

## 4. ZINC: HEALING AND IMMUNE POWER

Why It Matters: Zinc plays a crucial role in boosting immunity, healing wounds, and supporting DNA synthesis. Your body needs this mineral, especially during recovery or when facing illness.

Top Sources:

- Shellfish like oysters and crab

- Meat and poultry

- Legumes such as lentils and chickpeas

- Seeds like hemp and sesame

- Nuts, particularly cashews and almonds

How to Incorporate:

- Add a serving of shellfish or lean meat to your meals.

- Sprinkle seeds over salads, soups, or yogurt.

- Make legumes a staple in soups, stews, or side dishes.

## 5. CALCIUM: FOR STRONG BONES AND BEYOND

Why It Matters: Calcium isn't just for bones—it also supports muscle function and nerve signaling. Ensuring you get enough calcium is key to long-term health.

Top Sources:

- Dairy products like milk, cheese, and yogurt

- Leafy greens such as collard greens and broccoli

- Fortified plant milks (almond, soy)

- Sardines and canned salmon (with bones)

- Tofu

How to Incorporate:

- Start your day with fortified plant milk or dairy.

- Use tofu in stir-fries or salads.

- Add leafy greens to your meals or smoothies.

## 6. IRON: FUELING YOUR ENERGY AND BLOOD HEALTH

Why It Matters: Iron is essential for producing hemoglobin, which transports oxygen throughout the body. If you're feeling sluggish, low iron might be the culprit.

Top Sources:

- Red meat and poultry

- Seafood like clams and shrimp

- Leafy greens, especially spinach

- Legumes such as lentils and beans

How to Incorporate:

- Enjoy lean cuts of meat or seafood in your meals.

- Add legumes to soups, stews, or as sides.

- Use spinach in smoothies, salads, or as a side dish.

# 7. VITAMIN D: SUNSHINE FOR IMMUNITY AND BONES

Why It Matters: Known as the "sunshine vitamin," vitamin D is essential for maintaining immune health and strong bones. It also plays a role in reducing inflammation.

Top Sources:

- Fatty fish like salmon and mackerel

- Egg yolks

- Fortified foods (orange juice, cereals)

- Mushrooms exposed to sunlight

- Sunlight exposure itself

How to Incorporate:

- Spend 10-30 minutes in the sun several times a week.

- Include fatty fish in your meals.

- Use mushrooms and egg yolks in your cooking.

# 8. FOLATE: SUPPORTING CELL GROWTH AND REPAIR

Why It Matters: Folate is key for healthy cell growth, DNA synthesis, and tissue repair, making it especially important for pregnant women or those planning to conceive.

Top Sources:

- Leafy greens such as spinach and kale

- Citrus fruits like oranges and lemons

- Beans and legumes

- Fortified cereals and grains

How to Incorporate:

- Use leafy greens in salads or smoothies.

- Add citrus fruits to meals or snacks.

- Make legumes a regular part of soups, stews, and salads.

## 9. VITAMIN E: SKIN AND EYE HEALTH SUPERSTAR

Why It Matters: Vitamin E works as an antioxidant, protecting your cells from damage. It also plays a role in maintaining healthy skin and eyes.

Top Sources:

- Nuts and seeds, especially almonds and sunflower seeds

- Spinach and broccoli

- Vegetable oils like sunflower or safflower oil

- Avocado

How to Incorporate:

- Snack on nuts and seeds.

- Use vegetable oils in your salad dressings or cooking.

- Include spinach and broccoli in your meals.

## 10. PROBIOTICS: YOUR GUT'S BEST FRIEND

Why It Matters: Probiotics maintain a healthy gut microbiome, essential for digestion and immune health. They can even help balance mood and improve skin health.

Top Sources:

- Yogurt and kefir

- Fermented vegetables like sauerkraut and kimchi

- Miso and tempeh

- Kombucha


How to Incorporate:

- Enjoy yogurt or kefir as part of breakfast.

- Include fermented vegetables in your meals.

- Use miso in soups or as a seasoning.


Each nutrient is a building block in maintaining your health and warding off common ailments. By consciously incorporating these vital nutrients into your meals, you provide your body with the tools it needs for healing and longevity.


Let nature's pharmacy work in your favor—trust in the process and prioritize what you eat. In doing so, you will empower your journey toward holistic wellness, aligned with the teachings of Barbara O'Neill.


## ENERGIZING BREAKFAST RECIPES: START YOUR DAY WITH POWER AND NUTRITION


As a wellness coach and certified naturopath, drawing inspiration from the teachings of Barbara O'Neill, I believe breakfast should be a nourishing, energizing meal that supports your body's natural healing abilities.


Below are carefully curated breakfast recipes that not only taste great but also fuel your day with essential nutrients.


## AVOCADO AND SPINACH POWER SMOOTHIE

Preparation Time: 10 minutes

Servings: 2

**Ingredients:**

- 1 ripe avocado

- 2 cups fresh spinach

- 1 banana

- 1 cup unsweetened almond milk

- 1 tablespoon chia seeds

- 1 tablespoon flaxseeds

- 1 tablespoon honey (optional)

- 1 teaspoon spirulina powder (optional)

- Ice cubes

**Procedure:**

1. Slice the avocado and banana.

2. Combine all ingredients in a blender.

3. Blend until smooth and creamy.

4. Add ice cubes for a refreshing chill.

5. Serve immediately for an energy boost.

**Nutritional Information (per serving):**

- Calories: 280 kcal

- Protein: 5g

- Carbohydrates: 30g

- Fat: 18g

Rich in: Vitamin A, Vitamin C, Vitamin K, Folate

# QUINOA AND BERRY BREAKFAST BOWL

Preparation Time: 5 minutes

Cooking Time: 15 minutes

Servings: 2

**Ingredients:**

- 1 cup cooked quinoa

- 1/2 cup blueberries

- 1/2 cup sliced strawberries

- 1/4 cup almond slivers

- 1 tablespoon chia seeds

- 1 tablespoon honey or maple syrup

- 1 cup unsweetened almond milk

**Procedure:**

1. Cook quinoa according to package instructions.

2. Combine the cooked quinoa, berries, almonds, and chia seeds in a bowl.

3. Drizzle with honey or maple syrup.

4. Pour almond milk over the mixture, stir, and enjoy.

**Nutritional Information (per serving):**

- Calories: 350 kcal

- Protein: 10g

- Carbohydrates: 50g

- Fat: 12g

Rich in: Vitamin C, Vitamin E, Magnesium

# OVERNIGHT OATS WITH FLAXSEED AND APPLE

Preparation Time: 10 minutes (plus overnight soaking)

Servings: 2

## Ingredients:

- 1 cup rolled oats

- 1 cup unsweetened almond milk

- 1 grated apple

- 1 tablespoon flaxseed meal

- 1 tablespoon chia seeds

- 1 teaspoon cinnamon

- 1 tablespoon maple syrup (optional)

## Procedure:

1. Mix oats, almond milk, grated apple, flaxseed, chia seeds, and cinnamon in a jar.

2. Stir well to combine and refrigerate overnight.

3. In the morning, stir and add more almond milk if needed. Sweeten with maple syrup if desired.

Nutritional Information (per serving):

- Calories: 250 kcal

- Protein: 6g

- Carbohydrates: 45g

- Fat: 7g

Rich in: Vitamin C, Fiber, Vitamin B1, B2

# SCRAMBLED TOFU WITH VEGETABLES

Preparation Time: 10 minutes

Cooking Time: 10 minutes

Servings: 2

Ingredients:

- 1 block firm tofu, crumbled

- 1 diced bell pepper

- 1 cup chopped spinach

- 1 small onion, diced

- 1 garlic clove, minced

- 1 tablespoon olive oil

- 1 teaspoon turmeric

- 1/2 teaspoon black pepper

- Salt to taste

- Fresh herbs for garnish (optional)

Procedure:

1. Heat olive oil in a pan and sauté onion and garlic.

2. Add bell pepper and cook for 2-3 minutes.

3. Add crumbled tofu, spinach, turmeric, black pepper, and salt. Cook until heated through.

4. Garnish with herbs and serve warm.


Nutritional Information (per serving):

- Calories: 200 kcal

- Protein: 15g

- Carbohydrates: 10g

- Fat: 12g


Rich in: Vitamin C, Vitamin K, Folate

# CHIA SEED PUDDING WITH BERRIES

Preparation Time: 5 minutes (plus overnight chilling)

Servings: 2

## Ingredients:

- 1/2 cup chia seeds

- 2 cups unsweetened almond milk

- 1 teaspoon vanilla extract

- 1 tablespoon honey or maple syrup

- 1/2 cup mixed berries

## Procedure:

1. Mix chia seeds, almond milk, vanilla extract, and honey.

2. Stir well and refrigerate overnight.

3. In the morning, stir again and top with fresh berries.

Nutritional Information (per serving):

- Calories: 300 kcal

- Protein: 10g

- Carbohydrates: 40g

- Fat: 15g

Rich in: Omega-3, Vitamin C, Fiber

# SPINACH AND MUSHROOM OMELETTE

Preparation Time: 5 minutes

Cooking Time: 10 minutes

Servings: 1

## Ingredients:

- 2 eggs

- 1 cup chopped spinach

- 4 sliced mushrooms

- 1/2 onion, finely chopped

- 1 garlic clove, minced

- 1 tablespoon olive oil

- Salt and pepper to taste

## Procedure:

1. Sauté onion and garlic in olive oil until translucent.

2. Add mushrooms and spinach, cooking until softened.

3. Pour in beaten eggs, season with salt and pepper, and cook until eggs set.

4. Fold and serve hot.

## Nutritional Information (per serving):

- Calories: 320 kcal

- Protein: 18g

- Carbohydrates: 10g

- Fat: 22g

Rich in: Vitamin A, Iron, Folate

# SAVORY BREAKFAST QUINOA BOWL

Preparation Time: 5 minutes

Cooking Time: 20 minutes

Servings: 2

**Ingredients:**

- 1 cup quinoa

- 2 cups vegetable broth

- 1 diced avocado

- 1 cup halved cherry tomatoes

- 1/4 cup chopped red onion

- 1/2 lime, juiced

- Fresh cilantro

- Salt and pepper to taste

**Procedure:**

1. Cook quinoa in vegetable broth until liquid is absorbed.

2. Combine quinoa, avocado, tomatoes, and red onion.

3. Drizzle with lime juice, season with salt and pepper, and garnish with cilantro.

**Nutritional Information (per serving):**

- Calories: 380 kcal

- Protein: 10g

- Carbohydrates: 55g

- Fat: 15g

These breakfast recipes are designed to fuel your mornings with essential vitamins, minerals, and macronutrients that support energy, immunity, and overall health.

# ENERGY-BOOSTING LUNCH RECIPES

**Grilled Salmon with Avocado Salsa**

Preparation Time: 15 minutes

Cooking Time: 10 minutes

Servings: 2

**Ingredients:**

- 2 salmon fillets

- 1 tablespoon olive oil

- Salt and pepper to taste

- 1 avocado, diced

- 1 small red onion, finely chopped

- 1 jalapeño, seeded and chopped

- 2 tablespoons chopped cilantro

- Juice of 1 lime

**Instructions:**

1. Preheat your grill to medium-high heat.

2. Brush the salmon fillets with olive oil and season with salt and pepper.

3. Grill the salmon for about 5 minutes on each side or until fully cooked.

4. In a bowl, mix the diced avocado, red onion, jalapeño, cilantro, and lime juice to make the salsa.

5. Serve the grilled salmon topped with avocado salsa.

**Macronutrients per Serving:**

- Calories: 470 kcal

- Protein: 34g

- Carbohydrates: 14g

- Fat: 32g

## Quinoa Chickpea Salad

Preparation Time: 15 minutes

Servings: 2

### Ingredients:

- 1 cup cooked quinoa

- 1 cup chickpeas, drained and rinsed

- 1 cucumber, diced

- 1 bell pepper, diced

- 1/4 cup feta cheese, crumbled

- 2 tablespoons olive oil

- Juice of 1 lemon

- Salt and pepper to taste

- Fresh parsley, chopped

### Instructions:

1. In a large bowl, mix cooked quinoa, chickpeas, cucumber, and bell pepper.

2. Add crumbled feta, olive oil, lemon juice, salt, and pepper, then toss to combine.

3. Garnish with chopped fresh parsley before serving.

### Macronutrients per Serving:

- Calories: 410 kcal

- Protein: 18g

- Carbohydrates: 58g

- Fat: 14g

# TURKEY AND SPINACH WRAP

Preparation Time: 10 minutes

Servings: 2

## Ingredients:

- 2 whole wheat tortillas

- 4 slices turkey breast

- 1 cup fresh spinach leaves

- 1/4 cup hummus

- 1 carrot, grated

- 1/4 red onion, thinly sliced

## Instructions:

1. Spread hummus evenly over each tortilla.

2. Lay down the turkey slices over the hummus.

3. Add fresh spinach, grated carrot, and sliced onion.

4. Roll up the tortillas tightly, cut in half, and serve.

Macronutrients per Serving:

- Calories: 320 kcal

- Protein: 25g

- Carbohydrates: 35g

- Fat: 10g

# LENTIL SOUP WITH KALE

Preparation Time: 10 minutes

Cooking Time: 25 minutes

Servings: 4

**Ingredients:**

- 1 cup dried lentils, rinsed

- 4 cups vegetable broth

- 1 onion, chopped

- 2 carrots, diced

- 2 stalks celery, diced

- 2 cups kale, chopped

- 2 cloves garlic, minced

- 1 teaspoon thyme

- Salt and pepper to taste

- Olive oil

**Instructions:**

1. Heat olive oil in a large pot over medium heat.

2. Add onion, carrots, and celery, sauté until softened.

3. Stir in garlic and thyme, cooking until fragrant.

4. Add lentils and vegetable broth, bringing to a boil.

5. Lower the heat and simmer for 20 minutes.

6. Add chopped kale and simmer for another 5 minutes.

7. Season with salt and pepper, and serve hot.

**Macronutrients per Serving:**

- Calories: 235 kcal

- Protein: 14g

- Carbohydrates: 40g

- Fat: 3g

# GRILLED VEGETABLE AND HUMMUS PITA

Preparation Time: 10 minutes

Cooking Time: 10 minutes

Servings: 2

## Ingredients:

- 1 zucchini, sliced lengthwise

- 1 bell pepper, seeded and quartered

- 1 small eggplant, sliced

- 2 whole wheat pitas

- 1/2 cup hummus

- Olive oil

- Salt and pepper

## Instructions:

1. Preheat the grill to medium-high heat.

2. Brush the vegetables with olive oil, season with salt and pepper, then grill until tender and slightly charred.

3. Warm the pitas on the grill for about 1 minute on each side.

4. Spread hummus inside each pita and stuff with grilled vegetables.

5. Serve immediately.

## Macronutrients per Serving:

- Calories: 360 kcal

- Protein: 12g

- Carbohydrates: 55g

- Fat: 12g

# CHICKPEA AND AVOCADO SALAD

Preparation Time: 10 minutes

Servings: 2

**Ingredients:**

- 1 can chickpeas, rinsed and drained

- 1 ripe avocado, diced

- 1/2 red onion, finely chopped

- 1/2 cucumber, diced

- 10 cherry tomatoes, halved

- Juice of 1 lemon

- 2 tablespoons extra virgin olive oil

- Fresh cilantro, chopped

- Salt and pepper to taste

**Instructions:**

1. In a large bowl, combine chickpeas, avocado, red onion, cucumber, and cherry tomatoes.

2. Add lemon juice, olive oil, chopped cilantro, salt, and pepper, then toss gently.

3. Serve chilled or at room temperature.

**Macronutrients per Serving:**

- Calories: 380 kcal

- Protein: 10g

- Carbohydrates: 45g

- Fat: 20g

**Mango Chicken Wraps**

Preparation Time: 20 minutes

Servings: 2

Ingredients:

- 2 whole wheat tortillas

- 2 chicken breasts, cooked and sliced

- 1 ripe mango, peeled and sliced

- 1/4 cup Greek yogurt

- Handful of fresh spinach

- 1 tablespoon curry powder

- Salt and pepper to taste

Instructions:

1. Spread Greek yogurt on each tortilla and sprinkle with curry powder.

2. Lay down the sliced chicken and mango, then top with fresh spinach.

3. Roll up the tortillas tightly, slice in half, and serve.

Macronutrients per Serving:

- Calories: 345 kcal

- Protein: 28g

- Carbohydrates: 35g

- Fat: 10g

# ENERGIZING DINNER RECIPES FOR WELLNESS AND BALANCE

## PUMPKIN SOUP WITH A COCONUT TWIST

Preparation Time: 20 minutes

Cooking Time: 30 minutes

Servings: 4

**Ingredients:**

- 1 small pumpkin, peeled and cubed

- 1 onion, chopped

- 2 cloves garlic, minced

- 3 cups vegetable broth

- 1 teaspoon cumin

- 1/2 teaspoon nutmeg

- Salt and pepper to taste

- Coconut cream for garnish

**Procedure:**

1. Heat a large pot over medium heat and sauté the onion and garlic until soft.

2. Add the cubed pumpkin, vegetable broth, cumin, and nutmeg. Bring to a boil, then reduce to a simmer until the pumpkin is soft (about 20-25 minutes).

3. Blend the soup until smooth using a hand blender or carefully transfer it to a blender. Season with salt and pepper.

4. Serve hot, drizzled with coconut cream for a creamy finish.

**Nutritional Information (Per Serving):**

- Calories: 180 Kcal

- Protein: 3g

- Carbohydrates: 30g

- Fat: 6g

# QUINOA AND ROASTED VEGETABLE BOWL

Preparation Time: 15 minutes

Cooking Time: 20 minutes

Servings: 2

**Ingredients:**

- 1 cup quinoa

- 2 cups water

- 1 zucchini, cubed

- 1 bell pepper, cubed

- 1 small red onion, sliced

- 1 cup cherry tomatoes

- 2 tablespoons olive oil

- Salt and pepper to taste

- Fresh parsley, chopped

**Procedure:**

1. Rinse the quinoa under cold water, then bring 2 cups of water and quinoa to a boil. Reduce heat, cover, and simmer for about 15 minutes until all water is absorbed.

2. Preheat the oven to 425°F (220°C). Toss the zucchini, bell pepper, onion, and cherry tomatoes with olive oil, salt, and pepper. Spread on a baking sheet and roast for 20 minutes.

3. Once the quinoa and vegetables are done, combine them in a bowl and garnish with fresh parsley. Serve warm.

**Nutritional Information (Per Serving):**

- Calories: 495 Kcal

- Protein: 14g

- Carbohydrates: 70g

- Fat: 18g

# GRILLED SALMON WITH ASPARAGUS

Preparation Time: 10 minutes

Cooking Time: 10 minutes

Servings: 2

## Ingredients:

- 2 salmon fillets

- 1 bunch asparagus, trimmed

- 1 tablespoon olive oil

- Lemon slices

- Salt and pepper to taste

- Dill for garnish

## Procedure:

1. Preheat your grill to medium-high heat.

2. Brush both the salmon fillets and asparagus with olive oil, then season with salt and pepper.

3. Grill the salmon for about 4 minutes on each side, until fully cooked. Grill asparagus until tender and slightly charred.

4. Serve the salmon and asparagus together, garnished with lemon slices and fresh dill.

## Nutritional Information (Per Serving):

- Calories: 345 Kcal

- Protein: 34g

- Carbohydrates: 6g

- Fat: 20g

# TURKEY AND SWEET POTATO SKILLET

Preparation Time: 20 minutes

Cooking Time: 15 minutes

Servings: 4

**Ingredients:**

- 1 lb ground turkey

- 2 medium sweet potatoes, cubed

- 1 onion, diced

- 2 cloves garlic, minced

- 1 teaspoon smoked paprika

- 1/2 teaspoon cumin

- Salt and pepper to taste

- Olive oil for cooking

- Fresh cilantro for garnish

**Procedure:**

1. Heat olive oil in a large skillet over medium heat. Sauté the onion and garlic until translucent.

2. Add ground turkey to the skillet, breaking it up with a spatula. Season with smoked paprika, cumin, salt, and pepper. Cook until browned.

3. Stir in the cubed sweet potatoes, cover, and cook for about 15 minutes, or until the potatoes are tender.

4. Garnish with fresh cilantro and serve warm.

**Nutritional Information (Per Serving):**

- Calories: 320 Kcal

- Protein: 24g

- Carbohydrates: 28g

- Fat: 12g

# ROASTED CAULIFLOWER AND CHICKPEA CURRY

Preparation Time: 15 minutes

Cooking Time: 25 minutes

Servings: 4

## Ingredients:

- 1 head cauliflower, cut into florets

- 1 can chickpeas, drained and rinsed

- 2 tablespoons curry powder

- 1 can coconut milk

- 1 onion, diced

- 2 cloves garlic, minced

- Salt and pepper to taste

- Olive oil for cooking

- Fresh cilantro for garnish

## Procedure:

1. Preheat the oven to 400°F (200°C). Toss the cauliflower florets with olive oil, curry powder, and salt. Roast for 20-25 minutes until tender and golden.

2. In a skillet, sauté the onion and garlic with olive oil over medium heat. Add chickpeas and roasted cauliflower to the skillet.

3. Pour in coconut milk and simmer for 10 minutes. Season with salt and pepper to taste.

4. Serve hot, garnished with fresh cilantro.

## Nutritional Information (Per Serving):

- Calories: 300 Kcal

- Protein: 9g

- Carbohydrates: 29g

- Fat: 18g

**Mediterranean Chickpea Salad**

Preparation Time: 10 minutes

Servings: 4

Ingredients:

- 2 cans chickpeas, drained and rinsed

- 1 cucumber, diced

- 2 tomatoes, diced

- 1 red onion, finely chopped

- 1/4 cup olives, sliced

- 1/4 cup feta cheese, crumbled

- 2 tablespoons olive oil

- Juice of 1 lemon

- Salt and pepper to taste

- Fresh parsley, chopped

**Procedure:**

1. In a large bowl, combine the chickpeas, cucumber, tomatoes, red onion, olives, and feta cheese.

2. Drizzle with olive oil and lemon juice. Season with salt and pepper.

3. Toss to combine and garnish with fresh parsley.

**Nutritional Information (Per Serving):**

- Calories: 335 Kcal

- Protein: 12g

- Carbohydrates: 40g

- Fat: 15g

Each of these recipes is designed not only to provide nourishment but also to promote wellness through balanced nutrition. These meals are rich in whole foods, healthy fats, and plant-based ingredients, keeping you energized and supporting your overall health.

By incorporating these dishes into your regular meal rotation, you're not just feeding your body, but fueling it for optimal performance.

## SPICY SWEET POTATO AND BLACK BEAN CHILI

Prep Time: 15 minutes

Servings: 6

Ingredients:

- 2 large sweet potatoes, peeled and cubed

- 1 can black beans, drained and rinsed

- 1 onion, chopped

- 2 cloves garlic, minced

- 1 can diced tomatoes

- 2 tablespoons chili powder

- 1 teaspoon cumin

- Salt and pepper to taste

- 2 cups vegetable broth

- Olive oil

Instructions:

1. Heat a drizzle of olive oil in a large pot over medium heat. Add chopped onions and garlic, sautéing until softened and fragrant.

2. Add the cubed sweet potatoes, black beans, diced tomatoes, chili powder, cumin, salt, pepper, and vegetable broth.

3. Bring the mixture to a boil, then lower the heat to simmer for 25 minutes or until the sweet potatoes are fork-tender.

4. Serve hot, optionally topped with garnishes like avocado, sour cream, or fresh cilantro.

Macronutrients per Serving:

Calories: 210 Kcal | Protein: 8g | Carbohydrates: 40g | Fat: 3g

## Roasted Chicken with Rosemary and Root Vegetables

Prep Time: 15 minutes

Servings: 4

Ingredients:

- 4 chicken thighs

- 2 carrots, peeled and sliced

- 2 parsnips, peeled and sliced

- 1 sweet potato, peeled and cubed

- 4 sprigs of rosemary

- 3 tablespoons olive oil

- Salt and pepper to taste

Instructions:

1. Preheat the oven to 425°F (220°C).

2. Arrange the chicken thighs and the prepared vegetables in a roasting pan. Drizzle with olive oil, season with salt and pepper, and tuck rosemary sprigs between the chicken and vegetables.

3. Roast for 35-40 minutes, or until the chicken is golden brown and the vegetables are tender.

4. Serve warm, making sure each plate has a mix of the chicken and roasted vegetables.

Macronutrients per Serving:

Calories: 370 Kcal | Protein: 24g | Carbohydrates: 23g | Fat: 20g

# CHAPTER 24

## HEALTHY SNACKS AND SIDES FOR EVERYDAY ENJOYMENT

### CRUNCHY KALE CHIPS

Prep Time: 10 minutes

Ingredients:

- 1 bunch of kale, washed and torn into bite-sized pieces

- 2 tablespoons olive oil

- Sea salt, to taste

Instructions:

1. Preheat the oven to 350°F (175°C).

2. Remove kale stems and tear the leaves into small, bite-sized pieces.

3. Toss the kale with olive oil and spread the leaves on a baking sheet in a single layer. Sprinkle with sea salt.

4. Bake for 10-15 minutes, stirring halfway through, until the edges are brown but not burnt.

**Macronutrients per Serving:**

Calories: 58 Kcal | Protein: 2g | Carbohydrates: 5g | Fat: 4g

# AVOCADO AND TOMATO BRUSCHETTA

Prep Time: 10 minutes

Ingredients:

- 1 ripe avocado, diced

- 1 large tomato, diced

- 1/4 cup fresh basil, chopped

- 2 cloves garlic, minced

- Salt and pepper to taste

- Whole-grain baguette slices, toasted

Instructions:

1. In a bowl, mix together the diced avocado, tomato, basil, and minced garlic.

2. Season with salt and pepper to taste.

3. Spoon the mixture onto toasted baguette slices just before serving.

Macronutrients per Serving:

Calories: 95 Kcal | Protein: 2g | Carbohydrates: 13g | Fat: 5g

# SPICED ROASTED CHICKPEAS

Prep Time: 5 minutes

Ingredients:

- 1 can chickpeas, drained and rinsed

- 1 tablespoon olive oil

- 1 teaspoon smoked paprika

- 1/2 teaspoon garlic powder

- Salt and pepper to taste

Instructions:

1. Preheat the oven to 400°F (200°C).

2. Toss the chickpeas with olive oil, smoked paprika, garlic powder, salt, and pepper.

3. Spread the chickpeas in an even layer on a baking sheet.

4. Roast for 20-30 minutes, shaking the pan occasionally, until the chickpeas are crispy.

Macronutrients per Serving:

Calories: 134 Kcal | Protein: 5g | Carbohydrates: 20g | Fat: 4g

# SWEET POTATO AND BEETROOT SALAD

Prep Time: 15 minutes

Ingredients:

- 2 medium sweet potatoes, peeled and cubed

- 2 medium beetroots, peeled and cubed

- 2 tablespoons olive oil

- 1 tablespoon balsamic vinegar

- Salt and pepper to taste

- Fresh parsley, chopped, for garnish

Instructions:

1. Preheat the oven to 400°F (200°C).

2. Toss the sweet potatoes and beetroots with olive oil, salt, and pepper, then spread them on a baking sheet.

3. Roast for 25-30 minutes, or until tender.

4. Transfer the roasted vegetables to a serving bowl and drizzle with balsamic vinegar.

5. Garnish with fresh parsley and serve.

Macronutrients per Serving:

Calories: 123 Kcal | Protein: 2g | Carbohydrates: 23g | Fat: 3g

These recipes are perfect for anyone looking to enjoy delicious, wholesome meals that are packed with nutrients.

They're easy to make and are great options for maintaining energy levels throughout the day while staying aligned with holistic health practices.

# COCONUT CHIA PUDDING WITH TROPICAL TOPPINGS

Preparation Time: 5 minutes + chilling

Servings: 2

**Ingredients:**

- 1/4 cup chia seeds

- 1 cup coconut milk (full-fat or light, depending on your preference)

- 2 tablespoons honey or maple syrup, to taste

- 1/2 teaspoon vanilla extract

- Mango cubes and toasted coconut flakes for garnish

**Instructions:**

1. In a medium-sized bowl, whisk together the chia seeds, coconut milk, honey, and vanilla extract.

2. Let the mixture sit for 5 minutes, then stir again to prevent clumps.

3. Cover and refrigerate for at least 2 hours or overnight until the pudding has thickened to your desired consistency.

4. When ready to serve, top with fresh mango cubes and a sprinkle of toasted coconut flakes for a tropical touch.

**Nutritional Information (per serving):**

- Calories: 280

- Protein: 3g

- Carbohydrates: 20g

- Fat: 21g

# BAKED CINNAMON APPLES WITH HONEY AND PECANS

Preparation Time: 10 minutes

Servings: 4

Ingredients:

- 4 large apples, cored and sliced

- 2 tablespoons melted butter or coconut oil

- 4 tablespoons honey or maple syrup

- 1/2 teaspoon ground cinnamon

- 1/4 cup chopped pecans

Instructions:

1. Preheat your oven to 375°F (190°C).

2. Arrange the apple slices in a baking dish. Drizzle the melted butter over the apples and follow with honey.

3. Sprinkle the apples with cinnamon and chopped pecans.

4. Bake for 20-25 minutes, until the apples are tender and fragrant.

5. Serve warm, optionally paired with a dollop of Greek yogurt for added creaminess.

Nutritional Information (per serving):

- Calories: 210

- Protein: 1g

- Carbohydrates: 34g

- Fat: 9g

# ALMOND AND RASPBERRY THUMBPRINT COOKIES

Preparation Time: 20 minutes

Servings: 12 cookies

## Ingredients:

- 1 cup almond flour

- 1/4 cup melted coconut oil

- 1/4 cup maple syrup

- 1 teaspoon almond extract

- Raspberry jam for filling

## Instructions:

1. Preheat the oven to 350°F (175°C) and line a baking sheet with parchment paper.

2. In a bowl, combine almond flour, coconut oil, maple syrup, and almond extract until a dough forms.

3. Roll the dough into balls and place them on the prepared baking sheet. Press a thumbprint into the center of each ball and fill with raspberry jam.

4. Bake for 12-15 minutes or until the edges are golden brown. Allow the cookies to cool on the baking sheet.

5. Enjoy these treats warm or at room temperature.

## Nutritional Information (per cookie):

- Calories: 160

- Protein: 3g

- Carbohydrates: 14g

- Fat: 11g

# LEMON GINGER SORBET

Preparation Time: 5 minutes + freezing

Servings: 4

## Ingredients:

- 1/2 cup fresh lemon juice

- 2 cups water

- 1/3 cup honey or maple syrup

- 1 tablespoon freshly grated ginger

## Instructions:

1. In a saucepan, combine the water, honey, and ginger. Bring to a simmer and then remove from heat. Let it cool for a few minutes.

2. Stir in the fresh lemon juice, then strain the mixture to remove ginger pieces.

3. Pour the liquid into a shallow dish and place it in the freezer. Stir every 30 minutes to prevent large ice crystals from forming, until fully frozen (about 2-3 hours).

4. Blend the frozen mixture in a food processor for a smooth sorbet texture, and serve immediately.

## Nutritional Information (per serving):

- Calories: 100

- Protein: 0g

- Carbohydrates: 25g

- Fat: 0g

# CARROT CAKE ENERGY BALLS

Preparation Time: 20 minutes

Servings: 12 energy balls

## Ingredients:

- 1 cup shredded carrots

- 1 cup pitted dates

- 1/2 cup rolled oats

- 1/2 cup chopped walnuts

- 1/4 teaspoon cinnamon

- 1/8 teaspoon nutmeg

- Shredded coconut for coating

## Instructions:

1. In a food processor, combine the shredded carrots, dates, oats, walnuts, cinnamon, and nutmeg. Blend until the mixture starts to clump together.

2. Scoop the mixture and roll into small balls.

3. Roll each ball in shredded coconut for a delightful outer layer.

4. Refrigerate the energy balls for at least 1 hour to firm up before serving.

## Nutritional Information (per energy ball):

- Calories: 150

- Protein: 3g

- Carbohydrates: 18g

- Fat: 8g

# VEGAN CHOCOLATE PUDDING

Preparation Time: 10 minutes + chilling

Servings: 2

## Ingredients:

- 2 ripe avocados, peeled and pitted

- 1/4 cup raw cacao powder

- 1/4 cup almond milk

- 1/3 cup maple syrup

- 1 teaspoon vanilla extract

## Instructions:

1. Blend avocados, cacao powder, almond milk, maple syrup, and vanilla extract in a blender until smooth.

2. Divide the pudding between two dessert cups and refrigerate for at least 1 hour before serving.

3. Optional: Garnish with fresh berries or a sprinkle of cacao nibs for added texture.

## Nutritional Information (per serving):

- Calories: 240

- Protein: 3g

- Carbohydrates: 27g

- Fat: 15g

These nutrient-dense, flavor-packed recipes are crafted to satisfy your cravings while nourishing your body. With a blend of sweet, savory, and energizing options, you can enjoy the benefits of wholesome ingredients without compromising on taste.

Each recipe reflects the principles of a holistic, balanced approach to wellness, providing you with both sustenance and satisfaction.

# APPLE CIDER VINEGAR ELIXIR

Preparation Time: 5 minutes

**Ingredients:**

- 2 tablespoons apple cider vinegar

- 1 tablespoon honey

- Juice of 1 lemon

- 1 teaspoon ground cinnamon

- 2 cups water

**Instructions:**

1. In a large glass, mix together apple cider vinegar, honey, lemon juice, and ground cinnamon.

2. Add water and stir thoroughly to combine the ingredients.

3. Enjoy chilled or at room temperature for a refreshing, health-boosting drink.

**Nutritional Information (Per Serving):**

- Calories: 50

- Protein: 0g

- Carbohydrates: 13g

- Fat: 0g

# COCONUT WATER HYDRATION BOOST

Preparation Time: 3 minutes

Ingredients:

- 2 cups coconut water

- Juice of 1 lime

- A pinch of Himalayan pink salt

- 1 teaspoon honey

**Instructions:**

1. In a pitcher, combine coconut water, lime juice, Himalayan pink salt, and honey.

2. Stir well until the honey and salt are fully dissolved.

3. Serve chilled for a refreshing hydration boost.

**Nutritional Information (Per Serving):**

- Calories: 45

- Protein: 0.5g

- Carbohydrates: 11g

- Fat: 0.5g

# HERBAL HEALING BROTH

Preparation Time: 10 minutes

**Ingredients:**

- 3 cups vegetable broth

- 1 clove garlic, minced

- 1/2 inch ginger root, sliced

- 1/2 teaspoon turmeric powder

- A pinch of black pepper

- Fresh herbs (such as parsley or cilantro), chopped

**Instructions:**

1. Bring the vegetable broth to a boil in a saucepan.

2. Add minced garlic, ginger, turmeric, and black pepper to the broth.

3. Let it simmer for 5-7 minutes.

4. Remove from heat, add chopped fresh herbs, and let the broth steep for a few minutes.

5. Strain and serve warm for a soothing, immune-boosting drink.

**Nutritional Information (Per Serving):**

- Calories: 20

- Protein: 1g

- Carbohydrates: 4g

- Fat: 0g

# BERRY ANTIOXIDANT SMOOTHIE

Preparation Time: 5 minutes

Ingredients:

- 1/2 cup frozen blueberries

- 1/2 cup frozen raspberries

- 1 banana

- 1 cup spinach

- 1 cup almond milk

**Instructions:**

1. Combine all ingredients in a blender.

2. Blend until smooth.

3. Serve immediately for a delicious antioxidant boost.

**Nutritional Information (Per Serving):**

- Calories: 150

- Protein: 3g

- Carbohydrates: 34g

- Fat: 2g

# SOOTHING PEPPERMINT TEA

Preparation Time: 5 minutes

Ingredients:

- 1 tablespoon dried peppermint leaves

- 2 cups boiling water

## Instructions:

1. Place dried peppermint leaves in a tea infuser or directly in a teapot.

2. Pour boiling water over the leaves, cover, and steep for 5 minutes.

3. Strain into a cup and enjoy warm to aid digestion and promote relaxation.

## Nutritional Information (Per Serving):

- Calories: 0

- Protein: 0g

- Carbohydrates: 0g

- Fat: 0g

# CHAPTER 25

## 30-DAY NUTRITIOUS MEAL PLAN FOR BUSY LIVES

In today's fast-paced environment, prioritizing nutrition can often feel like a daunting challenge. However, maintaining a balanced and nourishing diet is crucial for optimal energy, focus, and long-term health.

Designed for individuals with busy schedules, this 30-day meal plan simplifies meal prep while ensuring that you get the right mix of nutrients to sustain your energy levels and support your overall well-being.

**What to Expect:**

This meal plan includes quick-to-make meals that are nutritionally balanced, flavorful, and easy to prepare. With approximately 1,800 calories per day, it includes breakfast, a mid-morning snack, lunch, a light dessert, and dinner—tailored to fit a variety of dietary preferences.

Each recipe includes simple ingredients and requires minimal time in the kitchen, making healthy eating more accessible for everyone, whether you're a busy professional, a parent on the go, or simply looking for efficient ways to improve your diet.

**Key Features:**

- **Efficiency:** Meals that require minimal prep and cook time.

- **Simplicity:** Uses ingredients that are easy to find at any grocery store.

- **Nutritional Balance:** Each meal provides a carefully calculated balance of proteins, fats, carbohydrates, vitamins, and minerals to support your energy and health.

- **Flexibility:** You can swap similar ingredients based on availability or personal preference without compromising the nutritional value of the meal.

- **Delicious Flavors:** All recipes are designed to be as tasty as they are healthy, ensuring that your meals remain satisfying throughout the 30 days.

This meal plan is perfect for anyone looking to enhance their nutrition while juggling a busy life. It offers both variety and convenience, ensuring that you can nourish your body without sacrificing time or flavor.

Each meal is designed to help you maintain energy, build immunity, and achieve your health goals seamlessly. Whether you're trying to improve your diet or simply seeking quick, healthy meals, this plan will guide you through 30 days of easy, nutritious eating.

This rewritten version enhances the structure, adjusts the tone to suit an American audience, and maintains a friendly yet informative style. It emphasizes the holistic health benefits, the convenience of the recipes, and the integration of Barbara O'Neill's teachings into practical, everyday nutrition.

# DAY 1: ENERGIZING KICKOFF

We're kicking off the 30-day plan with meals that pack both flavor and energy, ensuring you have the right nutrients to tackle your busy schedule.

**Breakfast: Quick Spinach and Feta Omelet with Whole Wheat Toast**

- Ingredients:

- 2 eggs

- 1 cup fresh spinach

- 30 grams feta cheese, crumbled

- 1 slice whole wheat toast

- 1 tsp olive oil

- Nutritional Characteristics:

- Calories: 350

- Rich in protein and fiber, high in iron and calcium to support strong muscles and bones.

**Morning Snack: Refreshing Greek Yogurt with Honey and Almonds**

- Ingredients:

- 1 cup Greek yogurt

- 1 tbsp honey

- 10 almonds, chopped

- Nutritional Characteristics:

- Calories: 200

- A protein-packed snack with healthy fats and calcium to keep you full and fueled.


## Lunch: Simple Quinoa Salad with Chickpeas, Avocado, and Sun-Dried Tomatoes

- Ingredients:

- 1 cup cooked quinoa

- ½ cup chickpeas, rinsed and drained

- ½ avocado, diced

- ¼ cup sun-dried tomatoes, chopped

- 2 tbsp olive oil

- Juice of 1 lemon

- Salt and pepper to taste

- Nutritional Characteristics:

- Calories: 500

- High in plant-based protein, healthy fats, fiber, and essential vitamins like potassium and Vitamin C.


## Dessert: Berry Delight

- Ingredients:

- 1 cup mixed berries (strawberries, blueberries, raspberries)

- Nutritional Characteristics:

- Calories: 70

- Rich in antioxidants and Vitamin C to boost immunity and fight inflammation.


## Dinner: Grilled Salmon with Asparagus and Brown Rice

- Ingredients:

- 150 grams salmon fillet

- 1 cup asparagus, trimmed

- ½ cup cooked brown rice

- 1 tbsp olive oil

- Lemon wedge

- Salt and pepper to taste

- Nutritional Characteristics:

- Calories: 680

- Packed with omega-3 fatty acids for heart health, plus complete protein and fiber for muscle support and digestion.


Total Calories for the Day: ~1800


## DAY 2: BALANCED BOOST


Today's menu emphasizes balance, with a mix of lean protein, healthy fats, and nutrient-dense veggies to keep you satisfied.


**Breakfast: Banana Nut Oatmeal**

- Ingredients:

- ½ cup rolled oats

- 1 cup almond milk

- 1 ripe banana, mashed

- 1 tbsp chopped walnuts

- 1 tsp cinnamon

- Instructions:

- Bring almond milk to a boil. Add oats and simmer until soft.

- Stir in banana, walnuts, and cinnamon, cooking for an additional minute.

- Serve warm.

- Nutritional Characteristics:

- Calories: 330

- High in fiber, heart-healthy fats, and naturally sweetened with banana.

**Morning Snack: Crunchy Carrot and Hummus**

- Ingredients:

- 1 large carrot, cut into sticks

- ¼ cup hummus

- Nutritional Characteristics:

- Calories: 150

- Provides fiber, beta-carotene for eye health, and plant-based protein from hummus.

**Lunch: Turkey and Avocado Wrap**

- Ingredients:

- 1 whole wheat tortilla

- 3 oz sliced turkey breast

- ¼ avocado, sliced

- Lettuce, tomato, and cucumber slices

- Mustard or a light spread of mayonnaise

- Instructions:

- Spread mustard or mayo on the tortilla, layer with turkey, avocado, lettuce, tomato, and cucumber.

- Roll tightly and cut in half.

- Nutritional Characteristics:

- Calories: 400

- Rich in lean protein and healthy fats, plus fiber from the veggies.

**Dessert: Apple Slices with Almond Butter**

- Ingredients:

- 1 medium apple, sliced

- 1 tbsp almond butter

- Nutritional Characteristics:

- Calories: 150

- A simple, fiber-packed snack with a boost of healthy fats.


**Dinner: Lemon Herb Chicken with Steamed Broccoli and Quinoa**

- Ingredients:

- 150 grams chicken breast

- 1 tbsp olive oil

- Herbs (basil, thyme, parsley)

- Juice of ½ lemon

- 1 cup broccoli, steamed

- ½ cup cooked quinoa

**- Instructions:**

- Marinate chicken in olive oil, lemon, and herbs for 30 minutes. Grill or bake until cooked.

- Serve with broccoli and quinoa.

- Nutritional Characteristics:

- Calories: 570

- High in lean protein, rich in fiber, vitamins, and iron for sustained energy.


Total Calories for the Day: ~1600


## DAY 3: REFRESH AND REPLENISH


Light, refreshing meals today will keep you feeling energized and nourished, with a focus on hydration and replenishment.


**Breakfast: Berry Yogurt Parfait**

- Ingredients:

- 1 cup Greek yogurt

- ½ cup mixed berries (blueberries, raspberries, strawberries)

- ¼ cup granola

- 1 tbsp honey

- Nutritional Characteristics:

- Calories: 310

- Packed with protein, antioxidants, and calcium for bone health.

**Morning Snack: Cucumber and Avocado Salad**

- Ingredients:

- 1 cucumber, sliced

- ½ avocado, diced

- Lemon juice, salt, and pepper

- Nutritional Characteristics:

- Calories: 180

- Hydrating and rich in healthy fats, with a dose of essential vitamins.

**Lunch: Grilled Chicken Caesar Salad**

- Ingredients:

- 150 grams chicken breast, grilled

- 2 cups romaine lettuce

- ¼ cup parmesan cheese

- Whole wheat croutons

- Caesar dressing (preferably low-fat)

- Nutritional Characteristics:

- Calories: 450

- High in protein and healthy fats, balanced with greens and calcium.

**Dessert: Dark Chocolate Squares**

- Ingredients:

- 2 squares of dark chocolate (70% or higher)

- Nutritional Characteristics:

- Calories: 100

- Rich in antioxidants for a mindful, indulgent treat.

**Dinner: Baked Cod with Sweet Potato Fries and Steamed Green Beans**

- Ingredients:

- 150 grams cod fillet

- 1 sweet potato, cut into fries

- 1 cup green beans

- Olive oil, sea salt, and pepper

- Nutritional Characteristics:

- Calories: 460

- Rich in omega-3s and protein, with fiber and vitamins from the sides.

Total Calories for the Day: ~1500

# DAY 4: POWER-PACKED START

We're focusing on power-packed meals today, giving your body a strong start and sustained energy throughout the day.

**Breakfast: Avocado Toast with Poached Egg**

- Ingredients:

- 2 slices whole grain bread

- 1 avocado

- 2 eggs, poached

- Optional toppings: chili flakes, radish

- Nutritional Characteristics:

- Calories: 400

- High in healthy fats, protein, and fiber to fuel your morning.


**Morning Snack: Mixed Nuts**

- Ingredients:

- ¼ cup mixed nuts (almonds, walnuts, cashews)

- Nutritional Characteristics:

- Calories: 170

- A great source of healthy fats, protein, and fiber.


**Lunch: Roast Beef Sandwich**

- Ingredients:

- 2 slices rye bread

- 100 grams roast beef

- 1 tbsp horseradish sauce

- Lettuce, tomato, and red onion slices

- Nutritional Characteristics:

- Calories: 350

- High in protein with essential vitamins and minerals.


**Dessert: Greek Yogurt with Blueberries**

- Ingredients:

- 1 cup Greek yogurt

- ½ cup fresh blueberries

- Nutritional Characteristics:

- Calories: 150

- Packed with protein and antioxidants.

**Dinner: Salmon Stir-Fry**

- Ingredients:

- 150 grams salmon, diced

- 1 cup bell peppers

- ½ cup broccoli florets

- 1 tbsp soy sauce

- 1 tsp sesame oil

- Garlic and ginger

- Nutritional Characteristics:

- Calories: 430

- Rich in omega-3s, antioxidants, and essential nutrients.

Total Calories for the Day: ~1500

# DAY 5: VIBRANT VEGGIE DAY

Welcome to Day 5 of your wellness journey—today is all about harnessing the power of vegetables to fuel and nourish your body. This plan is designed to be vibrant and nutrient-dense, giving you a healthy boost from morning to night, all while keeping the meals simple, delicious, and packed with whole foods.

Breakfast: Green Smoothie Bowl

Start your day with a refreshing and vibrant green smoothie bowl. It's rich in fiber, healthy fats, and antioxidants—designed to energize you and keep you feeling full throughout the morning.

- Ingredients:

- 1 ripe banana

- ½ avocado

- 1 cup fresh spinach

- ½ cup unsweetened almond milk

- 1 tbsp chia seeds

- Toppings: Sliced almonds, coconut flakes, fresh berries

- Instructions:

1. In a blender, combine the banana, avocado, spinach, and almond milk. Blend until smooth and creamy.

2. Pour the mixture into a bowl and top with chia seeds, sliced almonds, coconut flakes, and a handful of fresh berries.

- Nutritional Highlights:

- Calories: 350

- Benefits: High in fiber, packed with vitamins A, C, and E, and loaded with antioxidants to start your day strong.


Morning Snack: Veggie Sticks with Hummus

This light snack combines raw veggie sticks with creamy hummus for a satisfying crunch and nutrient-dense dip, offering fiber, healthy fats, and a solid dose of plant-based protein.


- Ingredients:

- Carrot sticks

- Celery sticks

- Cucumber slices

- ¼ cup hummus (preferably homemade or quality store-bought)

- Instructions:

- Prepare the vegetables by cutting them into sticks or slices.

- Serve with hummus for dipping.

- Nutritional Highlights:

- Calories: 150

- Benefits: A great mid-morning snack, rich in fiber and offering a balance of vitamins and plant protein.


Lunch: Tomato Basil Soup with Whole Grain Roll

A comforting yet light lunch, tomato basil soup delivers a rich dose of vitamins C and K, paired with a whole grain roll to provide fiber and keep you satisfied.

- Ingredients:

- 2 cups of tomato basil soup (preferably homemade or a high-quality store-bought version)

- 1 whole grain roll

- Instructions:

- Heat the soup in a saucepan over medium heat until warmed through.

- Serve with a warm whole grain roll on the side.

- Nutritional Highlights:

- Calories: 300

- Benefits: Rich in antioxidants from tomatoes and loaded with fiber, this meal is not only nourishing but supports heart health and digestion.

Dessert: Baked Pear with Cinnamon and Honey

This naturally sweet dessert is a simple, wholesome way to satisfy your sweet tooth without compromising your nutrition goals. Pears are a fantastic source of fiber, and the honey-cinnamon combination makes this feel like a treat.

- Ingredients:

- 1 pear, halved and cored

- Sprinkle of cinnamon

- Drizzle of honey

- Instructions:

1. Preheat your oven to 350°F (175°C).

2. Place pear halves on a baking sheet, sprinkle with cinnamon, and drizzle lightly with honey.

3. Bake for 15 minutes, or until the pear is tender and fragrant.

- Nutritional Highlights:

- Calories: 100

- Benefits: A fiber-rich dessert with a touch of natural sweetness, perfect to curb sugar cravings without the guilt.

Dinner: Chickpea Vegetable Curry

This hearty and satisfying dinner offers a flavorful blend of chickpeas and fresh vegetables in a creamy coconut curry. High in protein and fiber, this dish provides long-lasting energy and essential nutrients to close out your day.

- Ingredients:

- 1 tbsp coconut oil

- 1 onion, chopped

- 2 garlic cloves, minced

- 1 tbsp curry powder

- 1 can chickpeas, drained and rinsed

- 1 can diced tomatoes

- 1 cup coconut milk

- Assorted vegetables (e.g., bell pepper, zucchini, spinach)

- Instructions:

1. Heat the coconut oil in a large pan over medium heat. Add the onion and garlic, sauté until translucent.

2. Stir in the curry powder and cook briefly to release the aromas.

3. Add the chickpeas, diced tomatoes, and coconut milk. Bring to a simmer.

4. Toss in the vegetables and simmer until tender, about 10-15 minutes.

- Nutritional Highlights:

- Calories: 600

- Benefits: This dish is high in plant-based protein, fiber, and a variety of essential vitamins and minerals. The coconut milk adds creaminess while offering healthy fats to support brain function and energy.

Total Daily Caloric Intake: ~1500

# DAY 6: LEAN PROTEIN POWER

A day packed with lean protein to help build and repair tissues, keep you feeling full, and support sustained energy.

Breakfast: Scrambled Eggs with Spinach and Mushrooms

- Ingredients:

- 3 eggs

- 1 cup fresh spinach

- ½ cup sliced mushrooms

- 1 tbsp olive oil

- Salt and pepper to taste

- Instructions:

- Heat olive oil in a skillet over medium heat.

- Sauté mushrooms until they brown slightly, then add spinach and cook until wilted.

- Beat eggs and pour over the veggies, stirring until fully cooked.

- Season with salt and pepper.

- Nutritional Characteristics:

- Calories: 300

- High in protein and rich in iron and vitamins from the spinach and mushrooms.

## Morning Snack: Cottage Cheese with Pineapple

- Ingredients:

- ½ cup cottage cheese

- ½ cup chopped pineapple

- Nutritional Characteristics:

- Calories: 180

- A good source of protein and vitamin C, promoting muscle repair and immune support.

## Lunch: Turkey Lettuce Wraps

- Ingredients:

- 200 grams ground turkey

- Lettuce leaves (for wraps)

- 1 carrot, grated

- 1 bell pepper, thinly sliced

- 1 tbsp hoisin sauce

- 1 tsp olive oil

- Instructions:

- Cook ground turkey in olive oil until browned. Stir in hoisin sauce.

- Serve in lettuce leaves with grated carrot and sliced bell pepper.

- Nutritional Characteristics:

- Calories: 350

- High in lean protein, low in carbs, and packed with vitamins from fresh vegetables.

## Dessert: Kiwi and Strawberry Salad

- Ingredients:

- 2 kiwis, peeled and sliced

- 1 cup strawberries, halved

- Nutritional Characteristics:

- Calories: 90

- High in vitamin C and antioxidants, helping to fight free radicals and boost immunity.

## Dinner: Grilled Tilapia with Lemon Garlic Potatoes

- Ingredients:

- 150 grams tilapia fillet

- 1 cup diced potatoes

- 2 cloves garlic, minced

- Juice of 1 lemon

- 1 tbsp olive oil

- Parsley for garnish

- Instructions:

- Toss potatoes with olive oil, garlic, and half the lemon juice. Wrap in foil and grill with the tilapia until both are cooked through.

- Drizzle the remaining lemon juice over the fish and garnish with parsley.

- Nutritional Characteristics:

- Calories: 400

- Rich in omega-3 fatty acids, protein, and vitamin C, essential for heart and skin health.


Total Calories for the Day: ~1320


# DAY 7: REFRESHING AND LIGHT


A light yet satisfying day with nutrient-packed meals to refresh and rejuvenate.


**Breakfast: Chia Pudding with Mixed Berries**

- Ingredients:

- 3 tbsp chia seeds

- 1 cup almond milk

- 1 tbsp honey

- ½ cup mixed berries (blueberries, raspberries, blackberries)


- **Instructions:**

- Mix chia seeds with almond milk and honey, refrigerate for at least 4 hours or overnight. Top with mixed berries before serving.

- Nutritional Characteristics:

- Calories: 300

- High in fiber, omega-3 fatty acids, and antioxidants, supporting digestive and heart health.


**Morning Snack: Celery Sticks with Almond Butter**

- Ingredients:

- 3 celery stalks, cut into sticks

- 2 tbsp almond butter

- Nutritional Characteristics:

- Calories: 150

- A crunchy snack loaded with healthy fats and fiber for satiety.

## Lunch: Spinach and Quinoa Salad with Lemon Vinaigrette

- Ingredients:

- 1 cup cooked quinoa

- 2 cups fresh spinach

- ¼ cup chopped cucumber

- ¼ cup cherry tomatoes, halved

- ¼ cup crumbled feta cheese

- Dressing: 2 tbsp olive oil, juice of 1 lemon, salt, and pepper

- Instructions:

- Toss quinoa, spinach, cucumber, and tomatoes in a large bowl. Add vinaigrette and sprinkle with feta.

- Nutritional Characteristics:

- Calories: 400

- A protein-rich, vitamin-packed salad that's filling and refreshing.

## Dessert: Fresh Mango Slices

- Ingredients:

- 1 ripe mango, peeled and sliced

- Nutritional Characteristics:

- Calories: 100

- High in vitamin C and dietary fiber, supporting immune function and digestion.

**Dinner: Baked Lemon Herb Chicken with Steamed Vegetables**

- Ingredients:

- 150 grams chicken breast

- 1 tbsp olive oil

- Fresh herbs (rosemary, thyme, parsley)

- Juice of ½ lemon

- 1 cup mixed vegetables (carrots, broccoli, bell peppers)

- Instructions:

- Rub the chicken breast with olive oil, lemon juice, and herbs, bake at 375°F for 25-30 minutes. Steam the vegetables.

- Nutritional Characteristics:

- Calories: 350

- High in protein, low in fat, and rich in vitamins and minerals for balanced nutrition.


Total Calories for the Day: ~1300


# DAY 8: SUSTAINED ENERGY


A day centered around meals that will keep your energy levels high without weighing you down.


**Breakfast: Oatmeal with Flaxseeds and Maple Syrup**

- Ingredients:

- ½ cup rolled oats

- 1 cup water or milk

- 1 tbsp flaxseeds

- 1 tbsp maple syrup

- Nutritional Characteristics:

- Calories: 280

- High in fiber and omega-3 fatty acids, offering a slow release of energy to power your morning.

**Morning Snack: Greek Yogurt with Pumpkin Seeds**

- Ingredients:

- 1 cup Greek yogurt

- 2 tbsp pumpkin seeds

- Nutritional Characteristics:

- Calories: 190

- Rich in protein and magnesium, essential for muscle recovery and energy metabolism.

**Lunch: Lentil Soup with Whole Grain Bread**

- Ingredients:

- 2 cups lentil soup (homemade or store-bought)

- 1 slice whole grain bread

- Nutritional Characteristics:

- Calories: 360

- A hearty, fiber-rich lunch loaded with plant-based protein and iron.

**Dessert: Baked Cinnamon Apple**

- Ingredients:

- 1 apple, cored and sliced

- Sprinkle of cinnamon

- Nutritional Characteristics:

- Calories: 100

- Packed with natural sugars and fiber for a healthy sweet treat.

**Dinner: Grilled Turkey Burger with Avocado**

- Ingredients:

- 150 grams ground turkey

- 1 whole wheat bun

- ¼ avocado, sliced

- Lettuce, tomato, and onion

- Nutritional Characteristics:

- Calories: 500

- High in lean protein and healthy fats for long-lasting satiety and energy.

Total Calories for the Day: ~1430

# DAY 11: SOOTHING SIMPLICITY

A day designed to deliver wholesome, comforting meals that are easy to prepare while still being nutrient-dense.

**Breakfast: Almond Butter Toast with Banana Slices**

- Ingredients:

- 2 slices whole grain bread

- 2 tbsp almond butter

- 1 banana, sliced

- Instructions:

- Toast the bread slices until golden brown.

- Spread almond butter evenly on each slice.

- Top with banana slices and enjoy.

- Nutritional Characteristics:

- Calories: 400

- A balanced start to your day with healthy fats, fiber, and potassium from the bananas for heart health and energy.

**Morning Snack: Cottage Cheese with Fresh Peach Slices**

- Ingredients:

- ½ cup cottage cheese

- 1 peach, sliced

- Instructions:

- Top the cottage cheese with fresh peach slices.

- Nutritional Characteristics:

- Calories: 150

- Packed with protein and vitamin C for a refreshing, light snack that promotes muscle recovery and immune health.

**Lunch: Classic Chicken Salad**

- Ingredients:

- 150 grams cooked chicken breast, chopped

- ¼ cup celery, diced

- ¼ cup apple, diced

- ¼ cup mayonnaise

- 1 tbsp lemon juice

- Salt and pepper to taste

- Instructions:

- Mix chicken, celery, and apple in a bowl.

- Add mayonnaise, lemon juice, salt, and pepper.

- Chill in the fridge before serving.

- Nutritional Characteristics:

- Calories: 400

- High in protein with a refreshing blend of savory and sweet flavors. Provides a great balance of crunch and creamy textures.

**Dessert: Yogurt with Honey and Walnuts**

- Ingredients:

- 1 cup Greek yogurt

- 1 tbsp honey

- 2 tbsp chopped walnuts

- Instructions:

- Stir honey into the yogurt and top with walnuts.

- Nutritional Characteristics:

- Calories: 200

- A protein-packed dessert with healthy fats from walnuts and a touch of natural sweetness.


**Dinner: Lemon Garlic Pasta with Asparagus**

- Ingredients:

- 200 grams pasta (preferably whole wheat)

- 1 cup asparagus, trimmed and cut into pieces

- 2 cloves garlic, minced

- Juice of 1 lemon

- 2 tbsp olive oil

- Parmesan cheese for garnish

- Instructions:

- Cook pasta according to package instructions, adding asparagus in the last 3 minutes.

- Drain and return to the pot.

- Sauté garlic in olive oil, then mix into the pasta and asparagus.

- Stir in lemon juice and top with Parmesan cheese before serving.

- Nutritional Characteristics:

- Calories: 550

- A satisfying, fiber-rich dinner with a boost of vitamins from asparagus and a fresh, zesty flavor.


Total Calories for the Day: ~1700

# DAY 12: ENERGIZING ESSENTIALS

A day focused on meals that energize, sustain, and support overall well-being, perfect for busy days.

**Breakfast: Greek Yogurt Parfait with Granola and Honey**

- Ingredients:

- 1 cup Greek yogurt

- ½ cup granola

- 2 tbsp honey

- Optional: a handful of blueberries or sliced strawberries

- Instructions:

- Layer Greek yogurt, granola, and honey in a bowl or glass.

- Add fresh berries for a refreshing touch.

- Nutritional Characteristics:

- Calories: 420

- Rich in protein, calcium, and probiotics, with a sweet crunch from granola to keep you satisfied.

**Morning Snack: Sliced Cucumber and Hummus**

- Ingredients:

- 1 cucumber, sliced

- ¼ cup hummus

- Instructions:

- Serve cucumber slices with hummus for dipping.

- Nutritional Characteristics:

- Calories: 150

- A hydrating and fiber-filled snack, perfect for maintaining energy without excess calories.

**Lunch: Avocado Chicken Wrap**

- Ingredients:

- 1 whole wheat tortilla

- 100 grams cooked chicken breast, sliced

- ½ ripe avocado, sliced

- Mixed salad greens

- 2 tbsp Greek yogurt

- Instructions:

- Spread Greek yogurt on the tortilla.

- Layer chicken, avocado, and salad greens, then roll the tortilla tightly.

- Nutritional Characteristics:

- Calories: 500

- High in protein and healthy fats with fiber from the whole wheat tortilla and greens for digestive health.

## Dessert: Baked Apple with Cinnamon

- Ingredients:

- 1 apple, cored and sliced

- Sprinkle of cinnamon

- Instructions:

- Place apple slices in a baking dish, sprinkle with cinnamon, and bake at 350°F for about 20 minutes until soft.

- Nutritional Characteristics:

- Calories: 90

- A simple, fiber-rich dessert that satisfies your sweet tooth while keeping calories in check.

## Dinner: Quinoa and Black Bean Bowl

- Ingredients:

- 1 cup cooked quinoa

- ½ cup black beans, rinsed and drained

- ½ bell pepper, diced

- ¼ cup corn

- ¼ cup diced tomatoes

- 1 tbsp olive oil

- Juice of 1 lime

- Fresh cilantro for garnish

- Instructions:

- Combine quinoa, black beans, bell pepper, corn, and tomatoes in a bowl.

- Drizzle with olive oil and lime juice, toss to combine, and garnish with cilantro.

- Nutritional Characteristics:

- Calories: 440

- A nutrient-dense meal rich in protein, fiber, antioxidants, and healthy fats, keeping you fueled for the rest of the day.


Total Calories for the Day: ~1600


These meals are designed to balance nutrition and flavor, ensuring your energy levels remain stable and you feel satisfied throughout the day.


# DAY 13: FLAVORFUL FRESHNESS


**Breakfast: Berry Smoothie Bowl**

A bright, refreshing start to your day, this berry smoothie bowl is packed with antioxidants, fiber, and omega-3s.


- Ingredients:

- 1 cup mixed berries (blueberries, strawberries, raspberries)

- 1 banana

- ½ cup Greek yogurt

- ¼ cup almond milk

- 1 tablespoon chia seeds

- Toppings: Sliced almonds, shredded coconut, extra berries

- Instructions:

1. Blend the berries, banana, Greek yogurt, and almond milk until smooth.

2. Pour into a bowl and top with chia seeds, almonds, shredded coconut, and extra berries.

- Nutritional Highlights:

~350 calories. Rich in antioxidants, vitamins, and omega-3s from chia seeds.

## Morning Snack: Veggie Chips

A light and crispy snack that satisfies crunch cravings while staying nutritious.

- Ingredients:

- Sliced carrots, sweet potatoes, and beets

- 1 tablespoon olive oil

- Salt, to taste

- Instructions:

1. Toss vegetables in olive oil and salt.

2. Bake at 375°F for 20-25 minutes until crisp.

- Nutritional Highlights:

~150 calories. Low-calorie, rich in vitamins A and C.

## Lunch: Turkey Salad with Avocado

This fresh and hearty salad offers lean protein and heart-healthy fats for a balanced midday meal.

- Ingredients:

- 2 cups mixed greens (spinach, arugula, romaine)

- 100g cooked turkey breast, chopped

- ½ avocado, diced

- ¼ cup cherry tomatoes, halved

- 2 tablespoons balsamic vinaigrette

- Instructions:

1. Combine greens, turkey, avocado, and tomatoes.

2. Drizzle with balsamic vinaigrette and toss.

- Nutritional Highlights:

~400 calories. Packed with lean protein and healthy fats, this salad supports heart health.

**Dessert: Peach Yogurt Popsicles**

A sweet, cooling treat with a punch of protein and natural fruit sugars.

- Ingredients:

- 1 cup Greek yogurt

- 2 peaches, pureed

- 1 tablespoon honey

- Instructions:

1. Mix yogurt, peach puree, and honey.

2. Pour into molds and freeze until solid.

- Nutritional Highlights:

~100 calories. Low-fat, high in protein, with a refreshing fruity flavor.

**Dinner: Grilled Salmon with Asparagus and Quinoa**

A classic dinner featuring omega-3-rich salmon, fiber-filled quinoa, and tender asparagus.

- Ingredients:

- 150g salmon fillet

- 1 cup asparagus, trimmed

- ½ cup cooked quinoa

- 1 tablespoon olive oil

- Lemon wedges for garnish

- Instructions:

1. Preheat the grill to medium-high.

2. Brush salmon and asparagus with olive oil. Grill until the salmon is cooked and asparagus is tender.

3. Serve with quinoa and garnish with lemon wedges.

- Nutritional Highlights:

~600 calories. Rich in omega-3s, fiber, and protein, with an added boost of vitamins from the veggies.

Total Daily Calories: ~1600

# DAY 14: BALANCED DELIGHTS

Breakfast: Avocado and Egg Breakfast Sandwich

This protein-packed sandwich is a perfect blend of creamy avocado and hearty eggs on a toasted English muffin.

- Ingredients:

- 1 whole grain English muffin

- 1 ripe avocado, mashed

- 2 eggs, fried or poached

- Salt and pepper, to taste


- Instructions:

1. Toast the English muffin.

2. Spread mashed avocado on each half, then top with eggs.

3. Season with salt and pepper.


- Nutritional Highlights:

~450 calories. High in protein and healthy fats to keep you satisfied all morning.


## Morning Snack: Mixed Berry and Yogurt Parfait

A quick snack to keep you energized, full of antioxidants and protein.


- Ingredients:

- ½ cup Greek yogurt

- ½ cup mixed berries

- 1 tablespoon granola


- Instructions:

1. Layer the yogurt and berries in a glass.

2. Top with granola for crunch.


- Nutritional Highlights:

~200 calories. A refreshing and balanced snack with a good mix of protein and vitamins.


## Lunch: Spinach and Feta Stuffed Chicken Breast

This Mediterranean-inspired dish is rich in protein and minerals, perfect for a satisfying lunch.

- Ingredients:

- 150g chicken breast, butterflied

- ½ cup chopped spinach

- ¼ cup crumbled feta

- 1 tablespoon olive oil

- Salt and pepper, to taste

- Instructions:

1. Preheat the oven to 375°F.

2. Sauté spinach until wilted, then mix with feta and stuff inside the chicken breast.

3. Secure with toothpicks, brush with olive oil, and bake for 25-30 minutes.

- Nutritional Highlights:

~400 calories. Packed with lean protein, iron, and calcium.

**Dessert: Dark Chocolate and Nut Clusters**

A satisfying sweet treat that combines the richness of dark chocolate with heart-healthy nuts.

- Ingredients:

- 2 squares dark chocolate (70% or higher)

- ¼ cup chopped mixed nuts (almonds, walnuts, pecans)

- Instructions:

1. Melt the chocolate, mix in the nuts.

2. Spoon into clusters on parchment and refrigerate until set.

- Nutritional Highlights:

~150 calories. Rich in antioxidants and healthy fats.

**Dinner: Lemon Pepper Tilapia with Roasted Sweet Potatoes and Green Beans**

A wholesome, nutritious dinner combining lean tilapia, roasted veggies, and a hint of lemony freshness.

- Ingredients:

- 150g tilapia fillet

- 1 sweet potato, diced

- 1 cup green beans, trimmed

- 1 tablespoon olive oil

- Lemon pepper seasoning

- Instructions:

1. Preheat oven to 400°F.

2. Toss sweet potatoes and green beans with olive oil and lemon pepper seasoning.

3. Place the tilapia in the center of the baking sheet and roast for 20-25 minutes.

- Nutritional Highlights:

~500 calories. Provides lean protein, fiber, and healthy fats for a balanced meal.

Total Daily Calories: ~1700

# DAY 15: REFRESHING RECHARGE

**Breakfast: Cottage Cheese and Pineapple Bowl**

A simple yet protein-rich breakfast that includes digestive-friendly pineapple.

- Ingredients:

- 1 cup cottage cheese

- ½ cup chopped pineapple

- 1 tablespoon chia seeds

- Instructions:

1. Mix cottage cheese with pineapple, sprinkle with chia seeds.

- Nutritional Highlights:

~300 calories. High in protein and packed with digestive enzymes from the pineapple.

**Morning Snack: Carrot and Celery Sticks with Almond Butter**

This crunchy snack pairs fiber-rich veggies with creamy almond butter for a perfect balance of flavors.

- Ingredients:

- 1 large carrot, cut into sticks

- 2 celery stalks, cut into sticks

- 2 tablespoons almond butter

- Instructions:

1. Serve carrot and celery sticks with almond butter.

- Nutritional Highlights:

~180 calories. Rich in fiber and healthy fats.

**Lunch: Quinoa Salad with Roasted Vegetables**

This vibrant, fiber-rich salad is packed with roasted veggies and topped with tangy feta.

- Ingredients:

- 1 cup cooked quinoa

- ½ cup roasted bell peppers

- ½ cup roasted zucchini

- ¼ cup roasted red onions

- 2 tablespoons feta cheese

- Dressing: 1 tablespoon olive oil, juice of 1 lemon

- Instructions:

1. Combine quinoa and roasted vegetables.

2. Drizzle with olive oil and lemon, top with feta.

- Nutritional Highlights:

~400 calories. Provides a filling, nutrient-dense lunch with plenty of protein and vitamins.

## Dessert: Greek Yogurt with Honey and Cinnamon

A creamy dessert with a touch of sweetness and anti-inflammatory benefits.

- Ingredients:

- 1 cup Greek yogurt

- 1 tablespoon honey

- A sprinkle of cinnamon

- Instructions:

1. Mix yogurt with honey and cinnamon.

- Nutritional Highlights:

~150 calories. Rich in protein with anti-inflammatory properties from cinnamon.

**Dinner: Baked Lemon Herb Cod with Steamed Broccoli and Brown Rice**

A light, nutrient-rich dinner with a perfect balance of protein, fiber, and healthy fats.

- Ingredients:

- 150g cod fillet

- 1 cup steamed broccoli

- ½ cup cooked brown rice

- 1 tablespoon olive oil

- Herbs (parsley, dill, thyme)

- Juice of ½ lemon

- Instructions:

1. Preheat the oven to 375°F.

2. Marinate the cod with olive oil, lemon juice, and herbs, then bake for 12-15 minutes.

3. Serve with steamed broccoli and brown rice.

- Nutritional Highlights:

~500 calories. A high-protein, omega-3-rich dish with fiber from vegetables and grains.

Total Daily Calories: ~1530

# DAY 16: SUSTAINED SATISFACTION

**Breakfast: Nutty Oatmeal**

A hearty and nutritious breakfast to kick-start your day with sustained energy.

- Ingredients:

- ½ cup rolled oats

- 1 cup almond milk

- 1 tablespoon almond butter

- 1 tablespoon flaxseeds

- 1 banana, sliced

- Instructions:

1. Cook oats in almond milk as per package instructions.

2. Stir in almond butter, and top with banana slices and flaxseeds.

- Nutritional Highlights:

~350 calories. High in fiber, healthy fats, and protein for long-lasting energy.

**Morning Snack: Avocado and Tomato Slices**

A light yet filling snack that offers healthy fats and a fresh burst of flavor.

- Ingredients:

- 1 ripe avocado, sliced

- 1 tomato, sliced

- Salt and pepper to taste

- Instructions:

1. Arrange avocado and tomato slices, season with salt and pepper.

- Nutritional Highlights:

~200 calories. Packed with heart-healthy fats, vitamins C and E, and potassium.

**Lunch: Grilled Chicken Caesar Wrap**

A delicious wrap that balances lean protein and fresh greens with the rich flavor of Caesar dressing.

- Ingredients:

- 1 whole wheat tortilla

- 150 grams grilled chicken, sliced

- 1 cup romaine lettuce, chopped

- 2 tablespoons Caesar dressing

- 2 tablespoons grated Parmesan cheese

- Instructions:

1. Layer lettuce, chicken, dressing, and Parmesan on a tortilla.

2. Roll tightly, slice, and enjoy.

- Nutritional Highlights:

~450 calories. High in protein and fiber, offering a satisfying yet light lunch.

**Dessert: Mixed Berries with Mint**

A simple and refreshing dessert that's perfect for a midday treat.

- Ingredients:

- 1 cup mixed berries (strawberries, blueberries, raspberries)

- Fresh mint leaves

- Instructions:

1. Toss mixed berries with fresh mint leaves for a refreshing finish.

- Nutritional Highlights:

~100 calories. High in antioxidants and vitamins, offering a light, healthy dessert option.

**Dinner: Herb-Roasted Turkey Breast with Sweet Potatoes and Green Beans**

A hearty and nutrient-packed dinner to end the day with satisfaction.

- Ingredients:

- 200 grams turkey breast

- 1 sweet potato, cubed

- 1 cup green beans

- 1 tablespoon olive oil

- Mixed herbs (rosemary, thyme, sage)

- Instructions:

1. Preheat oven to 375°F.

2. Rub turkey with olive oil and herbs, place in roasting pan with sweet potatoes and green beans.

3. Roast for 25-30 minutes until turkey is cooked through and vegetables are tender.

- Nutritional Highlights:

~500 calories. High in protein and rich in essential vitamins and minerals from the vegetables.

Total Daily Calories: ~1600

# DAY 17: VIBRANT VARIETY

**Breakfast: Mango Coconut Chia Pudding**

This tropical-inspired chia pudding offers a refreshing, nutrient-dense start to your day.

- Ingredients:

- 3 tablespoons chia seeds

- 1 cup coconut milk

- ½ mango, diced

- 1 tablespoon shredded coconut

- Instructions:

1. Mix chia seeds with coconut milk and refrigerate overnight.

2. Stir the pudding and top with mango and shredded coconut in the morning.

- Nutritional Highlights:

~350 calories. Rich in fiber and healthy fats for a nutritious breakfast.

## Morning Snack: Roasted Chickpeas

A crunchy, protein-packed snack to keep you satisfied between meals.

- Ingredients:

- ½ cup chickpeas, drained and rinsed

- 1 tablespoon olive oil

- Spices (paprika or cumin), salt, and pepper to taste

- Instructions:

1. Toss chickpeas with olive oil and spices.

2. Roast at 400°F for 20-25 minutes until crispy.

- Nutritional Highlights:

~150 calories. High in protein and fiber, offering a satisfying crunch.

**Lunch: Avocado Shrimp Salad**

This light and flavorful salad delivers a fresh, zesty taste with plenty of healthy fats and protein.

- Ingredients:

- 150 grams cooked shrimp

- 1 avocado, diced

- 1 cup mixed greens

- ½ cucumber, sliced

- ¼ cup cherry tomatoes, halved

- Dressing: juice of 1 lime, 2 tablespoons olive oil, salt, and pepper

- Instructions:

1. Combine shrimp, avocado, mixed greens, cucumber, and cherry tomatoes.

2. Whisk together lime juice, olive oil, salt, and pepper. Toss salad with dressing.

- Nutritional Highlights:

~400 calories. High in healthy fats, lean protein, and packed with fresh flavors.

**Dessert: Baked Cinnamon Pears**

A warm, comforting dessert with natural sweetness and a touch of spice.

- Ingredients:

- 2 pears, halved and cored

- 1 tablespoon honey

- Cinnamon, to taste

- Instructions:

1. Drizzle pears with honey and sprinkle with cinnamon.

2. Bake at 350°F for 25 minutes until tender.

- Nutritional Highlights:

~150 calories. High in fiber and natural sugars, offering a satisfying, wholesome dessert.

**Dinner: Basil Pesto Pasta with Grilled Chicken**

A flavorful pasta dish that balances whole grains, lean protein, and the rich taste of pesto.

- Ingredients:

- 200 grams chicken breast, grilled and sliced

- 150 grams whole wheat pasta, cooked

- ¼ cup basil pesto

- ¼ cup grated Parmesan cheese

- Cherry tomatoes for garnish

- Instructions:

1. Toss pasta with basil pesto.

2. Top with grilled chicken, Parmesan, and cherry tomatoes.

- Nutritional Highlights:

~550 calories. High in protein and healthy fats, making for a satisfying and nourishing dinner.

Total Daily Calories: ~1600

# DAY 18: HEARTY HARVEST

**Breakfast: Pumpkin Spice Oatmeal**

This seasonal favorite brings warming spices and nutritious pumpkin for a comforting breakfast.

- Ingredients:

- ½ cup rolled oats

- 1 cup milk or water

- ¼ cup pumpkin puree

- 1 tablespoon maple syrup

- ½ teaspoon pumpkin spice

- Instructions:

1. Cook oats with milk or water.

2. Stir in pumpkin puree, maple syrup, and pumpkin spice.

- Nutritional Highlights:

~300 calories. High in fiber, vitamins, and metabolism-boosting spices.

**Morning Snack: Apple Slices with Peanut Butter**

A classic snack pairing that balances sweetness with a protein boost.

- Ingredients:

- 1 apple, sliced

- 2 tablespoons peanut butter

- Instructions:

1. Serve apple slices with peanut butter for dipping.

- Nutritional Highlights:

~200 calories. Rich in healthy fats, fiber, and protein.

## Lunch: Roasted Vegetable and Quinoa Salad

This hearty salad offers a blend of roasted vegetables, quinoa, and a touch of sweetness from dried cranberries.

- Ingredients:

- 1 cup cooked quinoa

- ½ cup roasted carrots

- ½ cup roasted Brussels sprouts

- ¼ cup dried cranberries

- 2 tablespoons balsamic vinaigrette

- Instructions:

1. Combine quinoa, roasted vegetables, and cranberries.

2. Drizzle with balsamic vinaigrette and toss.

- Nutritional Highlights:

~400 calories. High in fiber, antioxidants, and vitamins for a wholesome meal.

## Dessert: Greek Yogurt with Honey and Crushed Walnuts

A simple, nutritious dessert with a balance of protein, healthy fats, and natural sweetness.

- Ingredients:

- 1 cup Greek yogurt

- 1 tablespoon honey

- 2 tablespoons crushed walnuts


- Instructions:

1. Mix yogurt with honey and top with walnuts.


- Nutritional Highlights:

~250 calories. High in protein and healthy fats with a satisfying crunch.


## Dinner: Herb-Roasted Chicken with Sweet Potato Mash and Green Beans

A balanced dinner featuring lean protein, vitamin-rich sweet potatoes, and fiber-packed green beans.


- Ingredients:

- 150 grams chicken breast

- 1 sweet potato, peeled and cubed

- 1 cup green beans

- 1 tablespoon olive oil

- Herbs (rosemary, thyme, sage)


- Instructions:

1. Rub chicken with olive oil and herbs, roast for 25-30 minutes.

2. Boil sweet potatoes, mash with butter or milk, and season with salt.

3. Steam green beans until tender.


- Nutritional Highlights:

~450 calories. High in protein and vitamins, making for a hearty and nutritious meal.

# DAY 20: CLEAN EATING BOOST

**Breakfast: Avocado Berry Smoothie**

Kick off your day with a smoothie that's rich in nutrients, combining creamy avocado with antioxidant-packed berries and a dose of fiber.

- Ingredients:

- ½ ripe avocado

- ½ cup blueberries

- ½ cup strawberries

- 1 cup spinach

- 1 cup almond milk

- 1 tablespoon flaxseed

- Instructions:

1. Blend all ingredients until smooth and creamy.

- Nutritional Highlights:

~300 calories. This smoothie is a powerhouse of omega-3 fatty acids, fiber, and antioxidants, promoting heart health and providing sustained energy for the day.

**Morning Snack: Raw Nuts and Dried Fruit Mix**

A perfectly balanced snack, providing a blend of healthy fats and natural sugars for a mid-morning energy boost.

- Ingredients:

- ¼ cup mixed raw nuts (almonds, walnuts, cashews)

- ¼ cup mixed dried fruit (raisins, apricots, cranberries)


- Instructions:

1. Combine the nuts and dried fruits in a small bowl or pack in a snack bag.


- Nutritional Highlights:

~200 calories. Rich in protein, healthy fats, and antioxidants, this snack offers sustained energy with a natural sweetness.


## Lunch: Grilled Salmon Salad

A light yet satisfying salad that combines the protein power of salmon with the refreshing crunch of greens and cucumbers.


- Ingredients:

- 150 grams salmon fillet

- 2 cups mixed greens (arugula, spinach, romaine)

- ¼ cucumber, sliced

- ¼ red onion, thinly sliced

- 2 tablespoons olive oil

- 1 tablespoon balsamic vinegar


- Instructions:

1. Grill the salmon until fully cooked.

2. Toss the mixed greens, cucumber, and red onion with olive oil and balsamic vinegar.

3. Top the salad with grilled salmon.


- Nutritional Highlights:

~400 calories. High in omega-3 fatty acids and protein, this meal supports heart health and keeps you feeling full without weighing you down.

## Dessert: Coconut Chia Pudding

This creamy dessert is perfect for a mid-afternoon pick-me-up, providing healthy fats and fiber.

- Ingredients:

- 3 tablespoons chia seeds

- 1 cup coconut milk

- 1 tablespoon honey

- Instructions:

1. Mix chia seeds with coconut milk and honey. Let it sit for at least 3 hours or overnight in the fridge until it thickens.

- Nutritional Highlights:

~250 calories. High in fiber, healthy fats, and antioxidants, making it a digestion-friendly and satisfying treat.

## Dinner: Roasted Chicken and Vegetables

A simple, wholesome dinner that's rich in protein and nutrients, designed to fuel and nourish.

- Ingredients:

- 200 grams chicken breast

- 1 cup broccoli florets

- 1 carrot, sliced

- 1 bell pepper, sliced

- 2 tablespoons olive oil

- Herbs (rosemary, thyme, garlic powder)

- Salt and pepper to taste

- Instructions:

1. Preheat oven to 400°F.

2. Toss chicken and vegetables with olive oil, herbs, salt, and pepper.

3. Roast for 25-30 minutes, until the chicken is cooked through and the vegetables are tender.

- Nutritional Highlights:

~450 calories. A hearty and balanced meal that provides protein, fiber, vitamins, and minerals to cap off your day.

Total Calories for the Day: ~1600

# DAY 21: FIBER-FOCUSED FEAST

Breakfast: Steel-Cut Oats with Apples and Cinnamon

A warm, fiber-rich breakfast to fuel your morning with slow-burning energy.

- Ingredients:

- ½ cup steel-cut oats

- 1 cup water or milk

- 1 apple, diced

- 1 teaspoon cinnamon

- 1 tablespoon honey

- Instructions:

1. Cook the oats according to package instructions.

2. Stir in diced apple, cinnamon, and honey, and cook for an additional 2-3 minutes until the apples soften slightly.

- Nutritional Highlights:

~300 calories. High in fiber and slow-digesting carbohydrates, with cinnamon providing anti-inflammatory benefits.

**Morning Snack: Raw Veggie Sticks with Hummus**

A fiber-packed snack to keep you feeling full and satisfied between meals.

- Ingredients:

- Carrot sticks

- Celery sticks

- Bell pepper slices

- ¼ cup hummus

- Instructions:

1. Prepare a variety of raw vegetables and serve with hummus for dipping.

- Nutritional Highlights:

~150 calories. Provides a good source of fiber and protein, keeping your energy stable throughout the morning.

**Lunch: Black Bean and Avocado Burrito**

A fiber-rich burrito that combines the heart-healthy fats from avocado with the protein and fiber of black beans.

- Ingredients:

- 1 whole wheat tortilla

- ½ cup black beans, rinsed and drained

- ½ ripe avocado, sliced

- ¼ cup shredded lettuce

- 2 tablespoons salsa

- 1 tablespoon Greek yogurt (as a sour cream substitute)

- Instructions:

1. Warm the tortilla and layer it with black beans, avocado, lettuce, salsa, and Greek yogurt.

2. Roll the tortilla tightly to form the burrito.

- Nutritional Highlights:

~400 calories. A balanced meal with plenty of fiber and healthy fats to support digestive health and maintain satiety.

## Dessert: Fresh Berries with Mint

A light and refreshing dessert that's packed with antioxidants and vitamins.

- Ingredients:

- 1 cup mixed berries (blueberries, raspberries, strawberries)

- Fresh mint leaves for garnish

- Instructions:

1. Serve mixed berries garnished with fresh mint leaves.

- Nutritional Highlights:

~100 calories. High in antioxidants and vitamin C, with a refreshing touch from the mint.

## Dinner: Grilled Vegetable Pasta Salad

A fiber-rich pasta salad loaded with grilled vegetables and finished with a tangy dressing.

- Ingredients:

- 2 cups cooked whole wheat pasta

- 1 zucchini, sliced and grilled

- 1 bell pepper, sliced and grilled

- ½ cup cherry tomatoes, halved

- ¼ cup feta cheese, crumbled

- 2 tablespoons olive oil

- 1 tablespoon balsamic vinegar

- Instructions:

1. Toss grilled vegetables with cooked pasta and cherry tomatoes.

2. Drizzle with olive oil and balsamic vinegar, then top with crumbled feta.

- Nutritional Highlights:

~500 calories. Provides a satisfying balance of fiber, protein, and healthy fats, with plenty of nutrients from the variety of vegetables.

Total Calories for the Day: ~1450

# DAY 22: ENERGIZING EATS

**Breakfast: Kiwi Banana Smoothie**

A light yet energizing smoothie that's high in vitamin C and packed with potassium and fiber.

- Ingredients:

- 2 kiwis, peeled and sliced

- 1 banana

- 1 cup spinach

- 1 tablespoon flaxseed

- 1 cup almond milk

- Instructions:

1. Blend all ingredients until smooth.

- Nutritional Highlights:

~300 calories. Rich in vitamin C and potassium, this smoothie provides a refreshing and energizing start to the day.

## Morning Snack: Almonds and Dried Cranberries

A simple snack that offers a mix of healthy fats, fiber, and antioxidants.

- Ingredients:

- ¼ cup almonds

- ¼ cup dried cranberries

- Instructions:

1. Mix almonds and cranberries together for a quick and easy snack.

- Nutritional Highlights:

~200 calories. A balanced snack with protein, fiber, and antioxidants to keep your energy steady.

## Lunch: Chickpea Salad Sandwich

A plant-based sandwich that's both filling and nutritious, with a good balance of protein and fiber.

- Ingredients:

- 1 can chickpeas, drained and mashed

- 2 tablespoons mayonnaise or vegan alternative

- 1 tablespoon mustard

- 1 celery stalk, finely chopped

- 1 small onion, finely chopped

- Salt and pepper to taste

- 2 slices whole grain bread


- Instructions:

1. Mix mashed chickpeas with mayonnaise, mustard, celery, and onion.

2. Spread the mixture on whole grain bread and serve as a sandwich.


- Nutritional Highlights:

~400 calories. Packed with plant-based protein and fiber, this sandwich makes for a satisfying and nutritious lunch.


**Dessert: Greek Yogurt with Honey and Walnuts**

A protein-rich dessert with the added benefits of healthy fats and antioxidants from walnuts.


- Ingredients:

- 1 cup Greek yogurt

- 1 tablespoon honey

- 2 tablespoons chopped walnuts


- Instructions:

1. Top Greek yogurt with honey and sprinkle with chopped walnuts.


- Nutritional Highlights:


250 calories. High in protein, healthy fats, and a touch of natural sweetness.


**Dinner: Lemon Garlic Tilapia with Quinoa and Steamed Broccoli**

A light yet satisfying dinner that provides lean protein and essential nutrients.

- Ingredients:

- 150 grams tilapia fillets

- Juice of 1 lemon

- 1 garlic clove, minced

- 1 tablespoon olive oil

- 1 cup quinoa, cooked

- 1 cup broccoli, steamed

- Instructions:

1. Preheat oven to 375°F.

2. Marinate tilapia with lemon juice, garlic, and olive oil, then bake for 10-12 minutes.

3. Serve tilapia with cooked quinoa and steamed broccoli.

- Nutritional Highlights:

~450 calories. Provides high-quality protein, healthy fats, and a range of essential vitamins and minerals for a balanced meal.

Total Calories for the Day: ~1600

This meal plan emphasizes clean, nutritious ingredients to support energy, digestion, and overall wellness. Each dish is designed to be satisfying while providing essential nutrients in a balanced, flavorful way.

## DAY 23: PLANT-POWERED PLATES

**Breakfast: Spinach and Avocado Smoothie**

Start your day with a nutrient-packed smoothie that's brimming with healthy fats, fiber, and vitamins.

- Ingredients:

- 1 ripe avocado

- 1 cup fresh spinach

- 1 banana

- 1 tablespoon chia seeds

- 1 cup almond milk

- Instructions:

1. Blend all ingredients until smooth for a creamy, nutrient-dense start to your day.

- Nutritional Highlights:

~320 calories. This smoothie offers a perfect balance of fiber, healthy fats, and essential vitamins, designed to keep you energized and full throughout the morning.

**Morning Snack: Carrot Sticks with Beet Hummus**

Enjoy this colorful and antioxidant-rich snack to keep your energy levels steady.

- Ingredients:

- 1 large carrot, cut into sticks

- ¼ cup beet hummus

- Instructions:

1. Dip the carrot sticks into beet hummus for a vibrant and flavorful snack.

- Nutritional Highlights:

~150 calories. Packed with fiber and antioxidants, this snack supports gut health and offers a refreshing alternative to traditional hummus.

**Lunch: Vegan Lentil Soup**

Warm and comforting, this lentil soup is perfect for a hearty, plant-based lunch.

- Ingredients:

- 1 cup cooked lentils

- 1 small onion, diced

- 2 cloves garlic, minced

- 1 carrot, diced

- 1 celery stalk, diced

- 2 cups vegetable broth

- 1 teaspoon thyme

- Salt and pepper to taste

- Instructions:

1. In a large pot, sauté onion, garlic, carrot, and celery until softened.

2. Add lentils, broth, and thyme. Bring to a boil, then simmer for 20 minutes. Season to taste before serving.

- Nutritional Highlights:

~350 calories. Rich in plant-based protein and fiber, this soup is both filling and nutritious, promoting digestion and satiety.

## Dessert: Coconut Yogurt with Fresh Mango

A light and tropical treat that's dairy-free and full of probiotics.

- Ingredients:

- 1 cup coconut yogurt

- ½ mango, diced

- Instructions:

1. Top the coconut yogurt with diced mango for a fresh and satisfying dessert.

- Nutritional Highlights:

~200 calories. High in probiotics and vitamins, this dessert is great for digestive health and offers a naturally sweet indulgence.


**Dinner: Quinoa Stuffed Bell Peppers**

A vibrant, wholesome dinner that's rich in plant-based protein, fiber, and colorful nutrients.


- Ingredients:

- 2 bell peppers, halved and seeds removed

- 1 cup cooked quinoa

- ½ cup black beans, rinsed and drained

- ½ cup corn kernels

- ½ cup diced tomatoes

- 1 teaspoon cumin

- 1 teaspoon paprika

- ¼ cup shredded vegan cheese (optional)


- Instructions:

1. Preheat oven to 375°F.

2. Mix quinoa, black beans, corn, tomatoes, cumin, and paprika. Stuff this mixture into the bell pepper halves.

3. Top with vegan cheese (if desired) and bake for 25 minutes until the peppers are tender.


- Nutritional Highlights:

~380 calories. This dish is packed with fiber, protein, and a spectrum of vitamins and minerals, offering a satisfying plant-based meal.


Total Calories for the Day: ~1400 calories

# DAY 24: HEART-HEALTHY HIGHLIGHTS

Breakfast: Oatmeal with Walnuts and Berries

A heart-healthy breakfast rich in omega-3s, fiber, and antioxidants to start the day.

- Ingredients:

- ½ cup rolled oats

- 1 cup water or milk

- ¼ cup walnuts, chopped

- ½ cup mixed berries (blueberries, strawberries)

- 1 tablespoon honey

- Instructions:

1. Cook the oats in water or milk. Top with walnuts, berries, and a drizzle of honey.

- Nutritional Highlights:

~350 calories. A balanced breakfast that supports cardiovascular health with omega-3s from walnuts and antioxidants from the berries.

**Morning Snack: Celery Sticks with Almond Butter**

A crunchy and satisfying snack packed with fiber and healthy fats.

- Ingredients:

- 3 celery stalks, cut into sticks

- 2 tablespoons almond butter

- Instructions:

1. Dip celery sticks in almond butter for a satisfying crunch.

- Nutritional Highlights:

~180 calories. Almond butter provides heart-healthy fats, while celery adds fiber and hydration.

**Lunch: Grilled Turkey and Hummus Wrap**

This protein-rich wrap keeps things light yet filling, with heart-healthy ingredients.

- Ingredients:

- 1 whole wheat tortilla

- 100 grams turkey breast, grilled and sliced

- ¼ cup hummus

- Cucumber slices

- Tomato slices

- Lettuce

- Instructions:

1. Spread hummus on the tortilla, then add turkey, cucumber, tomato, and lettuce. Roll up and slice in half.

- Nutritional Highlights:

~400 calories. High in lean protein and fiber, this wrap promotes heart health while keeping you energized.

**Dessert: Dark Chocolate Squares**

Indulge in a heart-friendly dessert rich in antioxidants.

- Ingredients:

- 2 squares of dark chocolate (70% or higher)

- Instructions:

1. Enjoy two squares of dark chocolate as a mindful treat.

- Nutritional Highlights:

~100 calories. Dark chocolate is rich in flavonoids, which help improve blood flow and support heart health.

**Dinner: Baked Salmon with Asparagus and Quinoa**

A perfect heart-healthy dinner featuring omega-3-rich salmon and nutrient-dense vegetables.

- Ingredients:

- 150 grams salmon fillet

- 1 cup asparagus, trimmed

- ½ cup quinoa, cooked

- 1 tablespoon olive oil

- Lemon wedges for serving

- Instructions:

1. Preheat oven to 400°F. Arrange salmon and asparagus on a baking sheet, drizzle with olive oil, and bake for 15-20 minutes.

2. Serve with cooked quinoa and lemon wedges.

- Nutritional Highlights:

~470 calories. Salmon provides omega-3s, quinoa offers complete protein, and asparagus adds fiber, making this meal perfect for cardiovascular health.

Total Calories for the Day: ~1500 calories

# DAY 25: SIMPLE AND SATISFYING

**Breakfast: Greek Yogurt Parfait**

A balanced and easy breakfast that's high in protein and packed with fiber.

- Ingredients:

- 1 cup Greek yogurt

- ½ cup granola

- ½ cup fresh raspberries

- 1 tablespoon honey


- Instructions:

1. Layer Greek yogurt with granola and raspberries, then drizzle with honey.


- Nutritional Highlights:

~350 calories. Rich in protein and probiotics, this parfait supports gut health and keeps you satisfied.

**Morning Snack: Boiled Egg with Avocado**

A perfect combination of high-quality protein and healthy fats to keep you energized.


- Ingredients:

- 1 hard-boiled egg

- ½ avocado, sliced


- Instructions:

1. Slice the egg and avocado and enjoy them together.


- Nutritional Highlights:

~230 calories. This snack provides healthy fats and protein, ideal for sustained energy.


**Lunch: Chicken Salad with Mixed Greens**

A refreshing and balanced lunch with lean protein and vibrant vegetables.


- Ingredients:

- 150 grams cooked chicken breast, chopped

- 2 cups mixed salad greens

- ¼ cup cherry tomatoes, halved

- ¼ cucumber, sliced

- 2 tablespoons vinaigrette dressing

- Instructions:

1. Toss the chicken, salad greens, tomatoes, and cucumber together, and drizzle with vinaigrette.

- Nutritional Highlights:

~350 calories. This meal is high in lean protein and packed with vitamins from fresh vegetables, keeping you nourished.

## Dessert: Baked Pear with Cinnamon

A warm and comforting dessert with natural sweetness and anti-inflammatory benefits.

- Ingredients:

- 1 pear, halved and cored

- Sprinkle of cinnamon

- Instructions:

1. Sprinkle pear halves with cinnamon and bake at 350°F for 20 minutes until tender.

- Nutritional Highlights:

~150 calories. Rich in fiber and natural sugars, this dessert is comforting yet light, with a touch of anti-inflammatory cinnamon.

**Dinner: Grilled Veggie and Tofu Stir-Fry**

A satisfying, plant-based dinner full of protein and vitamins from a colorful array of vegetables.

- Ingredients:

- 200 grams tofu, pressed and cubed

- 1 bell pepper, sliced

- 1 zucchini, sliced

- 1 carrot, julienned

- 1 tablespoon soy sauce

- 1 tablespoon

sesame oil

- 1 garlic clove, minced

- 1 teaspoon grated ginger

- Instructions:

1. Heat sesame oil in a large pan or wok, and sauté garlic and ginger.

2. Add tofu and vegetables, stir-fry until the veggies are tender and tofu is golden.

3. Drizzle with soy sauce and toss to coat.

- Nutritional Highlights:

~420 calories. High in plant-based protein and loaded with vitamins, this dish is a great way to end the day on a light yet filling note.

Total Calories for the Day: ~1500 calories

This meal plan emphasizes balance, variety, and whole foods. The focus is on plant-based nutrition, healthy fats, lean proteins, and fiber-rich meals that keep you satisfied while promoting heart health and overall wellness.

Each dish is simple, yet packed with essential nutrients, making it easy to stick to a clean and wholesome eating routine.

# DAY 26: ENERGIZING ESSENTIALS

This day's meal plan is carefully designed to provide steady energy while nourishing your body with wholesome, nutrient-dense foods. With a balance of protein, healthy fats, and fiber, each meal is crafted to fuel your day from morning to night, keeping you satisfied and energized.

Breakfast: Blueberry Almond Overnight Oats

This make-ahead breakfast is a perfect blend of creamy oats, almond butter, and the antioxidant power of blueberries. It's packed with fiber, protein, and healthy fats to jumpstart your morning with long-lasting energy.

Ingredients:

- ½ cup rolled oats

- ½ cup almond milk

- ¼ cup Greek yogurt

- 1 tablespoon almond butter

- ½ cup fresh blueberries

- 1 tablespoon honey

Instructions:

1. In a jar or bowl, mix the oats, almond milk, Greek yogurt, and almond butter until well combined.

2. Top with blueberries and drizzle with honey.

3. Cover and refrigerate overnight for an easy, grab-and-go breakfast.

Nutritional Highlights:

Calories: 350

This breakfast is rich in fiber and protein, providing a perfect balance of nutrients to sustain your energy throughout the morning.

Morning Snack: Cottage Cheese with Sliced Peaches

A refreshing and light snack, this cottage cheese and peach pairing delivers a satisfying blend of creamy and sweet flavors while keeping you energized between meals.

Ingredients:

- ½ cup cottage cheese

- 1 ripe peach, sliced

Instructions:

1. Place cottage cheese in a bowl and top with fresh peach slices.

Nutritional Highlights:

Calories: 150

This snack is high in protein and packed with vitamins, particularly vitamin C from the peaches, making it a refreshing and nourishing mid-morning bite.

Lunch: Turkey Spinach Wrap

A simple yet satisfying wrap that's packed with lean protein and leafy greens. This turkey-spinach wrap with creamy avocado and hummus delivers a balanced meal with plenty of fiber and healthy fats to keep you fueled for the rest of the day.

Ingredients:

- 1 whole wheat tortilla

- 100 grams sliced turkey breast

- 1 cup fresh spinach

- ¼ avocado, sliced

- 2 tablespoons hummus

Instructions:

1. Spread hummus evenly over the tortilla.

2. Layer the sliced turkey, fresh spinach, and avocado.

3. Roll up the tortilla tightly and slice it in half for easy eating.

Nutritional Highlights:

Calories: 400

This lunch is loaded with protein and healthy fats, giving you a well-balanced meal that keeps you energized without feeling weighed down.

---

Dessert: Dark Chocolate and Walnut Bites

For an afternoon treat, these dark chocolate and walnut bites offer a healthy indulgence. They're rich in antioxidants and omega-3s, providing not only a satisfying snack but also supporting brain and heart health.

Ingredients:

- 2 squares of dark chocolate (70% or higher)

- ¼ cup chopped walnuts

Instructions:

1. Melt the dark chocolate in a microwave or over a double boiler.

2. Stir in the chopped walnuts until fully coated.

3. Spoon small clusters onto a parchment paper-lined tray.

4. Refrigerate until the chocolate has set, and enjoy.

Nutritional Highlights:

Calories: 200

These bites combine the mood-boosting power of dark chocolate with the heart-healthy benefits of walnuts, making for a delicious yet nutrient-dense dessert.

Dinner: Baked Cod with Herb Roasted Potatoes and Asparagus

A lean, nutrient-rich dinner to round out your day, featuring baked cod alongside herb-roasted potatoes and asparagus. This dish provides a clean source of protein with plenty of fiber and essential vitamins from the vegetables.

Ingredients:

- 150 grams cod fillet

- 1 cup potatoes, cubed

- 1 cup asparagus, trimmed

- 1 tablespoon olive oil

- Fresh herbs (dill, parsley, garlic powder)

- Salt and pepper to taste

Instructions:

1. Preheat the oven to 400°F (200°C).

2. Toss the potatoes and asparagus with olive oil, herbs, salt, and pepper.

3. Place the cod fillet on a baking sheet and surround it with the seasoned vegetables.

4. Bake for 20-25 minutes until the cod is flaky and the vegetables are tender.

Nutritional Highlights:

Calories: 400

This meal is rich in lean protein and fiber, offering a perfect combination of nutrients to support recovery and keep you feeling satisfied through the evening.

Total Calories for the Day: ~1500

With each meal crafted to support sustained energy and overall wellness, this day's menu provides a perfect balance of nutrients. Whether you're starting your day with fiber-packed oats or finishing with a lean, protein-rich dinner, Day 26 keeps you nourished and energized while maintaining a light and refreshing feel.

## DAY 27: FRESH AND FLAVORFUL

**Breakfast: Spinach and Mushroom Scramble**

Kick off your day with a protein-packed scramble that combines fresh vegetables with fluffy eggs, delivering a nutritious, energy-boosting breakfast.

- Ingredients:

- 3 eggs

- 1 cup fresh spinach

- ½ cup mushrooms, sliced

- 1 tablespoon olive oil

- Salt and pepper to taste

- Instructions:

1. Heat olive oil in a skillet over medium heat.

2. Sauté the mushrooms until browned.

3. Add spinach and cook until wilted.

4. Beat eggs, pour over vegetables, and stir until eggs are cooked.

5. Season with salt and pepper.

- Nutritional Highlights:

~300 calories. This breakfast provides a great source of protein, along with vitamins A and D, and is rich in antioxidants from the spinach and mushrooms.

**Morning Snack: Greek Yogurt with Honey and Almonds**

A simple, satisfying snack rich in calcium and protein, topped with almonds for added crunch.

- Ingredients:

- 1 cup Greek yogurt

- 1 tablespoon honey

- 2 tablespoons almonds, chopped


- Instructions:

1. Mix Greek yogurt with honey and top with almonds.


- Nutritional Highlights:

~250 calories. Packed with protein and healthy fats, this snack is also a good source of calcium, supporting bone health and muscle recovery.


## Lunch: Quinoa and Black Bean Salad

This fiber-filled salad is a plant-powered lunch with vibrant flavors, offering a balance of complex carbs, protein, and a light dressing.


- Ingredients:

- 1 cup cooked quinoa

- ½ cup black beans, rinsed and drained

- ½ bell pepper, diced

- ¼ cup corn

- ¼ cup cilantro, chopped

- Dressing: Juice of 1 lime, 1 tablespoon olive oil, salt, and pepper


- Instructions:

1. Combine quinoa, black beans, bell pepper, corn, and cilantro.

2. Whisk together lime juice, olive oil, salt, and pepper, and pour over the salad.

3. Toss to combine and chill before serving.

- Nutritional Highlights:

~400 calories. High in fiber and plant-based protein, this dish also provides vitamins and minerals, making it a nutritious and flavorful meal.

## Dessert: Fresh Fruit Salad

A light and refreshing dessert that is naturally sweet and bursting with vitamins.

- Ingredients:

- 1 cup mixed fresh fruits (strawberries, kiwi, pineapple, mango)

- Instructions:

1. Chop fruits into bite-sized pieces and mix in a bowl.

- Nutritional Highlights:

~120 calories. This dessert is packed with antioxidants and vitamins A and C, promoting overall wellness.

## Dinner: Grilled Lemon Herb Chicken with Steamed Green Beans and Carrots

A zesty and satisfying dinner that's high in protein and loaded with nutrient-rich vegetables.

- Ingredients:

- 150 grams chicken breast

- 1 tablespoon olive oil

- Juice of 1 lemon

- 1 teaspoon mixed dried herbs (thyme, rosemary, parsley)

- 1 cup green beans

- 1 cup carrots, sliced

- Instructions:

1. Marinate the chicken in olive oil, lemon juice, and herbs for at least 30 minutes.

2. Grill the chicken until fully cooked.

3. Steam the green beans and carrots until tender.

4. Serve chicken with steamed vegetables on the side.

- Nutritional Highlights:

~430 calories. This meal is rich in lean protein, vitamins, and minerals, and provides a satisfying flavor from the lemon and herbs.

Total Calories for the Day: ~1500 calories

# DAY 28: WHOLESOME HARMONY

**Breakfast: Chia Seed Pudding with Mixed Berries**

This omega-3 rich breakfast provides a light, fiber-filled start to the day, complemented by the natural sweetness of fresh berries.

- Ingredients:

- 3 tablespoons chia seeds

- 1 cup almond milk

- 1 tablespoon maple syrup

- ½ cup mixed berries (blueberries, raspberries, blackberries)

- Instructions:

1. Mix chia seeds, almond milk, and maple syrup in a bowl or jar and refrigerate overnight to thicken.

2. Top with mixed berries before serving.

- Nutritional Highlights:

~300 calories. High in omega-3 fatty acids, fiber, and antioxidants, this breakfast supports heart health and digestion.

## Morning Snack: Raw Veggie Sticks with Avocado Dip

A crunchy and healthy snack served with a creamy avocado dip rich in vitamins and healthy fats.

- Ingredients:

- 1 carrot, cut into sticks

- 1 celery stalk, cut into sticks

- ½ avocado, mashed

- Juice of ½ lime

- Salt and pepper to taste

- Instructions:

1. Mix mashed avocado with lime juice, salt, and pepper to create a dip.

2. Serve with carrot and celery sticks.

- Nutritional Highlights:

~150 calories. A nutrient-packed snack offering fiber, vitamins, and heart-healthy fats.

## Lunch: Mediterranean Tuna Salad

This protein-rich salad delivers a burst of Mediterranean flavors with fresh veggies and a light, zesty dressing.

- Ingredients:

- 1 can tuna, drained

- ½ cup chickpeas, rinsed and drained

- ¼ cup diced cucumber

- ¼ cup halved cherry tomatoes

- ¼ cup sliced red onion

- 2 tablespoons olive oil

- 1 tablespoon lemon juice

- Salt and pepper to taste


- Instructions:

1. Mix tuna, chickpeas, cucumber, tomatoes, and onion in a bowl.

2. Dress with olive oil and lemon juice, then season with salt and pepper.


- Nutritional Highlights:

~400 calories. High in protein and omega-3s, this salad supports cardiovascular health and is light yet filling.


## Dessert: Baked Cinnamon Apples

A warm and comforting dessert, naturally sweetened with honey and cinnamon for a cozy finish to any meal.


- Ingredients:

- 2 apples, cored and sliced

- ½ teaspoon cinnamon

- 1 teaspoon honey


- Instructions:

1. Place apple slices in a baking dish, sprinkle with cinnamon and drizzle with honey.

2. Bake at 375°F for 20 minutes or until tender.


- Nutritional Highlights:

~120 calories. This dessert is rich in fiber and antioxidants, with natural sweetness and a touch of spice.

**Dinner: Herb-Roasted Turkey Breast with Quinoa and Roasted Brussels Sprouts**

A wholesome, protein-packed dinner featuring tender turkey breast and roasted vegetables for a balanced, nutrient-dense meal.

- Ingredients:

- 200 grams turkey breast

- 1 cup quinoa, cooked

- 1 cup Brussels sprouts, halved

- 1 tablespoon olive oil

- Mixed herbs (thyme, sage, rosemary)

- Salt and pepper to taste

- Instructions:

1. Preheat oven to 375°F.

2. Rub turkey breast with olive oil and herbs, then season with salt and pepper.

3. Place turkey and Brussels sprouts on a baking tray and roast for 25-30 minutes until the turkey is cooked through and the sprouts are caramelized.

4. Serve with cooked quinoa.

- Nutritional Highlights:

~530 calories. This meal is high in lean protein, complex carbs, and fiber-rich vegetables, making it both nutritious and satisfying.

Total Calories for the Day: ~1500 calories

These meal plans emphasize whole foods and balanced nutrition, designed to fuel your body while keeping you satisfied. Each dish is nutrient-dense and easy to prepare, making them perfect for a lifestyle that focuses on clean, wholesome eating.

# DAY 29: A LIGHT AND ENERGIZING MENU

As we near the end of your wellness journey, Day 29 offers a meal plan that's designed to keep you feeling light yet nourished, with every dish delivering vital nutrients while being easy to prepare. This day focuses on heart-healthy fats, lean proteins, and plenty of fiber, ensuring you remain energized and satisfied throughout the day.

Breakfast: Pear and Walnut Oatmeal

Start your day with this warm, satisfying oatmeal that combines the comforting texture of oats with the natural sweetness of pear and the crunch of walnuts. It's a fiber-packed breakfast that supports heart health while providing essential omega-3 fatty acids.

Ingredients:

- ½ cup rolled oats

- 1 cup water or milk (for extra creaminess)

- 1 pear, diced

- 2 tablespoons walnuts, chopped

- 1 tablespoon honey or maple syrup (optional for a hint of sweetness)

Instructions:

1. Cook the oats in water or milk according to package directions.

2. During the last minute of cooking, stir in the diced pear and chopped walnuts.

3. Once the oats are fully cooked, drizzle with honey or maple syrup for added sweetness.

Nutritional Highlights:

Calories: 350

This heart-healthy breakfast is rich in fiber, healthy fats, and vitamins, making it an energizing start to the day without weighing you down.

Morning Snack: Cottage Cheese with Sliced Tomatoes

A quick snack that's simple, light, and packed with protein. Cottage cheese provides a creamy base, while juicy tomatoes bring a burst of flavor and a dose of vitamin C.

Ingredients:

- ½ cup cottage cheese

- 1 ripe tomato, sliced

- Salt and pepper to taste

Instructions:

1. Place the cottage cheese in a bowl and top with tomato slices.

2. Season with salt and pepper to your liking.

Nutritional Highlights:

Calories: 150

High in protein, this snack offers a satisfying option between meals, keeping your energy steady and your muscles fueled. The tomatoes add a boost of antioxidants and vitamin C.

Lunch: Chicken Avocado Salad

This lunch is as refreshing as it is nourishing. Grilled chicken provides lean protein, while avocado offers heart-healthy fats. The mixed greens add an additional punch of vitamins and minerals.

Ingredients:

- 150 grams grilled chicken breast, sliced

- 1 ripe avocado, diced

- 2 cups mixed greens (spinach, arugula, or lettuce)

- ¼ cup cucumber, sliced

- 2 tablespoons olive oil

- 1 tablespoon balsamic vinegar

Instructions:

1. Combine the sliced chicken, avocado, mixed greens, and cucumber in a large bowl.

2. Drizzle with olive oil and balsamic vinegar, and toss everything together gently.


Nutritional Highlights:

Calories: 400

This salad is a perfect balance of lean protein, healthy fats, and fresh veggies, making it a fulfilling meal that keeps you feeling light but nourished.


Dessert: Mango Sorbet


A light, tropical dessert that satisfies your sweet tooth without any added sugars. The natural sweetness of mango pairs beautifully with a zesty touch of lime for a refreshing treat.


Ingredients:

- 1 ripe mango, peeled and diced

- Juice of 1 lime


Instructions:

1. Blend the diced mango and lime juice until smooth.

2. Transfer to a container and freeze for at least 4 hours, stirring occasionally to achieve a smooth sorbet texture.


Nutritional Highlights:

Calories: 150

This dessert is rich in vitamins A and C, providing a nutritious boost while keeping things light.


Dinner: Baked Trout with Asparagus and Sweet Potatoes

Dinner wraps up the day with a nutrient-packed meal that features omega-3-rich trout, vibrant asparagus, and comforting sweet potatoes. It's a well-balanced dinner that feels indulgent without being heavy.

Ingredients:

- 150 grams trout fillet

- 1 cup asparagus, trimmed

- 1 small sweet potato, sliced thin

- 1 tablespoon olive oil

- Fresh herbs (dill, parsley)

- Salt and pepper to taste

Instructions:

1. Preheat the oven to 400°F (200°C).

2. Place the trout, asparagus, and sweet potato slices on a baking sheet. Drizzle with olive oil and sprinkle with fresh herbs, salt, and pepper.

3. Bake for 20-25 minutes, or until the trout flakes easily with a fork and the vegetables are tender.

Nutritional Highlights:

Calories: 450

With omega-3 fatty acids from the trout, fiber-rich sweet potatoes, and the antioxidant power of asparagus, this dinner is both delicious and highly nutritious.

Total Calories for the Day: ~1500

This menu is designed to be both light and energizing, providing just the right amount of calories to sustain your energy without leaving you feeling sluggish. It's packed with essential nutrients like omega-3s, fiber, and vitamins, making it an excellent choice for those looking to maintain a balanced, healthy lifestyle.

# DAY 30: NUTRITIOUS FINALE

As we wrap up this nourishing journey, Day 30 focuses on balanced, wholesome meals that will leave you feeling satisfied and energized. With an emphasis on healthy fats, proteins, and fiber, today's menu is designed to support your overall wellness.

**Breakfast: Avocado and Egg Toast**

Start your day with a classic combination that delivers a perfect blend of creamy avocado and protein-rich eggs. It's a simple, satisfying, and nutrient-dense breakfast.

- Ingredients:

- 2 slices of whole-grain bread

- 1 ripe avocado, mashed

- 2 eggs (poached or fried)

- Salt and pepper to taste

- Optional: a sprinkle of red pepper flakes for added heat

- Instructions:

1. Toast the whole-grain bread slices until they're golden and crisp.

2. Spread mashed avocado evenly on each slice.

3. Top each toast with a poached or fried egg, seasoned with salt, pepper, and optional red pepper flakes.

- Nutritional Highlights:

~400 calories. This dish provides a balance of healthy fats from the avocado and high-quality protein from the eggs, giving you sustained energy to power through your morning.

**Morning Snack: Greek Yogurt with Mixed Nuts**

This protein-packed snack keeps hunger at bay while offering a delicious combination of creamy yogurt and crunchy nuts.

- Ingredients:

- 1 cup Greek yogurt

- ¼ cup mixed nuts (almonds, walnuts, pistachios)

- Instructions:

1. Stir the mixed nuts into the Greek yogurt for a satisfying, nutrient-dense snack.

- Nutritional Highlights:

~200 calories. Rich in protein and healthy fats, this snack is perfect for maintaining stable energy levels and supporting muscle recovery.

## Lunch: Quinoa Vegetable Stir-Fry

For lunch, enjoy a vibrant and hearty quinoa vegetable stir-fry that's packed with fiber, plant-based protein, and essential micronutrients.

- Ingredients:

- 1 cup cooked quinoa

- 1 cup mixed vegetables (broccoli, bell peppers, carrots)

- 1 tablespoon olive oil

- 2 tablespoons soy sauce (or tamari for a gluten-free option)

- 1 garlic clove, minced

- Instructions:

1. Heat olive oil in a pan over medium heat.

2. Add minced garlic and vegetables, stir-frying until the vegetables are tender but still crisp.

3. Stir in the cooked quinoa and soy sauce, cooking for another 2-3 minutes until everything is evenly heated.

- Nutritional Highlights:

~350 calories. This stir-fry is full of fiber and essential nutrients from the quinoa and mixed vegetables, making it a wholesome and flavorful midday meal.

## Dessert: Fresh Fruit Salad

A refreshing and light dessert, this fresh fruit salad is bursting with natural sweetness and packed with vitamins.

- Ingredients:

- 1 cup chopped mixed fruits (pineapple, strawberries, kiwi, grapes)

- Instructions:

1. Combine the chopped fruits in a bowl and toss lightly to mix.

- Nutritional Highlights:

~120 calories. Loaded with antioxidants and vitamins A and C, this fruit salad provides a healthy and naturally sweet treat.

## Dinner: Grilled Salmon with Roasted Brussels Sprouts and Wild Rice

End the day with a nutrient-dense dinner featuring omega-3-rich salmon, fiber-filled Brussels sprouts, and hearty wild rice.

- Ingredients:

- 150 grams salmon fillet

- 1 cup Brussels sprouts, halved

- ½ cup wild rice, cooked

- 1 tablespoon olive oil

- Lemon wedges for serving

- Instructions:

1. Preheat the grill for the salmon.

2. Toss Brussels sprouts with olive oil and roast in the oven at 400°F for 20-25 minutes until crispy and caramelized.

3. Grill the salmon for 6-8 minutes per side, or until it's fully cooked.

4. Serve the grilled salmon alongside the roasted Brussels sprouts and wild rice. Squeeze fresh lemon over the salmon for an added burst of flavor.

- Nutritional Highlights:

~530 calories. This meal offers a rich source of omega-3 fatty acids from the salmon, fiber and antioxidants from the Brussels sprouts, and complex carbohydrates from the wild rice, making it a perfectly balanced dinner.

Total Calories for the Day: ~1600 calories

This meal plan is a fitting conclusion to a month of mindful eating. The emphasis on whole grains, lean proteins, healthy fats, and fresh produce ensures that you're fueling your body with nutrient-dense foods that promote long-term wellness.

With a final day full of balanced, delicious dishes, you can finish strong, feeling nourished and energized.

## WEEKLY SHOPPING GUIDE FOR OPTIMAL HEALTH

This shopping list is designed to provide one week's worth of meals for one to two people, based on the 30-day meal plan.

The goal is to purchase fresh, nutrient-rich ingredients without overbuying, so adjust quantities as needed to match your personal consumption habits and ensure freshness.

## FRUITS:

- Bananas: 5

- Apples: 3

- Pears: 3

- Mixed Berries (blueberries, strawberries, raspberries): 1 pound

- Mangoes: 2

- Kiwi: 3

- Pineapple: 1

- Lemons: 4


## VEGETABLES:

- Avocados: 3

- Spinach: 1 large bag

- Mixed Salad Greens: 1 large bag

- Broccoli: 2 heads

- Asparagus: 1 bunch

- Green Beans: 1 pound

- Bell Peppers (varied colors): 3

- Carrots: 1 pound

- Cucumbers: 2

- Cherry Tomatoes: 1 pint

- Brussels Sprouts: 1 pound

- Zucchini: 2

- Sweet Potatoes: 2

- Onions: 2

- Garlic: 1 bulb

- Ginger: 1 piece


## FRESH HERBS:

- Parsley: 1 bunch

- Cilantro: 1 bunch

- Dill: 1 bunch

- Thyme: 1 bunch

- Rosemary: 1 bunch

## PROTEIN SOURCES:

- Eggs: 12

- Greek Yogurt: 32 oz

- Cottage Cheese: 16 oz

- Chicken Breast: 2 lbs

- Salmon Fillets: 1 lb

- Turkey Breast: 1 lb

- Canned Tuna: 4 cans

- Cod Fillets: 1 lb

- Tilapia Fillets: 1 lb

- Ground Turkey: 1 lb

- Tofu: 1 block

- Chickpeas (canned or dried): 2 cans or 1 lb dried

- Black Beans (canned or dried): 2 cans or 1 lb dried

- Lentils: 1 lb

## DAIRY & ALTERNATIVES:

- Almond Milk: 1 gallon

- Coconut Milk: 2 cans

- Feta Cheese: 8 oz

- Parmesan Cheese: 8 oz

- Vegan Cheese (optional): 1 package

## GRAINS & NUTS:

- Rolled Oats: 1 lb

- Quinoa: 1 lb

- Whole Wheat Bread: 1 loaf

- Whole Wheat Tortillas: 1 package

- Whole Grain Pasta: 1 lb

- Wild Rice: 1 lb

- Granola: 1 lb

- Almonds: ½ lb

- Walnuts: ½ lb

- Mixed Nuts: ½ lb

- Chia Seeds: ½ lb

- Flaxseeds: ½ lb

## PANTRY STAPLES:

- Olive Oil: 1 small bottle

- Coconut Oil: 1 small jar

- Balsamic Vinegar: 1 small bottle

- Soy Sauce: 1 small bottle

- Maple Syrup: 1 small bottle

- Honey: 1 small bottle

- Spices: Check stock and replenish as needed (salt, pepper, cinnamon, nutmeg, pumpkin spice, chili flakes)

- Vegetable Broth: 2 cartons

- Baking Essentials: As needed for recipes

## SNACKS & EXTRAS:

- Hummus: 1 tub

- Dark Chocolate (70% or higher): 1 bar

- Dried Fruits: ½ lb

- Almond Butter: 1 small jar

- Peanut Butter: 1 small jar

# CHAPTER 26

## 15 TRANSFORMATIVE JUICE BLENDS FOR DETOX, ENERGY, AND IMMUNITY

Juicing is a highly effective way to pack essential nutrients into your diet. Below are five of 15 revitalizing juice recipes tailored for detoxification, increased energy, and immune support. Enjoy them fresh for maximum nutrient absorption.

### 1. GREEN DETOX DELIGHT

- Ingredients: 2 cups spinach, 1 green apple (cored and sliced), ½ cucumber, 1 celery stalk, juice of ½ lemon, 1-inch piece of ginger (peeled)

- Instructions:

1. Wash all produce.

2. Peel the lemon and ginger.

3. Juice all ingredients, starting with the ginger for maximum yield.

4. Stir in the lemon juice for added detox power. Enjoy immediately.

- Benefits: Packed with antioxidants, supports liver detoxification and digestion.

### 2. TROPICAL ENERGY BOOSTER

- Ingredients: 1 cup fresh pineapple chunks, 1 orange (peeled), ½ mango (peeled and pitted), ½ banana

- Instructions:

1. Juice the pineapple, orange, and mango.

2. Blend with banana for a smooth texture.

3. Enjoy as a refreshing start to your day.

- Benefits: High in Vitamin C and natural sugars, provides an energy boost and hydration.

### 3. BEETROOT IMMUNITY ELIXIR

347

- Ingredients: 1 medium beet (peeled), 1 carrot (peeled), 1 apple (cored), juice of ½ lemon, 1-inch turmeric piece (peeled)

- Instructions:

1. Juice the beet, carrot, apple, and turmeric.

2. Stir in lemon juice for extra zing.

3. Drink immediately to support immune function.

- Benefits: Enhances blood flow and reduces inflammation with a potent dose of vitamins.

## 4. ANTIOXIDANT BERRY FLUSH

- Ingredients: 1 cup blueberries, 1 cup strawberries (hulled), ½ cup raspberries, 1 cup water or coconut water

- Instructions:

1. Wash all berries.

2. Juice or blend the berries, then strain if necessary.

3. Mix with water or coconut water and serve.

- Benefits: Rich in antioxidants, this juice aids detoxification and supports skin health.

## 5. SPICY CITRUS IMMUNE BOOST

- Ingredients: 2 oranges (peeled), 1 grapefruit (peeled), ½ lime (peeled), ½-inch ginger piece (peeled), pinch of cayenne pepper

- Instructions:

1. Juice the oranges, grapefruit, lime, and ginger.

2. Stir in cayenne pepper.

3. Consume for a vitamin-packed, metabolism-boosting drink.

- Benefits: Strengthens the immune system and stimulates metabolism with Vitamin C and anti-inflammatory spices.

These juices are a fantastic addition to your daily routine, providing a concentrated source of nutrients that promote wellness. Whether you're looking for a detox, a morning pick-me-up, or an immune booster, these blends offer a quick and effective solution.

# 6. COOLING CUCUMBER MINT CLEANSE

This refreshing juice offers a hydrating and cleansing experience, perfect for hot days or post-workout recovery. The combination of cucumber, mint, and lime creates a cooling sensation, while the ginger aids digestion and adds a hint of spice.

Ingredients:

- 1 large cucumber

- 1 green apple, cored and sliced

- ½ cup fresh mint leaves

- ½ lime, peeled

- 1-inch piece of ginger, peeled

Instructions:

1. Prepare Ingredients: Wash the cucumber, apple, mint, and lime thoroughly.

2. Juicing: Run the cucumber, apple, ginger, and lime through the juicer.

3. Add Mint: Add the mint leaves last to extract their refreshing flavor.

4. Serve Chilled: Pour the juice into a glass and serve chilled for the best results.

Benefits:

- Hydration: The cucumber and lime provide hydration and electrolytes.

- Digestion: Ginger helps soothe the digestive system and may reduce bloating.

- Cooling Effect: Mint and cucumber offer a cooling sensation, ideal for warm days or after intense physical activity.

# 7. SWEET POTATO SUNRISE

Start your morning with this nutrient-packed, vibrant juice that provides a natural boost of energy. Sweet potato and carrots offer a sweet, earthy flavor, while orange and cinnamon add a warming, zesty twist. This juice is rich in beta-carotene and promotes eye health and immune function.

Ingredients:

- 1 medium sweet potato, peeled and sliced

- 2 large carrots, peeled

- 1 orange, peeled

- ½ teaspoon cinnamon

Instructions:

1. Juice: Juice the sweet potato, carrots, and orange together.

2. Add Cinnamon: Stir in the cinnamon for a warming spice touch.

3. Serve: Enjoy this nutrient-dense juice first thing in the morning for a gentle yet energizing start to your day.

Benefits:

- Eye Health: High in beta-carotene, which supports vision and reduces oxidative stress.

- Immune Support: Vitamin C from the orange boosts immunity, while cinnamon adds anti-inflammatory benefits.

## 8. POWER GREEN KICK

Packed with leafy greens and detoxifying herbs, this potent green juice provides a natural energy lift and is loaded with antioxidants. The kale, parsley, and cucumber work synergistically to detoxify and hydrate, while ginger and lemon enhance flavor and digestion.

Ingredients:

- 2 cups kale leaves

- ½ cup parsley

- 1 green apple, cored and sliced

- 1 cucumber

- ½ lemon, peeled

- 1-inch piece of ginger, peeled

Instructions:

1. Prep Ingredients: Thoroughly wash the kale, parsley, apple, cucumber, and lemon.

2. Juice: Juice the kale, parsley, apple, cucumber, lemon, and ginger one after the other.

3. Stir: Mix well and consume immediately to maximize the nutrient content.

Benefits:

- Detoxification: Kale and parsley are powerful detoxifiers, promoting liver function and overall vitality.

- Energy Boost: Rich in chlorophyll and essential vitamins, this juice supports energy levels throughout the day.

- Antioxidants: Provides a hefty dose of antioxidants to combat free radicals, boosting overall wellness.

## 9. RED RADIANCE BOOSTER

Ingredients:

- 1 medium beet, peeled and sliced

- 1 red apple, cored and sliced

- ½ cup red cabbage, chopped

- ½ lemon, peeled

- 1 carrot, peeled

Instructions:

1. Prepare all ingredients by peeling and slicing as needed.

2. Juice the beet, apple, cabbage, lemon, and carrot.

3. Mix well and enjoy this vibrant, nutrient-dense drink.

Benefits:

This juice is a powerhouse of antioxidants and Vitamin C, supporting heart health and reducing inflammation. The combination of beet and red cabbage also boosts energy levels, making this a fantastic juice for a midday pick-me-up or pre-workout drink.

# 10. PINEAPPLE GINGER HYDRATOR

Ingredients:

- 1 cup pineapple chunks

- ½ cucumber

- 1-inch piece of ginger, peeled

- ½ lime, peeled

Instructions:

1. Prepare and slice all ingredients.

2. Juice the ginger first, followed by the pineapple, cucumber, and lime to balance flavors.

3. Drink fresh for an invigorating and tropical refreshment.

Benefits:

This juice is ideal for hydration and recovery, particularly after exercise. Pineapple contains bromelain, which supports digestion, while ginger's anti-inflammatory properties aid in reducing soreness and inflammation. Perfect for staying hydrated and energized throughout the day.

# 11. CITRUS CARROT GLOW

Ingredients:

- 3 large carrots, peeled

- 2 oranges, peeled

- 1 lemon, peeled

- 1-inch piece of turmeric, peeled

Instructions:

1. Wash and peel all ingredients.

2. Juice the carrots, oranges, lemon, and turmeric together.

3. Stir well and serve immediately.

Benefits:

This juice is a great source of Vitamin A from the carrots and Vitamin C from the citrus, which are essential for immune support and skin health. The turmeric adds an anti-inflammatory boost, making this juice a fantastic option for maintaining a healthy glow and supporting overall wellness.

## 12. SPICED APPLE DELIGHT

Ingredients:

- 2 red apples, cored and sliced

- 1-inch piece of ginger, peeled

- ½ teaspoon cinnamon

- ¼ teaspoon nutmeg

- ¼ cup water

Instructions:

1. Juice the apples and ginger.

2. In a blender, combine the juice with water, cinnamon, and nutmeg. Blend until smooth.

3. Serve chilled or over ice for a warming, spiced treat.

Benefits:

The combination of apples and ginger aids digestion, while cinnamon and nutmeg provide warming spices that help boost metabolism. This drink is perfect for a cozy afternoon break, balancing comfort and health.

# 13. BERRY BEET BLAST

Ingredients:

- 1 medium beet, peeled and sliced

- 1 cup strawberries

- ½ cup blueberries

- ½ cup raspberries

- Juice of ½ lemon

Instructions:

1. Wash and prepare the berries and beet.

2. Juice the beet and berries together.

3. Stir in lemon juice and enjoy immediately.

Benefits:

This vibrant juice is packed with antioxidants, making it a perfect drink to support detoxification and heart health. The berries provide a potent mix of vitamins and minerals that reduce inflammation and support cardiovascular function.

# 14. TROPICAL GREENS FUSION

Ingredients:

- 1 cup fresh pineapple chunks

- ½ cup kale leaves

- ½ cup spinach leaves

- ½ cucumber

- ½ lime, peeled

Instructions:

1. Wash and prep all the ingredients.

2. Juice the pineapple, kale, spinach, cucumber, and lime.

3. Stir well and enjoy this tropical blend.

Benefits:

This refreshing fusion combines the sweetness of pineapple with nutrient-rich greens like kale and spinach. It's a great way to boost detoxification while infusing your body with vitamins and minerals that promote overall health.

## 15. CUCUMBER MELON REFRESHER

Ingredients:

- 1 cup honeydew melon chunks

- ½ cucumber

- ½ green apple, cored and sliced

- Juice of ½ lime

- Fresh mint leaves (optional)

Instructions:

1. Prep and wash the melon, cucumber, and apple.

2. Juice all the ingredients together.

3. Stir in the lime juice and garnish with fresh mint if desired.

Benefits:

Perfect for hot days, this light and hydrating juice is rich in vitamins and antioxidants that detoxify and replenish your body. The refreshing blend of cucumber and melon makes it an excellent choice for staying cool and hydrated.

# CHAPTER 27

## HERBAL TEAS AND INFUSIONS

### GINGER LEMON DETOX TEA

Ingredients:

- 1-inch piece of fresh ginger, peeled and sliced

- Juice of 1 lemon

- 2 cups water

- 1 teaspoon honey (optional)

Instructions:

1. Bring water to a boil.

2. Add sliced ginger and reduce heat to simmer for 10 minutes.

3. Remove from heat, add lemon juice, and stir in honey if using.

4. Strain and serve warm.

Benefits:

This detox tea is ideal for improving digestion and reducing inflammation. Ginger's soothing properties, combined with the immune-boosting benefits of lemon, make this a great choice for starting your day on a healthy note.

### PEPPERMINT CHAMOMILE SOOTHING TEA

Ingredients:

- 1 tablespoon dried peppermint leaves

- 1 tablespoon dried chamomile flowers

- 2 cups water

- Honey (optional)

Instructions:

1. Boil water.

2. Place the peppermint and chamomile in a teapot or infuser.

3. Pour boiling water over the herbs and let steep for 5-7 minutes.

4. Strain and enjoy with honey if desired.

Benefits:

This calming blend is perfect for reducing stress and promoting relaxation. Chamomile helps improve sleep quality, while peppermint soothes digestion, making it a great evening drink to wind down.

## TURMERIC GINGER IMMUNITY BOOST TEA

Ingredients:

- 1 teaspoon turmeric powder or 1-inch piece of fresh turmeric, peeled and sliced

- 1-inch piece of fresh ginger, peeled and sliced

- 2 cups water

- 1 teaspoon honey

- Dash of black pepper

Instructions:

1. Boil water and add turmeric and ginger.

2. Simmer for 10 minutes.

3. Stir in honey and a dash of black pepper to increase turmeric absorption.

4. Strain and serve.

Benefits:

A potent anti-inflammatory tea that supports the immune system. The turmeric and ginger work together to aid digestion and reduce inflammation, making this an excellent remedy for colds or flu.

# LAVENDER LEMON BALM RELAXATION TEA

Ingredients:

- 1 tablespoon dried lavender flowers

- 1 tablespoon dried lemon balm leaves

- 2 cups water

- Honey (optional)

Instructions:

1. Boil water.

2. Add lavender and lemon balm to a teapot or infuser.

3. Pour boiling water over the herbs and steep for 5-7 minutes.

4. Strain and add honey if desired.

Benefits:

This soothing tea helps reduce anxiety and promotes relaxation. Lavender calms the mind, while lemon balm supports sleep and stress relief, making it ideal for unwinding before bed.

# ROSEMARY SAGE MEMORY BOOST TEA

Ingredients:

- 1 tablespoon fresh rosemary leaves or 1 teaspoon dried rosemary

- 1 tablespoon fresh sage leaves or 1 teaspoon dried sage

- 2 cups water

- Lemon slices (optional)

- Honey (optional)

Instructions:

1. Boil water and add rosemary and sage.

2. Steep for 5-7 minutes.

3. Strain and serve with lemon slices and honey, if desired.

Benefits:

This aromatic tea enhances memory and concentration. Both rosemary and sage are known for their cognitive benefits, making this tea a great choice for mental clarity and focus.

## HIBISCUS CINNAMON HEART HEALTH TEA

Ingredients:

- 2 tablespoons dried hibiscus flowers

- 1 cinnamon stick

- 2 cups water

- Honey or agave syrup to taste (optional)

Instructions:

1. Bring water to a boil.

2. Add the hibiscus flowers and cinnamon stick to the boiling water.

3. Lower the heat and let the mixture simmer for about 10 minutes.

4. Remove from heat, strain the tea into a cup, and sweeten with honey or agave syrup if desired.

Benefits:

This tea is an excellent source of antioxidants, particularly anthocyanins found in hibiscus, which can help lower blood pressure and support cardiovascular health. The cinnamon adds not only warmth and flavor but also aids in regulating blood sugar levels, making this a beneficial tea for heart health.

## LEMON GINGER TURMERIC DIGESTIVE TEA

Ingredients:

- 1-inch piece of fresh ginger, peeled and sliced

- 1-inch piece of fresh turmeric, peeled and sliced

- Juice of 1 lemon

- 2 cups water

- Honey to taste (optional)


Instructions:

1. Bring water to a boil.

2. Add the ginger and turmeric slices, and lower the heat to simmer for 10 minutes.

3. Remove from heat, add the lemon juice, and stir in honey if desired.

4. Strain into a cup and enjoy while warm.


Benefits:

This soothing tea promotes digestion, reduces inflammation, and supports immune health. Ginger and turmeric are both powerful anti-inflammatory agents, while lemon provides a boost of Vitamin C and helps with digestion. A great option for mornings or after meals.


## ELDERBERRY ECHINACEA IMMUNE SUPPORT TEA


Ingredients:

- 1 tablespoon dried elderberries

- 1 tablespoon dried echinacea leaves or flowers

- 2 cups water

- Honey to taste (optional)


Instructions:

1. Bring water to a boil.

2. Add the elderberries and echinacea to the boiling water.

3. Lower the heat and simmer for 10-15 minutes.

4. Strain the tea into a cup and sweeten with honey if desired.

Benefits:

This tea is a powerful immune booster, combining the antiviral properties of elderberries with echinacea's ability to enhance the immune system. It's an excellent remedy to help prevent or speed recovery from colds and flu.

## ROOIBOS VANILLA ANTIOXIDANT TEA

Ingredients:

- 2 tablespoons rooibos tea leaves

- 1 vanilla bean, split and seeds scraped out (or 1 teaspoon vanilla extract)

- 2 cups water

- Honey to taste (optional)

Instructions:

1. Bring water to a boil.

2. Add rooibos tea leaves and the vanilla bean or vanilla extract to the boiling water.

3. Reduce heat and let simmer for 5-7 minutes.

4. Strain the tea into a cup and sweeten with honey if desired.

Benefits:

Rich in antioxidants, this tea helps combat inflammation and promotes relaxation. The rooibos offers heart health benefits, while the vanilla adds a soothing flavor that encourages calm and relaxation, making this an ideal tea for the evening.

## SPEARMINT NETTLE DETOX TEA

Ingredients:

- 1 tablespoon dried spearmint leaves

- 1 tablespoon dried nettle leaves

- 2 cups water

- Lemon slices for garnish (optional)

- Honey to taste (optional)

Instructions:

1. Boil the water.

2. Add spearmint and nettle leaves to the boiling water.

3. Reduce heat and simmer for 5-7 minutes.

4. Strain the tea into a cup, and garnish with lemon slices and honey if desired.

Benefits:

This refreshing detox tea supports the body's natural detoxification process, reduces inflammation, and promotes digestive health. Nettle is known for its ability to cleanse the system, while spearmint adds a cooling, soothing element to the tea.

# CHAPTER 28

## SMOOTHIE RECIPES FOR HEALTH AND VITALITY

### GREEN POWER SMOOTHIE

Ingredients:

- 1 cup spinach leaves

- 1 banana

- ½ avocado

- ½ cup Greek yogurt

- 1 cup almond milk

- 1 tablespoon chia seeds

Instructions:

1. Add all ingredients to a blender.

2. Blend until smooth.

3. Pour into a glass and enjoy immediately.

Benefits:

Packed with healthy fats, protein, and vitamins, this smoothie is a great way to start your day with sustained energy. Spinach provides iron, while chia seeds offer omega-3s and fiber for digestive health.

### BERRY ANTIOXIDANT BLAST

Ingredients:

- ½ cup blueberries

- ½ cup strawberries

- ½ cup raspberries

- 1 cup coconut water

- 1 tablespoon flaxseed

- 1 tablespoon honey


Instructions:

1. Combine all ingredients in a blender.

2. Blend until smooth.

3. Pour into a glass and enjoy.


Benefits:

This smoothie is loaded with antioxidants from the berries, which help fight free radicals, support immune function, and promote skin health. The addition of coconut water hydrates while the flaxseeds provide added fiber and omega-3s.


## TROPICAL IMMUNITY BOOSTER


Ingredients:

- 1 cup pineapple chunks

- ½ mango, peeled and diced

- 1 orange, peeled and segmented

- ½ cup carrot juice

- 1 tablespoon fresh ginger, grated

- ½ cup coconut milk


Instructions:

1. Add all ingredients to a blender.

2. Blend until smooth.

3. Serve and enjoy.

Benefits:

This tropical smoothie is packed with Vitamin C from the pineapple, mango, and orange, while the ginger adds anti-inflammatory benefits. Carrot juice provides beta-carotene for eye health, and coconut milk adds a creamy texture and healthy fats.

## CHOCOLATE PEANUT BUTTER PROTEIN SHAKE

Ingredients:

- 1 banana

- 2 tablespoons natural peanut butter

- 1 tablespoon cocoa powder

- 1 scoop chocolate protein powder

- 1 cup almond milk

- 1 teaspoon honey

Instructions:

1. Add all ingredients to a blender.

2. Blend until smooth.

3. Pour and savor the rich flavor.

Benefits:

A great post-workout shake, this smoothie provides protein for muscle recovery, healthy fats from peanut butter, and potassium from the banana to help replenish electrolytes.

## DETOXIFYING GREEN TEA SMOOTHIE

Ingredients:

- 1 cup brewed green tea, cooled

- ½ cucumber, peeled and sliced

- ½ green apple, cored and sliced

- ½ avocado

- Juice of ½ lemon

- 1 tablespoon honey

Instructions:

1. Brew the green tea and let it cool.

2. Add all ingredients to a blender.

3. Blend until smooth.

4. Serve chilled.

Benefits:

This smoothie is perfect for detoxifying the body and boosting metabolism. Green tea is rich in antioxidants and aids fat burning, while cucumber and apple provide hydration and fiber. The avocado offers healthy fats for a creamy texture.

## MANGO SPINACH SMOOTHIE

Ingredients:

- 1 cup fresh spinach leaves

- 1 cup frozen mango chunks

- ½ banana

- ½ cup Greek yogurt

- 1 cup orange juice

- 1 tablespoon chia seeds

Instructions:

1. Combine all ingredients in a blender.

2. Blend until smooth.

3. Pour into a glass and enjoy.

Benefits:

This vitamin-packed smoothie is a refreshing way to boost your immune system and improve digestion. Mango and spinach provide a dose of Vitamins A and C, while chia seeds offer omega-3s for heart health.

## COCONUT BLUEBERRY BLISS SMOOTHIE

Ingredients:

- 1 cup blueberries (fresh or frozen)

- ½ cup coconut milk

- ½ cup water

- 1 banana

- 1 tablespoon flaxseed

- 1 tablespoon honey

Instructions:

1. Add all ingredients to a blender.

2. Blend until smooth.

3. Serve immediately.

Benefits:

This smoothie is rich in antioxidants, healthy fats, and fiber, making it ideal for supporting heart health and digestion. The combination of blueberries and coconut milk creates a creamy, satisfying treat that's also nutritious.

# AVOCADO LIME SMOOTHIE

Ingredients:

- 1 avocado

- ½ cucumber, peeled and sliced

- Juice of 1 lime

- ½ cup coconut water

- 1 tablespoon fresh mint leaves

- 1 tablespoon honey

Instructions:

1. Add all ingredients to a blender.

2. Blend until smooth.

3. Pour into a glass and enjoy fresh.

Benefits:

This hydrating and refreshing smoothie supports healthy skin and digestion. Avocado provides healthy fats, while lime and mint offer a zesty, cooling finish. It's a perfect option for a light, nutritious snack.

# STRAWBERRY BANANA OAT SMOOTHIE

Ingredients:

- ½ cup rolled oats

- 1 cup strawberries (fresh or frozen)

- 1 banana

- 1 cup almond milk

- 1 tablespoon almond butter

- 1 teaspoon vanilla extract

Instructions:

1. Add all ingredients to your blender.

2. Blend until the mixture is smooth and creamy.

3. Serve immediately for best texture and flavor.

Benefits:

This smoothie is not only delicious but also packed with essential nutrients. The oats and almond butter provide a good dose of fiber and healthy fats, while the banana and strawberries add natural sweetness along with vitamins and antioxidants.

It's an ideal option for breakfast or a post-workout recovery drink, offering sustained energy and nutrition to fuel your day.

## PUMPKIN SPICE SMOOTHIE

Ingredients:

- ½ cup pumpkin puree

- 1 banana

- 1 cup almond milk

- ½ cup Greek yogurt

- 1 tablespoon maple syrup

- ½ teaspoon pumpkin pie spice

Instructions:

1. Place all ingredients into a blender.

2. Blend until smooth and creamy.

3. Pour into a glass and enjoy the warm, comforting flavors of fall.

Benefits:

Rich in fiber, vitamins, and antioxidants, this smoothie brings the cozy flavors of pumpkin spice into a healthy, nourishing drink. The pumpkin puree is an excellent source of Vitamin A and fiber, while the Greek yogurt adds protein and probiotics, supporting gut health and digestion. It's the perfect seasonal treat with the added bonus of supporting overall wellness.

# APPENDICES

## TECHNIQUES TO PRESERVE HEALTHY NUTRIENTS

### STEAMING VEGETABLES

Method: Use a steamer basket placed over boiling water.

Details: Place your vegetables in the basket, cover, and let them steam until they are tender yet vibrant in color.

Benefits: Steaming helps to retain essential nutrients by keeping vegetables out of direct contact with water, preventing the leaching of water-soluble vitamins like Vitamin C and B-vitamins.

### BLANCHING

Method: Boil vegetables briefly, then cool quickly in an ice bath.

Details: Submerge vegetables in boiling water for 1-2 minutes, then immediately transfer them to an ice bath to halt cooking.

Benefits: This method is excellent for preserving the bright color, flavor, and nutrients in vegetables. It's also useful for preparing vegetables before freezing, locking in their nutrients for longer-term storage.

### STORING IN AIRTIGHT CONTAINERS

Method: Use clean, dry, and airtight containers for food storage.

Details: After washing and cutting fruits and vegetables, store them in the refrigerator in sealed containers to reduce exposure to air and moisture.

Benefits: Keeping food in airtight containers helps preserve its freshness and nutrient content by minimizing the breakdown caused by oxygen and humidity.

### USING LOW HEAT FOR COOKING

Method: Opt for slow cooking methods or use sous-vide techniques.

Details: Cook foods at low temperatures over longer periods of time to retain more nutrients.

371

Benefits: This technique helps preserve heat-sensitive vitamins and minerals that are often lost in high-heat cooking, making it a better option for nutrient retention.

## AVOIDING OVERCOOKING

Method: Cook vegetables to a tender-crisp state.

Details: Use a timer to ensure you don't overcook, which can degrade vitamins and minerals.

Benefits: By cooking vegetables until they are just tender, you maintain their texture, flavor, and nutrient profile, keeping them rich in vitamins like C and K.

## QUICK STIR-FRYING

Method: Use high heat for a short duration.

Details: Stir-fry vegetables and proteins quickly in a hot pan, ensuring they stay crisp and nutrient-rich.

Benefits: The brief cooking time helps to retain vitamins and antioxidants, while also enhancing the flavors and textures of your ingredients.

## FREEZING FRESH PRODUCE

Method: Freeze produce soon after harvesting or purchasing.

Details: Wash, peel, and cut fruits and vegetables, then freeze them in airtight containers or bags.

Benefits: Freezing locks in nutrients at their peak, preventing spoilage and allowing you to enjoy fresh produce year-round without significant nutrient loss.

## USING MINIMAL WATER FOR COOKING

Method: Boil or simmer with the least amount of water necessary.

Details: Use just enough water to cover the food when boiling or simmering.

Benefits: Using less water minimizes the loss of water-soluble vitamins, which can be leached into the cooking liquid and lost.

# OPTING FOR FRESH OR FROZEN OVER CANNED

Method: Choose fresh or frozen produce over canned when possible.

Details: Fresh produce or frozen options without added preservatives retain more nutrients than canned foods, which may lose some of their vitamins and minerals during the preservation process.

Benefits: Both fresh and frozen produce provide higher nutritional value compared to canned options, which are often loaded with sodium and may have undergone nutrient-depleting processing.

# PROPER STORAGE OF OILS

Method: Store oils in cool, dark places.

Details: Keep oils away from heat and light to prevent oxidation, and always use them within their recommended shelf life.

Benefits: Properly storing oils ensures that their essential fatty acids, especially omega-3s, remain intact and provide their full health benefits.

By incorporating these nutrient-preserving techniques, you can ensure that your food maintains its maximum nutritional value, in line with the principles of holistic health.

Whether you're steaming, stir-frying, or storing your produce, paying attention to how you prepare and preserve your food will help you get the most out of every meal.

# CHAPTER 29

## CONVERSION CHARTS FOR EASY REFERENCE

Understanding measurement conversions is key to successfully following recipes, especially when switching between different units of measurement.

This guide provides simple conversion charts to help you navigate between volume, weight, temperature, and ingredient measurements, ensuring your cooking and baking is precise.

### VOLUME CONVERSIONS

| Teaspoons (tsp) | Tablespoons (tbsp) | Cups | Milliliters (ml) | Liters (L) | Fluid Ounces (fl oz) | Pints (pt) | Quarts (qt) | Gallons (gal) |
|---|---|---|---|---|---|---|---|---|
| 1 | 0.333 | 0.0208 | 4.93 | 0.00493 | 0.17 | 0.0104 | 0.0052 | 0.0013 |
| 3 | 1 | 0.0625 | 14.79 | 0.01479 | 0.50 | 0.03125 | 0.0156 | 0.0039 |
| 48 | 16 | 1 | 236.59 | 0.23659 | 8 | 0.5 | 0.25 | 0.0625 |
| 96 | 32 | 2 | 473.18 | 0.47318 | 16 | 1 | 0.5 | 0.125 |
| 192 | 64 | 4 | 946.35 | 0.94635 | 32 | 2 | 1 | 0.25 |
| 384 | 128 | 8 | 1892.71 | 1.89271 | 64 | 4 | 2 | 0.5 |
| 768 | 256 | 16 | 3785.41 | 3.78541 | 128 | 8 | 4 | 1 |

# WEIGHT CONVERSIONS

| Grams (g) | Kilograms (kg) | Ounces (oz) | Pounds (lb) |
|---|---|---|---|
| 1 | 0.001 | 0.0353 | 0.0022 |
| 100 | 0.1 | 3.5274 | 0.2205 |
| 200 | 0.2 | 7.0548 | 0.4409 |
| 500 | 0.5 | 17.637 | 1.1023 |
| 1000 | 1 | 35.274 | 2.2046 |

# TEMPERATURE CONVERSIONS

| Celsius (°C) | Fahrenheit (°F) |
| --- | --- |
| 0 | 32 |
| 10 | 50 |
| 20 | 68 |
| 30 | 86 |
| 40 | 104 |
| 50 | 122 |
| 60 | 140 |
| 70 | 158 |
| 80 | 176 |
| 90 | 194 |
| 100 | 212 |
| 150 | 302 |
| 200 | 392 |
| 250 | 482 |

# DRY INGREDIENT CONVERSIONS (APPROXIMATE)

| Cups | Grams (g) | Ounces (oz) | Ingredient |
|------|-----------|-------------|------------|
| 1/4 | 30 | 1 | All-purpose flour |
| 1/3 | 40 | 1.4 | All-purpose flour |
| 1/2 | 60 | 2 | All-purpose flour |
| 1 | 120 | 4.2 | All-purpose flour |
| 1/4 | 50 | 1.75 | Sugar |
| 1/3 | 65 | 2.3 | Sugar |
| 1/2 | 100 | 3.5 | Sugar |
| 1 | 200 | 7 | Sugar |
| 1/4 | 20 | 0.7 | Cocoa powder |
| 1/3 | 25 | 0.9 | Cocoa powder |
| 1/2 | 40 | 1.4 | Cocoa powder |
| 1 | 80 | 2.8 | Cocoa powder |

# COMMON INGREDIENT CONVERSIONS (APPROXIMATE)

| Ingredient | 1 Cup (grams) | 1 Cup (ounces) |
|---|---|---|
| All-purpose flour | 120 | 4.2 |
| Sugar | 200 | 7 |
| Brown sugar | 220 | 7.8 |
| Powdered sugar | 125 | 4.4 |
| Cocoa powder | 80 | 2.8 |
| Butter | 227 | 8 |
| Honey | 340 | 12 |
| Milk | 240 | 8.5 |
| Water | 240 | 8.5 |

Whether you're following a recipe or converting your favorite dish to suit different measurements, these charts provide a reliable reference for volume, weight, temperature, and common ingredient conversions.

By keeping these handy, you can ensure precision and consistency in your cooking, no matter which system of measurement you're using.

# CHAPTER 30

## REAL LIFE STORIES OF TRANSFORMATION

### A JOURNEY TO WELLNESS: SARAH'S STORY

#### EARLY STRUGGLES

At 42, Sarah was a mother of two, juggling the demands of her career and home life. The constant stress took a toll on her health. She suffered from chronic fatigue, persistent digestive issues, and overwhelming anxiety. Despite seeking help from conventional medicine, nothing seemed to work. Feeling stuck, Sarah feared she'd never regain her vitality.

#### THE TURNING POINT

One evening, a close friend suggested she watch a series of lectures by Barbara O'Neill, an expert in natural healing. Skeptical but hopeful, Sarah began listening to Barbara's teachings. For the first time, she felt a flicker of hope. Barbara's emphasis on the body's natural ability to heal itself resonated deeply with Sarah, and she became determined to give a holistic approach a chance.

#### EMBRACING A HOLISTIC APPROACH

Inspired by Barbara's wisdom, Sarah started implementing changes in small, manageable steps:

1. Detoxification: Sarah began with a gentle 14-day detox, focusing on cleansing foods like dandelion greens and lemon water. She followed Barbara's recommendation to drink warm water with apple cider vinegar every morning. This simple habit left her feeling less bloated and more energized.

2. Nutritional Overhaul: Gradually, Sarah transformed her diet. She included more whole foods like leafy greens, berries, and nuts, following Barbara's advice on reducing inflammation. Ingredients like turmeric and ginger became staples, helping to ease the inflammation that had plagued her for years.

3. Herbal Remedies: Guided by Barbara's lectures, Sarah began using herbal teas and supplements tailored to her health concerns. Peppermint and chamomile tea soothed her digestive issues, while adaptogenic herbs like ashwagandha and rhodiola helped combat her chronic fatigue.

4. Stress Management: Realizing the impact stress had on her health, Sarah incorporated daily meditation and mindfulness into her routine. She created a calming space at home where she could meditate, breathe deeply, and reflect. Yoga and light physical activity became part of her daily routine, helping to balance her mental and emotional well-being.

## THE TRANSFORMATION

Over the next six months, Sarah experienced a remarkable transformation. Her digestive issues subsided, her energy levels soared, and her anxiety diminished. She lost weight and felt lighter both physically and emotionally. Her skin, once dull, now glowed with vitality.

While there were challenging days, Sarah consistently turned to Barbara's teachings for support. She journaled her progress, reflecting on her journey and celebrating each milestone, no matter how small.

## INSPIRING OTHERS

As Sarah's health improved, friends and family took notice. They marveled at her transformation and began seeking her advice. Sarah embraced her role as a wellness advocate, eager to share the holistic principles that had changed her life.

## A NEW BEGINNING

Sarah's journey wasn't just about physical healing; it was a shift in how she lived her life. She learned to listen to her body, nourish it with natural remedies, and prioritize self-care. Her story is a powerful reminder that the human body has an incredible ability to heal, especially when given the right tools and support.

# FROM DESPAIR TO VITALITY: JOHN'S PATH TO HEALING

## INITIAL CHALLENGES

At 55, John had always considered himself in decent health. But years of a sedentary lifestyle and a diet high in processed foods began to catch up with him. He developed joint pain, high blood pressure, and bouts of depression. Despite multiple doctor visits and a list of medications, John saw little improvement. Frustrated and desperate, he knew something had to change.

## DISCOVERING A NEW APPROACH

One day, while searching online for alternatives, John discovered Barbara O'Neill's videos on natural healing. Her calm, practical approach caught his attention. She spoke about the body's inherent ability to heal, and John was particularly drawn to her holistic approach that encompassed both physical and mental health.

## MAKING THE SHIFT

Determined to regain control of his health, John began implementing Barbara's guidance with three key changes:

1. Healing Diet: John overhauled his diet, eliminating processed foods and introducing whole, nutritious meals. His mornings started with green smoothies packed with spinach, kale, and berries. Following Barbara's advice, he embraced anti-inflammatory foods like turmeric and ginger, which brought relief from his joint pain.

2. Herbal Remedies: John researched herbal solutions to his specific health issues. Hibiscus tea became his go-to for managing high blood pressure, while a mix of turmeric and ginger supplements helped with joint pain. To address his depression and anxiety, John added ashwagandha to his routine.

3. Physical Activity: Understanding that movement was key to his recovery, John began incorporating exercise. He started with daily walks, eventually working up to swimming and yoga. These activities not only improved his physical condition but also had a profound effect on his mental well-being.

## OVERCOMING SETBACKS

John's journey wasn't without its challenges. He struggled to break old habits, and there were moments when he felt overwhelmed. But Barbara's teachings reminded him to view setbacks as part of the process, not as failures. He also found support through a local wellness group, which helped him stay motivated.

## A REMARKABLE TRANSFORMATION

After a year of dedication, John experienced a profound transformation. His blood pressure normalized, his joint pain became manageable, and his mood improved significantly. He lost weight, built muscle, and regained the energy he hadn't felt in years.

His improved health fostered a deeper connection with his family as well. John began cooking healthy meals, engaging his wife and children in his wellness journey.

Together, they discovered new recipes inspired by Barbara's teachings and enjoyed family walks and activities.

## SPREADING THE WORD

John's remarkable story spread through his community. Friends and neighbors, impressed by his transformation, sought his advice. John embraced his new role as a wellness advocate, hosting workshops and sharing his experiences to help others embark on their own healing journeys.

## EMBRACING A NEW LIFE

For John, this wasn't just about physical healing—it was about reclaiming his life. He discovered the joy of mindful living, of nurturing his body and spirit. Barbara O'Neill's teachings had given him the tools to embrace a new path, proving that it's never too late to transform your health and well-being.

These real-life stories highlight the incredible power of natural remedies and holistic health practices. Sarah and John, both inspired by Barbara O'Neill's teachings, demonstrate that healing is possible at any stage of life.

Through dedication, education, and support, they overcame significant health challenges and rediscovered vibrant, fulfilling lives. Their stories serve as inspiration for anyone seeking to improve their health through holistic practices.

# A JOURNEY TO HOLISTIC HEALING: EMILY'S STORY

## THE STRUGGLE

At 38, Emily was a dedicated mother of two and a passionate teacher. Like many, she had spent years prioritizing her family and career, often at the expense of her own health. The relentless stress, coupled with irregular eating habits and a lack of self-care, had gradually worn her down.

Emily found herself battling chronic migraines, digestive problems, and an overwhelming sense of fatigue. Despite numerous visits to doctors and specialists, the solutions offered only temporary relief. Prescribed medications dulled her symptoms but came with concerning side effects and left her feeling reliant on a medical system that wasn't addressing the root of her issues.

## TURNING POINT

One evening, while browsing social media, Emily stumbled upon a video by Barbara O'Neill, a naturopath and advocate for holistic health. Barbara's calm, practical approach to natural remedies struck a chord with Emily. She was inspired by the idea that the body has an innate ability to heal when given the right tools and attention. Intrigued, Emily dove deeper into Barbara's teachings, watching lectures and reading about holistic healing methods over the next few weeks.

# A NEW BEGINNING

With newfound hope and a sense of empowerment, Emily decided to take control of her health by making meaningful changes. The first step was transforming her diet and lifestyle, drawing from Barbara O'Neill's recommendations for natural healing.

1. Revamping Her Diet: Emily began by eliminating processed foods and introducing nutrient-rich, whole foods into her daily routine. She embraced anti-inflammatory ingredients like leafy greens, berries, nuts, and seeds, as well as fermented foods like sauerkraut and kimchi to support gut health. Every morning, she adopted the habit of drinking warm water with lemon and ginger, following Barbara's advice to aid digestion and cleanse her system.

2. Embracing Herbal Remedies: In her quest for natural relief, Emily researched herbal remedies to target her specific ailments. For her migraines, she discovered the benefits of feverfew and butterbur supplements, which reduced the frequency and intensity of her headaches. To address her digestive issues, she incorporated peppermint tea and slippery elm into her routine. Ashwagandha, an adaptogenic herb, became part of her daily regimen to help manage stress and boost her energy levels.

3. Prioritizing Self-Care: Recognizing the importance of nurturing her mind and body, Emily carved out time each day for self-care. She turned to mindfulness and meditation, often using Barbara's guided meditation sessions to help calm her mind and foster inner peace. Yoga became another essential practice, helping her relax and build physical strength, while also serving as a stress-relief tool during busy days.

# OVERCOMING CHALLENGES

Emily's journey wasn't without difficulties. Old habits occasionally resurfaced, and the pressures of balancing work and family often made it hard to stay on track. But she found solace in Barbara O'Neill's teachings, which emphasized self-compassion and forgiveness.

Emily came to understand that setbacks were a natural part of the healing process. Instead of viewing them as failures, she saw them as opportunities to learn and grow, gradually building resilience and commitment.

# TRANSFORMATIVE RESULTS

Six months into her journey, Emily experienced a profound transformation. Her migraines, once a constant burden, had become less frequent and much more manageable. Her digestive issues improved significantly, and she felt a newfound sense of energy that replaced the chronic fatigue that had once dominated her life. She was no longer simply getting through her days—she was thriving.

Emily's lifestyle changes didn't go unnoticed by her family. Her husband and children observed the positive shifts in her health and well-being and became curious about the changes she was making.

Over time, her family began to adopt healthier eating habits, incorporating more whole foods into their meals. Outdoor activities became a regular part of their routine, creating a happier, healthier home environment.

## A NEW PERSPECTIVE

Emily's journey wasn't just about addressing her physical ailments; it was a complete shift in how she approached life. She learned to live with intention, making self-care a priority and nurturing her body, mind, and spirit.

Barbara O'Neill's teachings had provided her with the tools to reclaim her health and live a balanced, vibrant life. The result wasn't just a healthier body—it was a deeper connection to her loved ones and a more fulfilling way of life.

Emily's story is a testament to the power of natural remedies and holistic health. Through dedication and a willingness to embrace new practices, she was able to overcome her chronic health challenges and rediscover vitality.

Her journey encourages others to believe in the body's innate ability to heal and to explore the profound benefits of holistic healing for both the body and mind.

# GET YOUR EXCLUSIVE BONUS HERE!

SCAN THIS QR CODE:

OR

COPY AND PASTE THIS URL:

https://drive.google.com/drive/folders/1LC5h-TwSCLFfU0-IoJ7JrtAkguW8ajRP?usp=drive_link

Made in the USA
Columbia, SC
22 November 2024

47236457R00213